Devi and Her Avatars

Dr Alka Pande is one of India's leading authors, art historians and curators. Her prominent books include *108 Portraits of Indian Culture and Heritage* (2024) and *Body Sutra* (2019). Currently, she serves as a consultant art advisor and curator of the Visual Arts Gallery at the India Habitat Centre in New Delhi.

Her honours include the Knight of the Order of Arts and Letters (2006), the Australia-India Council Special Award (2009), and the Amrita Sher-Gil Samman (2015). Recently, she received the Culture Champion Award (Global) and the CIMA Lifetime Achievement Award (2023) for her contribution to Indian art.

Connect with the author at
https://alkapande.com/
https://x.com/DrAlkaPande
https://instagram.com/alka.pande

Devi and Her Avatars

ALKA PANDE

RUPA

Published by
Rupa Publications India Pvt. Ltd 2025
7/16, Ansari Road, Daryaganj
New Delhi 110002

Sales centres:
Bengaluru Chennai Hyderabad
Jaipur Kathmandu Kolkata
Mumbai Prayagraj

Copyright © Alka Pande 2025

The author gratefully acknowledges ArputhaRani Sengupta for permission to reprint extracts from *Cult of the Goddess*.

While every effort has been made to trace copyright holders and obtain permission, this has not been possible in all cases; any omissions brought to our attention will be remedied in future editions.

The views and opinions expressed in this book are the author's own and the facts are as reported by her, which have been verified to the extent possible, and the publishers are not in any way liable for the same. The publisher has used its best endeavours to ensure that URLs for external websites referred to in this book are correct and active at the time of going to press. However, the publisher has no responsibility for the websites and can make no guarantee that a site will remain live or that the content is or will remain appropriate.

All rights reserved.
No part of this publication may be reproduced, transmitted or stored in a retrieval system, in any form or by any means, electronic, mechanical, photocopying, recording or otherwise, without the prior permission of the publisher.

P-ISBN: 978-93-6156-426-0
E-ISBN: 978-93-6156-272-3

First impression 2025

10 9 8 7 6 5 4 3 2 1

The moral right of the author has been asserted.

Printed in India

This book is sold subject to the condition that it shall not, by way of trade or otherwise, be lent, resold, hired out or otherwise circulated, without the publisher's prior consent, in any form of binding or cover other than that in which it is published.

To my mother Kamala,
whose *shakti* drives my work.

Contents

Foreword ix
Preface xi

Mahadevi 1
Sati 7
Parvati 17
Durga Mahishamardini 26
Navadurgas 33
Girija 39
Gajalakshmi 45
Kali 49
Chamunda 56
Saraswati 62
Sharada 66
Vagadevi 70
Aranyani 75
Bhudevi 79
Momai 84
Tulsi 89
Jyestha 93
Kamadhenu 97
Kamakshi 101
Lajja Gauri 106
Manasa 110
Matangi 116
Meenakshi 120

Mumba	125
Renuka	128
Sandhya	133
Shitala	138
Santoshi	141
Vana Devi	147
Aditi	152
Annapurna	155
Gayatri	160
Katyayani	165
Ganga	170
Hariti	175
Prakriti	179
Chhinnamasta	185
Lalita	190
Shakambhari	195
Ushas	199
Shashthi	204
Vindhyavasini	210
Mohini	215
Dasa Mahavidyas	220
Sapta Matrikas	229
Chausath Yoginis	238
Yellamma	244
Salabhanjika	249
Prajnaparamita	253
Isakki Amman	259
Bharat Mata	264
Notes	270
Acknowledgements	281
Bibliography	282

Foreword

Ya Devi Sarva Bhuteshu...Devi and Her avatars reside everywhere.

Writer and historian Dr Alka Pande has chosen some of the most revered and fascinating avatars from the *Devi Bhagavata Purana* and the *Durga Saptashati*—the two key texts in which the many forms of Devi are celebrated—and explored their origins as well as the local lore and legends surrounding them in her latest book, *Devi and Her Avatars*.

From Adi Shakti to Shiva Shakti to Mahadevi, from the Vedic to the Puranic to the tribal goddesses, from Vindhyavasini to Durga to the *kuladevi*s, the Goddess is worshipped in different forms and each avatar symbolises an aspect of Her that her worshippers seek. In the East, she is Tantric goddess Kamakhya; in the West, She is Momai Mata; in the South, She could be Bhagavathi, or the fertility goddess Mariamman or Pochamma or Yellamma; in the North, She is Parvati, the consort of Shiva and the mother of Ganesha—and many other forms besides.

This fascinating book traces how and why Devi resides amongst us and how Her presence has been experienced and revered by Her believers for many millennia. It is a tribute to the goddess principle in Hinduism, a religion of astonishing breadth and variety, which absorbed an eclectic mix of ancient customs, traditions and narratives over the centuries into a harmonious whole. Oral traditions, scriptures, and Vedic texts are equally revered by Hindus, who accept all paths as equally significant, and multiple forms and names of Devi as equally sacred manifestations of Shakti.

Alka Pande also delves into the subliminal elements behind the rituals followed by people of various sects of Hinduism, from ancient times to the present. For each of the fifty-one avatars of Devi she mentions in the text, Her iconography is depicted, along with specific *stotras* and verses from sacred texts where She is cited and venerated, together with an erudite discussion of their significance.

This book is a fascinating and comprehensive account of Devi that provides a deep and rewarding insight into the primordial Goddess of Hinduism. I commend it warmly to all who wish to open their eyes, minds and hearts to Her.

Shashi Tharoor
Author and Member of Parliament

Preface

या देवी सर्वभूतेषु शान्तिरूपेण संस्थिता।
या देवी सर्वभूतेषु शक्तिरूपेण संस्थिता।
या देवी सर्वभूतेषु सिद्धिदात्रीरूपेण संस्थिता।
नमस्तस्यै नमस्तस्यै नमस्तस्यै नमो नम:॥
या देवी सर्वभूतेषु माँ बुद्धिरूपेण संस्थिता।
नमस्तस्यै नमस्तस्यै नमस्तस्यै नमो नम:॥

*The Goddess who is omnipresent
as the symbol of peace
The Goddess who is omnipresent
as the embodiment of power
The Goddess who is omnipresent
as the personification of the Universal Mother
I bow to her, I bow to her, I bow to her again and again.
O Devi, who resides everywhere,
in all living beings, as intelligence, beauty and consciousness
I salute you. I offer my salutations again and again.*

—*Durga Saptashati,*
Chapter 5, Verses 20–22, 32–34, 47–49

*T*his particular Devi *stotra* invokes the power residing within the worshippers of the Divine Feminine. In Hinduism, Devi is a power to be reckoned with, permeating the collective imagination of every God-fearing Hindu. For a person of faith and belief—especially one who is inclined towards Indic wisdom—in a country with 33 million gods and goddesses and innumerable sects, even if they become atheists, non-believers, rationalists or liberals tutored in Western liberal order, all rational thought flies out of the window when it comes to the process of acculturation, and what remains is the itihasa (history) or stories from our mythic past.

Coming from a Shakta household, where adulation, adoration and worship were a part of my everyday existence, the concept of Devi as an all-encompassing force guiding our lives was the underlying philosophy of life itself. At this point, I wish to clarify who the Shaktas are; they are those who worship the goddess as the Supreme Deity. Both Vaishnavites and Shaivites also worship the feminine principle, i.e. Devi, in Her manifestations as Lakshmi and Parvati.

However, for the Shaktas, Devi is equal to Deva. So, it was interesting to see my grandfather spending the last few years of his life reading the Ramcharitmanas as part of his *dincharya* (everyday routine). Later, my father continued the tradition, quoting extensively from the Ramayana, except during Navaratri when Devi came alive in our homes. It was fascinating to observe my mother, who came from a staunch Vaishnava tradition, reading the *Devi Bhagavata Purana* (also known as the *Srimad Bhagavatam*) and assimilating numerous stories, informing us that there was plenty to learn from this particular text. My mother and father were both deeply religious people, having strong affinities with their respective beliefs. But somewhere in the midst of all this Narayana bhakti came the fierce, all-powerful, all-pervasive, all-nurturing Devi, who is the Ultimate Mother before whom we all bow as she vanquishes our demons, material or otherwise.

The supremacy of the feminine principle will naturally

enter the text time and again, whether it be through study, discourse, mythology, theology, the belief and understanding of Shakti, or the pre-eminence of the feminine power. She resides in the macrocosm as well as the microcosm. The discovery and development of Shakti, the psychic energy in man, is the aim of the *Mantra Shastra*. The Shakti which resides in man, and the development of which is one of the aims of the *Yoga Shastra*, is called the Kundalini Shakti, and the place where it resides is called the *muladhara*.[1]

∽

As young children, we were woken up at 4.00 a.m. on the day of Mahalaya, the eve of Navaratri, to hear the *Chandipath* being narrated by the iconic Birendra Krishna Bhadra as it was broadcast on All India Radio from Calcutta (now Kolkata). Bhadra's powerful and resonant voice was like a bugle that announced the commencement of the nine days of Devi worship. It was as if Goddess Saraswati resided on the tip of his tongue. His rendition of the *Chandipath* continues to be broadcast in its pre-recorded format even today. Such was the magic and sway of his alluring, bhakti-laden voice. The three important aspects of the *Chandipath* are the *devi kavacham*, considered to be the *beej* (seed) of the *Durga Saptashati* (also known as the *Devi Mahatmya*), the *argala*, personified as Shakti, and the *keelakam*, the invocation recited before reading the *Durga Saptashati*.

शिव: शक्त्या युक्तो यदि भवति शक्त: प्रभवितुं
न चेदेवं देवो न खलु कुशल: स्पन्दितुमपि ।
अतस्त्वामाराध्यां हरिहरविरिञ्चादिभिरपि
प्रणन्तुं स्तोतुं वा कथमकृतपुण्य: प्रभवति

Only when Shiva joins with you, O Shakti,
can he exert his powers as the Lord.
On his own he has not even the power to stir.

You are worshipped by Shiva, Vishnu, Brahma and other gods. How dare I, a meritless mortal, offer you reverence and praise?

—*Saundarya Lahari*, Ananda Lahari, Verse 1

This was also the time we went 'pandal-hopping'. After the Durga idol was placed in it, the pandal became a temporary temple where the neighbourhood community enjoyed dance and music performances and ate the *bhog*² to celebrate the arrival of the goddess. My memories of eating *maach* (fish) and khichdi in the packed pandals remain as vivid as ever. Durga is worshipped in the form of a married daughter coming to earth with her children to visit her parents. On the ninth day of her stay, she prepares to return to her home on Mount Kailash. The *visarjan* happens on the tenth day, which entails the enactment of sending her back home through the practice of submerging the idol into the nearest water body.

∽

Durga is worshipped in all her nine forms—Navadurga—during Navaratri such that one of the forms sits in the centre and each of the remaining eight on a lotus on the eight points of a compass. The central figure has 18 hands, large breasts and big thighs, all adorned with numerous ornaments. This form is the boon-bestowing goddess.

Enveloped in myths, folktales and Pauranic itihasa, where oral and received wisdom form the overarching narrative of religious discourse, Shakti—the primal energy underlying all creation, knowledge, nurturing and destruction—is said to stem from the collective energy of Brahma, Vishnu and Mahesh. Shakti Puja, a convergence of divine energies, centres on this concept, giving rise to Devi.

I wish to emphasise here that the generic word 'shakti' encompasses many interpretations as well as manifestations of the great goddess culture in Hindu thought. Many of these goddesses are not even related. Some are maternal, some sexual, while some are completely non-feminine, having a more male aspect to them. So, the Great Goddess is omnipresent throughout the Indian subcontinent, with a specific representation of each of the various manifestations of Shakti according to the respective geographical context.

Shakti and Her Many Forms

महाविद्या महामाया महामेधा महास्मृतिः।
महामोहा च भवती महादेवी महेश्वरी॥
प्रकृतिस्त्वं च सर्वस्य गुणत्रयविभाविनी।
कालरात्रिर्महारात्रिर्मोहरात्रिश्च दारुणा॥

You are the supreme knowledge as well as the great nescience,
the great intellect and contemplation,
as also the great delusion,
the Great Goddess, as also the great demon.
You are the primordial cause of everything,
bringing into force the three qualities (sattva, rajas and tamas).
You are the dark night of periodic dissolution,
you are the great night of final dissolution
and the terrible night of delusion.

—*Durga Saptashati*, Chapter 1, Verses 77–79

The concept of Shakti, which is the prime focus of this book, is a deeply personal and subjective interpretation of the cosmic force that runs as an amorphous thread throughout the Indian subcontinent. As I, with the help of other scholars and believers of Hinduism, will emphasise, *ekam sadvipra bahudha vadanti*. It means that there is only one truth, which learned people call by many names. This is how I too have perceived the truth of Devi in my long and profoundly intimate journey of understanding the concept of Shakti and adoring Devi as a mother and a power which resides primarily in women. Thus, among the many manifestations of the universal power, I will explore each of the three major masculine and feminine principles.

While Brahma, Vishnu and Mahesh form the mighty triumvirate, and patriarchy takes precedence, each of the gods has their respective consort who traces their lineage to the primal forces of Devi. Facing the powerful trinity is the all-encompassing supreme female power of Shakti, known as Adi Shakti, who is further divided into the material form of Shakti as Prakriti (or Parvati), Vidya Shakti as Kali and Maya Shakti as Yoga Maya.

Adi Shakti, the primordial force, represents the ultimate feminine principle or the zero energy, without which there would be no manifested universe. Thus, all forms of activity are ultimately reducible to the primordial Shakti (Adi Shakti), whence every other form of power emanates.

Devi is right at the top, even above Brahma, the creator, Vishnu, the preserver, and Shiva, the destroyer. The Shaktas believe that it is the divine Shakti, the female force, that drives the three primordial gods. Each of their consorts is the very embodiment of Devi herself in her numerous manifestations—Saraswati, the consort of Brahma, Lakshmi, the consort of Vishnu, and Parvati, the consort of Shiva.

Earlier, I used to think that Devi and Shakti were synonymous, but as I delved deeper into their study in a Vaishnava Shakta household, I started to explore the concept of Devi and, more importantly, Shakti that resides within Devi. The latter is artistically represented in Indian sculptures and paintings, featured in the calendars that used to hang in many Indian homes, particularly in the kitchen and puja rooms. Among them, Lakshmi, seated atop a lotus, was a familiar icon, and

Kali standing atop Shiva with a dripping red tongue and a *mundamala* around her neck, was popular too. These visual representations led me to some vital questions.

Who is Shakti?
What is shakti?
Where is Shakti?

The word 'shakti' symbolises the energy of contemporary Indian women who lead empowered lives on their own terms, prioritising ethics, dignity and freedom. Shakti embodies the universe and is often referred to as Devi, 'the shining one' in Sanskrit, who represents life-giving forces. Devi is worshipped both independently, as the Supreme Deity, especially in Shaivism, and in association with Shiva in Shaivism and Vishnu in Vaishnavism. Devi, when worshipped as Shakti, is interrelated to the worship of Shiva, which is evident in Devi iconography. The followers of Shakti worship, known as the Shaktas, perceive her as the ultimate reality. Shakta philosophy emphasises rituals for venerating various forms of the universal energy personified as goddesses.

In the concept of Ardhanarishvara, which I explored during my doctoral work, there is complete gender parity between Purusha and Prakriti; rather, it leans towards Shakti within Shiva. While the Shaivites believe that Shiva created Shakti, the Shaktas feel that Shiva without Shakti is a *shava* (corpse), and that is the belief I follow in my personal thought process as well.

The concept of Shakti has been well-documented and researched by a number of priests, art historians, scholars of the cult of Shakti, and tantra specialists. As these people are experts in their respective areas, they often tend to have specific stances, which can be quite inflexible. However, for a theoretical understanding of the concept of Shakti from a more personalised space of family worship, I leaned on the academic interpretations by a cross-section of intellectuals. Studying works such as the *Saundarya Lahari*, the *Lalita Sahasranama* as well as more modern texts[3] is how I enriched my home-grown initiation into the worship of Devi, in whom is vested the primordial Shakti, who is the very core of this book. Shakti and Devi are often mentioned synonymously; however, I am clearly demarcating the two concepts. Shakti, for me, symbolises the primordial energy which is the very essence of the vital life source that is present in every living organism. Devi, on the other hand, can either be the prefix or the suffix for, or the many manifestations of the primordial power, Adi Shakti.

The Shaivites believe that all goddesses are incarnations of Uma, while the Vaishnavites believe that Vishnu's power lies in Yoga Nidra. However, it is Vindhyavasini, the local goddess associated with Krishna's birth story, who is the virginal Shakti. Unlike Uma, her power was not controlled or diminished by a more powerful husband. Vindhyavasini was thus capable of providing the nuclear origin for the cult of the unmarried and virgin Great Goddess, who was understood as Adi Shakti, the world's primeval power. Vindhyavasini's modern devotees still maintain that she is Adi Shakti and they say that Uma is but an incarnation of this power. Thus, as Uma claims to absorb Vindhyavasini, so Vindhyavasini claims to absorb Uma.[4]

Some of the most important Sanskrit texts, including the Mahabharata and the *Harivamsa*, allude to Mahadevi as the one who lives in the Vindhyas, akin to the nomenclature of Vindhyavasini, the goddess who incarnates in the form of Mahadevi for Vishnu. Through the Shaivite discourse, she is also Tridevi, synonymous with Parvati, who is the wife of Mahadeva. The feminine force is to be reckoned with, and for the Shaktas, the fiercest deity in Hinduism is Kali, who symbolises *kala* ('time' in Sanskrit). She is Adi Shakti, the other half of Lord Shiva who symbolises pure consciousness and is also described using the name Sacchidananda.

I soon discovered that Devi was also becoming part of an important feminist discourse not just in India but also globally, wherein female religious icons were becoming part of emerging knowledge systems in comparative religion and theology. Thus, the innumerable Hindu myths and diverse cultural traditions of our land become essential to the understanding and unravelling of the mystique around Adi Shakti, Parashakti, Mahashakti and Mahadevi, which will be referred to in the course of this book.

Devi in Myths and Scriptures

त्वयैतद्धार्यते विश्वं त्वयैतत् सृज्यते जगत्।
त्वयैतत् पाल्यते देवि त्वमत्स्यन्ते च सर्वदा

By you this universe is born,
By you this world is created,
O Devi, by you it is protected.

—*Durga Saptashati*, Chapter 1, Verses 75–76

Because of their long-standing existence, myths abound in the Indian subcontinent, whether in the form of stories that were handed down orally or through hand-inscribed verses etched on rock paintings and wayside shrines. Hindu myths are mainly found in Hindu texts such as the Vedas and the Puranas.

I have divided India into four geographical regions on the basis of the rituals of Devi (Shakti) worship associated with each of them. In North India, Shakti appears as Devi Mahamaya; in the West, as Durga; in the East, as Chandi or Kali; and in the South, as Bhadrakali or Amman.

One of the most famous and endearing myths is that of

Sati. Entrenched in Puranic literature, the legend is central to this book. In the Shakta tradition, Sati is an important manifestation of the Divine Feminine in the likeness of a human being.

Another great myth which has been celebrated in its multiple versions is that of the primordial energy Shakti, or Devi, within the Indian tradition. In one of her manifestations, Goddess Mahishasuramardini is the killer of the demon Mahisha. She is thus considered to echo a woman warrior's fierce virginal autonomy. In the *Devi Mahatmya* ('Glory of the Goddess'), we have the first detailed account in Sanskrit of the goddess' role in the demise of the asuras Madhu, Kaitabha, Mahisha, Shumbha and Nishumbha. The *Devi Bhagavatam* quotes another story of Mahishasuramardini in which the buffalo demon Mahisha could be killed only by a woman.

The idea underlying Durga's cosmic interventions and the structure of the different demon-slaying myths conform to well-known ideas in Hindu thought. The idea of a deity descending to the world in various forms from time to time to maintain the cosmic order is a central Vaishnavite idea. We will further explore Devi in myths and scriptures in this text.

Iconography of Shakti

अहं रुद्रेभिर्वसुभिश्चराम्यहमादित्यैरुत विश्वदेवैः।
अहं मित्रावरुणोभा बिभर्म्यहमिन्द्राग्नी अहमश्विनोभा॥१॥
अहं सोममाहनसं विभर्म्यहं त्वष्टारमुत पूषणं भगम्।
अहं दधामि द्रविणं हविष्मते सुप्राव्ये यजमानाय सुन्वते॥२॥

I move along with the Rudras, the Vasus,
the Adityas, also with the Vishvedevas.
I hold both Mitra and Varuna, both Indra and Agni

> *and both the Ashvin brothers.*
> *I bear the pressed-out Soma,*
> *also Tvashtri, Pushan and Bhaga.*
> *I grant wealth to the possessor of oblation,*
> *to the mindful institutor of sacrifice*
> *and to the performer of Soma sacrifice.*

—*Rig Veda*, Book 10, Chapter 125, Verses 1–2

The iconography of Devi has been well-documented in the *Shilpa Shastras* and traditional texts on sculptures and paintings. One that often comes to mind here is Navadurga, as she is an important *rupa* (form) of Devi.

The first female representation in the ancient period was that of the Mother Goddess, with large pendulous breasts and thick thighs. They were votive figures in terracotta, where the female form was depicted as Prakriti (nature), Prithvi (earth) and Devi (the Mother Goddess). From the Harappan dancing girl, the woman evolved into the sensuous *yakshi* (the female nature spirit, similar to a fairy), like the Chulakoka yakshis beneath an Ashoka tree on a pillar at the Bharhut stupa, located in Satna district of Madhya Pradesh.

As Mahishasuramardini, Durga stands out with a distinct individuality. She should have 10 hands, according to the *Shilparatna*, which describes her further as having three eyes; she should wear on her head a *jatamukuta* (matted crown), and in it there should be the *chandrakala* (the digit of the moon). The colour of her body should be like that of the *atasi* flower, and the eyes should resemble the *nilotpala* (blue lotus); she should have high breasts and a thin waist and there should be three bends in her body. In her right hands, she should carry the trishula, *khadaga, shaktyayudha, chakra* and stringed bow, and in her left hands, the *pasha, ankusha, khetaka, parasu* and bell.[5] At her feet should lie a buffalo with its head cut off and blood gushing from its neck. From within this neck should be visible the half-emerged real asura, bound down by Devi's *nagapasha* (the noose of serpents).

From Mother Goddess to Amman

As I mentioned earlier, having been raised in a traditional Brahmin household, the rituals of worship were an important part of our everyday existence, along with the narration of the Puranic texts, in which were embedded numerous stories that we children used to accept as the gospel truth. From demons to gods, from nymphs to goddesses, my imagination knew no bounds. This book is a result of the many stories and legends that I heard during my childhood.

As I grew up, imbibing a rational, more Western education, I found these stories bordering on the phantasmagorical. Nature, nurture and cultural ethos have almost an uncanny way of rearing their heads. After many years of following Cartesianism, I returned to my childhood memories and the shaping of my own aesthetic and religious philosophy. Devi plays an integral role in my life, with our family being Shakta. During every Navaratri, there were nine days of intense Devi worship. The *Devi Bhagavata Purana* was regularly read by my mother, who insisted that whatever we witnessed and experienced in our lives had already been revealed in that particular text.

Over the years, the many manifestations of Devi were revered in our home. As a child, I heard many stories from the *Devi Bhagavata Purana*, and then later, I studied more of those stories while pursuing my doctoral work.

For the purposes of this particular book, I have picked fifty-one goddesses from both the higher and lower positions in the hierarchy, including the Vedas, the Upanishads, the

Brahmanas and the Puranas. This knowledge consists of folk, tribal, sectarian and cultic practices. From Mahadevi to Yellamma, there is an unbroken tradition of Devi worship, along with innumerable legends about her.

As I mentioned earlier, Devi is also the primordial mother and the origins of the Devi pantheon therefore begin with the worship of the Mother Goddess. She is variously addressed as Ambe Mata, Maa Durga, Amman and Matrika. What is even more interesting to me is the many rupas (manifestations) and *swarupa*s (own forms) of the Mother Goddess. She is loving, adoring, nurturing, protective, ferocious and a slayer of demons. She is also Chhinnamasta, one of the Chausath Yoginis, belonging to the esoteric tradition of tantra, which is both enigmatic and powerful.

I have attempted to explore the parallel trajectories of myths and legends and the cultic interpretations of the Mother Goddess, as the fountainhead of all feminine power, the Eternal Goddess, sits supreme at the top of the triad of Brahma, Vishnu and Mahesh.

Mahadevi

नमो देव्यै महादेव्यै शिवायै सततं नमः।
नमः प्रकृत्यै भद्रायै नियताः प्रणताः स्म ताम्॥

Salutations to Devi, to Mahadevi;
Salutations always to Her who is one with Shiva
(the auspicious one);
Salutations to Her who is the primordial source of creation
and controller of everything; we bow always to Her.

—*Durga Saptashati*, Chapter 5, Verse 9

In the Hindu pantheon, Devi is also venerated as Mahadevi, the Great Goddess. To me, she is the all-embracing Mother Goddess, that is, Bhagavati, or the primordial source of feminine energy, or the creative force. It is important to understand that before the Hindu trinity of Brahma, Vishnu and Mahesh took shape and Devi took the form of Adi Parashakti, there existed a primordial goddess. She was Mahadevi, who came to represent the female energy that went on to become Adi Shakti.

There is a fascinating myth that is associated with the relationship between Vishnu and Mahadevi. The tale is as follows: Once, Vishnu, when only a baby, resting in the cradle of a fig leaf, questioned himself as to who he was, who created him and how he should act. Suddenly, he heard a celestial voice announcing, 'All that is, is me. There is nothing eternal but me.' (*Devi Bhagavata*, Skanda 1). He was unable to locate the source of this celestial voice. When so puzzled, there appeared before him a heavenly female with four hands, holding a conch, a disc, a club and a lotus flower. She was clad in divine clothes and ornaments and was attended by 21 celestial powers. Some of the important ones were *rati*, the erotic; *bhuti*, the riches and prosperity; *buddhi*, the wisdom and intellect; *kirti*, the reputation and credibility; *smriti*, the memory and remembrance; *nidra*, the sleep; *daya*, the compassion and sympathy; *gati*, the movement and pace; *tushti*, the contentment; *pushti*, the growth and affirmation; *kshama*, the forbearance and tolerance; *lajja*, the grace and coy demeanour; and *tandra*, the lethargy. Vishnu instantly realised that she was none other than Adi-Sakti Mahadevi and paid his respects to her.[1]

I think it is beautiful to see this continuity in the mythos of Adi Shakti. If we go deep into the roots of Hinduism, we find her in one form or another. Today, we may know her as Saraswati, Lakshmi and Parvati, as her attributes often make her interchangeable with the trinity goddesses, while in some legends, the three are together considered Mahadevi. Even in the Vedic period, she existed as the force that gave the deities the power to access their cosmic energy.

Devi's most notable characteristic is perhaps her dual nature, which, in one form or another, can be seen in all her manifestations, including even the gentle, docile and domestic goddesses. To me, Mahadevi has always been representative of both the light and the dark, for she is existence itself—the complete embodiment of the very nature of the universe which is both good and bad. Therefore, while she is Uma, the benevolent one, she is also Durga, the inaccessible one. However, one must note here that even in Mahadevi's form, the goddess' most popular association is with Durga, or her more fierce personification Kali.

As the primordial creative energy, she has been given a myriad of names perhaps because she manifests in various forms: Vindhyavasini (the daughter of the Vindhyas), Kanya (the virgin girl), Mahamaya (the illusion), and the quaint Bhutanayaki (the queen of the *bhuta*s). In each form, she has an association with Shiva as the one channelling his energy. For instance, as Bhutanayaki, Mahadevi is the keeper of the secrets of life and death, as told to her by Lord Shiva, the *aghori* (a tantric practitioner), who dwells in graveyards and crematoriums. As Vindhyavasini, she brings the worship of Shiva, along with meditative practices and the yogic tradition, to the South, a region that was historically largely Vaishnavite. Now, many of these embodiments and attributes are also a result of the sociocultural evolution of India. In one version of the myth, it is stated that:

> Mahamuni Narada, on behalf of the gods, subsequently narrated to Mahadevi the humiliation the gods had to suffer at the hands of Mahisasura. She immediately came to their rescue and killed Mahisasura in a fierce battle (16.7). The event is recorded in the *Skanda*, the *Varaha*, the *Vamana*, and the *Siva Purana* and Devi-Mahatmya of the *Markandeya Purana*. The legend gets shaped with some difference at different hands and in different centuries, yet the nucleus of the myth remains by and large the same.[2]

In the worship of Devi, her devotees seek to appease her and sometimes wield her dark power with blood and animal sacrifice and the performance of wild, almost pagan-like rituals. These are, in fact, a part of some Durga Puja celebrations in the eastern states. I think what is truly remarkable in the worship of Mahadevi is the sense of agency left to the devotee. Turning to a darker form of worship is not frowned upon and one has the right to choose their path for uniting with the Divine. It is as if to say that we decide the world that we create through the ultimate creative force of Devi; will this world be one that is good and benevolent or one that is dark and destructive? I think this independence and ability to direct one's own journey towards a spiritual awakening and enlightenment is what draws countless devotees to the mystery of Mahadevi. Even the *tantrikas* have found an association with the goddess' sexual and magical powers, finding shelter at her feet in a world where their practices and ways of being are often shunned.

Devi has appeared in numerous episodes of the Mahabharata and the Puranic texts. In the Mahabharata, she is the strength and destructive force behind Draupadi, who fights for her honour with the same autonomy that Mahadevi embodies for all women. In the *Devi Mahatmya*, which is part of the *Markandeya Purana*, one of her most well-known legends is that of the end of Mahisha, the buffalo demon. It is a legend that is attributed to Durga, who is but a principal form of Mahadevi. Mahisha, who wanted to take over the world, had become a menace to all the three lokas. He had a boon from Brahma—he could not be killed by a man or an animal—and because of it, he imagined himself to be immortal.

Mahisha had never considered women to be of much worth and it hadn't even occurred to him that it was possible for a woman to bring about his end. When he saw the beautiful Durga, he proposed marriage, but when Durga moved away unimpressed, he tried to force her. This, in turn, led to the well-known battle between Devi and Mahishasura, immortalised by the *Mahishasura Mardini*

Stotra. The gods created Durga with their collective powers and the creative cosmic energies of Mahadevi. They gave her all their weapons; armed and ready for battle, Mahadevi brought an end to the menace that was Mahisha. This also marked the culmination of the thought process that minimised the strength of a woman and underestimated her ability to stand up for herself and take action to protect herself.

In her iconography, Mahadevi is depicted as an ethereal woman riding a lion into battle. In contrast, we also see her sometimes as Mahadevi Kali, with harsh features, skin gleaming a dark midnight blue, blood-red mouth and her lolling tongue dripping with fresh blood. In the Bengali Lokayata Shakta tradition, she is commonly described as Shyama, as the invocation goes:

> *Crazy is my Father, crazy is my Mother,*
> *And I, their son, am crazy too!*
> *Shyama is my Mother's name.*
> *My Father strikes His cheeks and makes a hollow sound:*
> *Ba-ba-boom! Ba-ba-boom!*
>
> *And my Mother, drunk and reeling,*
> *Falls across my Father's body!*
> *Shyama's streaming tresses hang in vast disorder;*
> *Bees are swarming numberless*
> *about Her crimson Lotus Feet.*
> *Listen, as She dances, how Her anklets ring!*[3]

This form is particularly popular with the worshippers of Shaktism and Shaivism. One of her earliest representations is in a cave near Mallapuram, dating all the way back to the 7th or 8th century CE. Similarly, another depiction from the mid-8th century CE at the Kailashanatha temple at Ellora shows her as Durga in the action of slaying Mahisha. This kind of iconography has been so popularised in India for its empowering imagery that it has been canonised and embedded into the artistic, cultural and architectural traditions, which vary from region to region. Durga, or Mahadevi, is known and loved by her fervent devotees in her most powerful form, as she is shown in the relief sculpture at Kailashanatha—a four-armed goddess atop her lion trampling the evil followers of Mahisha as she faces the buffalo demon, ready to brandish her many weapons.

Sati

मानसे दक्षहस्तो मे देवी दाक्षायणी हर।
अमरो भैरवस्तत्र सर्वसिद्धिप्रदायक:॥

My right hand fell at Manasa;
Devi there is known as Dakshayani.
There is the immortal Bhairava;
Devi there is the giver of all spiritual accomplishments.

—Shakti Peetha Stotra

The myths and legends in Hindu culture teach devotees lessons in morality, strength, tolerance, patience and bravery. These quaint anecdotes of *devi*s and *devata*s, sometimes interspersed with distractingly attractive *apsara*s up to no good or with raging sages, both entertain and teach us lessons about the complexities of living in an ever-changing and tough society. The story of Devi Sati is one that embodies the struggles of the human world, namely, the struggles of being a fiercely independent woman in a society that is not yet ready to accept such independence. Sati was the first consort of Lord Shiva; she was extremely fierce and known equally for her frightening temper and loving, gentle nature.

According to legend, Sati and Parvati were but different aspects of Devi who manifested as humans to guide Shiva away from his ascetic isolation and involve him in the ways of samsara, the material world. While both Sati and

Parvati loved Shiva, their ways of expressing it seem to have conformed to different social expectations. Where Sati appears to symbolise wild and uncontrolled energy, Parvati, who follows later, seems to be tinged with a gentler domesticity, a benevolent power that perseveres with patience. Not to say that Devi Parvati did not have a sense of agency—episodes such as the birth of Ganesha and Kartikeya, which will be discussed later in the text, certainly speak to the independence and agency of the goddess. However, it is correct to assume that both the forms of Devi, Sati and Parvati, symbolise self-determination, an indomitable will, perseverance, passion and a fiery nature. This is perhaps why, among the 51 legends associated with Shakti, Devi Sati plays an important role.

> As David Kinsley writes, two other temples whose primary deity is not a Mahavidya are interesting because they are related to Sati and the origin of the Mahavidyas. The temple of Jvalamukhi-devi in Himachal Pradesh prominently depicts the Mahavidyas on the walls of a large pavilion, separate from the main shrine, which houses an image of Durga. Jvalamukhi-devi's temple is said to be the place where the goddess Sati's tongue fell when her body was chopped up by Visnu and so is one of the *sakta pithas*, sacred goddess sites, scattered all over India.[1]

According to the *Shiva Purana*, Devi Sati was also known as Dakshayani, the daughter of Daksha—the *prajapati* who was the creator of living beings. One of Lord Brahma's sons, Daksha was responsible for populating the earth and establishing the earliest of human civilisations. Prajapati Daksha and his queen consort Prasuti had for long desired to have a daughter. They turned to Lord Brahma to show them the way and, on his advice, donned the ochre robes of sages and *tapasvi*s, undergoing a long and rigorous penance to please Devi Adi Parashakti. Deep in the forest, they chose a bare spot for practising meditation, bearing the brunt of the harsh elements and wilderness in all their primitive charm, never once letting any external stimuli shift their focus from their goal of appeasing the Devi.

After a sufficiently long test of patience, Devi Adi Parashakti finally appeared before the couple. She is described in the Puranic texts as having an effulgent form, bearing a thousand arms that held infinite weapons. Draped in a blood-red sari and bedecked with intricate ornaments studded with gems, the goddess wore armour made of pure gold and a crown atop her bright forehead. She was pleased with the couple's worship, granting them any boon they wished. Daksha asked the goddess for a daughter and the Devi granted the boon, informing them that she herself would be born to them. With her boon also came a warning: if she were ever to be insulted or disrespected, she would return to her original form, leaving behind her human body and the ties to that human form.

There are two notable points of interest here. The first is the purity of the relationship between the Divine and the devotee. There are numerous tales in Hindu mythology that show us example after example of divine boons gone wrong. This makes us wonder: if the gods, as omnipresent beings, already know of the possible pitfalls of a boon, why do they go through with the exercise at all? It is here that we must acknowledge the sanctity of the bond between the Divine and the worshipper. There is unconditional love and devotion, capable of seeing the highest potential in even the most flawed humans. It is this highest potential that the gods bestow their grace upon. The second point of note is the agency already given to Devi Sati even before her birth to have the option to leave her mortal form should she feel insulted or disgraced; this agency is lacking in the mythos of Devi Parvati and is, in some ways, indicative of the societal values of the time.

Soon after Prajapati Daksha and Queen Prasuti returned to the palace happily, Devi Adi Parashakti was born to the king and queen, as per her promise. The human incarnations of each of the trinity gods—Brahma, Vishnu and Shiva—occur to perform certain karmas in the mortal world; accordingly, Devi Adi Shakti was born as a woman to begin a new cycle of karma, one which was closely related to Lord Shiva. It was Adi Parashakti's will to bring Shiva out of ascetic penance, involving him closely with the matters of the human world. Shiva symbolised pure energy, and through Devi, this energy was harnessed for creation. So, the union of Shiva and Shakti was not only necessary but also inevitable for the future of mankind.

Even as a young girl, Sati felt a pull towards Shiva, spending her days immersed in his stories, legends and songs. Whenever Sage Narada would come by the palace to pay his respects to his brother, Prajapati Daksha, he would share a new story with Sati, cementing in her a deep devotion to Shiva. As she grew older, she received many marriage proposals from kings and princes from all across the lands, but she was adamant that if she were to get married, it would only be to Shiva.

The *Shiva Purana* describes Sati's journey to winning Shiva over, drawing parallels with the journey of a man seeking union with the Divine. It is for this reason that the stories of Sati and Parvati bear such significance in Hindu mythology. They show the path of bhakti, *tapas* and self-determination as a way of achieving salvation. Sati, having left the comforts of the palace, went deep into the forest to undergo severe austerities in her bid to appease Shiva and win his love. It is here that the stories of Sati and Parvati are virtually interchangeable, with most versions detailing Parvati's similar journey of ascetic penance in the icy cold caves of the Himalayas. The deeper the goddess meditated, the more severe became her tapas, renouncing food and water and sustaining herself on a single leaf per day, which she eventually gave up. She forsook her clothes and any other form of covering herself, bearing the harsh elements and earning the epithet of Aparna—the one who sustained on nothing but a leaf.

So much heat was generated by Devi's tapas that the gods started to worry that the concentration of the energies might end up destroying the world, and a world destroyed by Adi Shakti herself would be impossible to rebuild. They turned to Shiva, who had been keeping an eye on this strangely determined young woman seeking him as her consort. He finally agreed to accept her as his bride, in turn recognising her as the rupa of Shakti.

However, Prajapati Daksha was not happy with the news of the union. It is here that we see the earliest example of a bifurcation in Hinduism, dividing the followers into sects of Vaishnavite worshippers, who worshipped Vishnu, and of Shaivite worshippers, who worshipped Shiva, each with separate traditions, ways of worship, rituals and lifestyles. As a Vaishnavite, Daksha could not bear his favourite daughter marrying, in his opinion, a lowly ascetic such as Shiva. Unable to deter his daughter from her choice, he watched her wed Shiva and leave for her marital home in Kailash. The grief was too much to bear and he cut all ties with his daughter and her husband.

Not long after the wedding, Daksha organised a grand yajna (sacrificial ritual) at his palace in honour of Vishnu, inviting everyone including kings, princes, gods, goddesses, Brahma and Vishnu. But Shiva and his wife Devi Sati were excluded from this occasion. Sati, on hearing about the yajna, turned to Shiva, begging him to join her in attendance. However, Shiva refused to go and advised Sati against it too, knowing full well the intentions with which Daksha had chosen to not extend them an invitation. Determined to be present at this great, most auspicious event, a forlorn Sati defied her husband's wishes and left for her father's kingdom all on her own. This is a fascinating point in the tale as it is representative of Devi's agency and independent nature, using which she made choices that were true to herself; first, she defied her father to marry the man of her own choosing, and second, she defied her husband to do what she believed to be her right as a daughter, i.e., attending a grand event in her father's home. When we follow Devi Parvati's story, not only do we find a father who willingly facilitated his daughter's quest for Shiva, but we also find a woman who chose diplomacy over outright rebellion to attain her wishes. Shiva, knowing well enough that Sati would be humiliated, sent his *gana*s after her to protect her, according to some sources, and to bring her back, according to others.

On seeing Sati arrive at the yajna, Daksha became furious, hurling insult after insult to humiliate not only Devi but also her beloved husband Shiva. Sati tried to plead with her father and placate him, but he refused to listen and continued to insult her in front of everyone assembled for the yajna. Finally, Sati, unable to tolerate any more of her father's insults, flew into a fearsome rage, embracing her primal form as Adi Parashakti. Before all those assembled at the inauspicious yajna, she reintroduced herself to Daksha as the eternal power of creation, whom he had disrespected. She stated that as a result of his insult, she would give up her mortal form by jumping into the sacrificial fire, rendering it inauspicious.

It is this earliest example of self-immolation that is said

to have set the precedent for the Indian practice of sati. The tradition infamously came to be seen as representative of Devi's intense love, devotion and loyalty towards her husband that made it impossible for her to tolerate his being disrespected by her father. In India, this controversial practice of sati continued for a long time in rural areas, wherein widows would jump onto their deceased husbands' funeral pyres. This was supposedly done so that the widow could uphold her honour, as well as that of her husband and his family, but also so that she did not become what was considered a 'burden' upon the family. It was justly abolished in 1829 through the efforts of Raja Ram Mohan Roy.

Nowadays, people tend to associate the sati practice with the Rajputs, especially after Roop Kanwar was forced to immolate herself in an act of sati,[2] although there are notable exceptions. Romila Thapar has noted that the sati practice is most common among the Kshatriyas, who have a relatively 'high status'.[3] There are satis in other communities too, but higher castes are often leery of lower-caste satis.[4] This century has witnessed the rise of large inter-caste cults devoted to satis from various communities.[5]

On learning about Sati's sacrifice, an enraged and grief-stricken Shiva stormed the yajna and performed *tandava* (the dance of destruction), which created a concentration of negative cosmic energies, destroying everything in its wake. He pulled one of his *jata*s, from which sprang Virabhadra, Shiva's fierce and destructive manifestation. Dark and frightful, he had eight hands, each holding a weapon. From another jata arose Bhadrakali, the dark incarnation of Devi. Working together, the couple destroyed everything in sight, fuelled by Lord Shiva's boundless grief. According to some accounts, they were joined by eight other goddesses, all forms of the supreme Devi—Chamundi, Ishaani, Kali,

Mundamardini, Bhadra, Katyayani, Vaishnavi and Twarita.

According to the *Devi Bhagavata Purana*, Virabhadra severed Daksha's head for instigating the whole episode. The other goddesses attacked the assembly and all those who were present there. The destruction continued through the night till Devi's primordial form eventually appeared to Shiva, appealing to him to stop the destruction, restore what had been torn apart, and bring back those he had slain, for it was already destined that she would return. Shiva, in turn, restored everything to as it had been and brought back Daksha by substituting his head with that of a goat as a humbling reminder of his grave mistake for the entirety of his life. This gesture of forgiveness and grace on Shiva's part transformed Daksha into a devotee of Lord Shiva—a faith he would continue to follow for the rest of his life.

Shiva, too grief-stricken to partake in the human world, held tight the lifeless body of Sati, roaming the three lokas and bemoaning his loss. According to one legend in the *Shiva Purana*, Vishnu dismembered Sati's body by cutting it into several pieces with his Sudarshana Chakra. These 51 body parts became a manifestation of her primordial energy wherever they fell on earth and came to be known as the Shakti Peethas. This was the only way in which Shiva would truly let go of Sati, his beloved wife and consort. Later, when Shiva regained his senses, he created a *bhairava* for each Shakti Peetha, protecting and preserving the goddess' form and also creating a union between Shakti and Shiva.

> According to Kinsley, the Mahavidyas have a dual role in Shiva's life. On one hand, it appeases Shiva, and on the other, it terrifies Shiva as well, varying from one version to the other of the Mahavidyas. As he writes, in versions 1 and 2, the Mahavidyas emerge against a background of male–female tensions, and there may

be the implication of such tension in version 3 as well. This tension arises when the goddess feels abused, ignored, or insulted by her father or husband. In version 1, Sati becomes furious and transforms herself into such a horrible, frightening being that Siva can barely stand to look at her. The Mahavidyas are forms of this being, further personifications of Shati's wrath. Version 1 makes clear, and versions 2 and 3 imply, that the goddess, Shiva's spouse in each case, has a will of her own and is perfectly capable of exercising that will even if it means going against her husband or father. The point cannot be missed in version 1: Sati is not content to remain a passive, obedient, submissive wife if she is sufficiently provoked. She contains aspects and powers that easily overwhelm and frighten her husband.[6]

The tale of Sati raises many questions for a reader or student of Hindu mythology. Why did Sati choose to take her own life? Why did she not choose to walk away? The riddle reveals a different answer with each rendering of the myth. Sati is an enigma. Having led a life of immense discipline, devotion and tapas, she had attained yogic siddhis. However, her intention was never the renunciation of the world; it was rather a creative embrace of all the desires of the material world through the life of a householder.

Shiva, the ascetic, was as far from being a householder as one could imagine, and to attain her goal, Sati adopted the austerity of the ascetic way. Daksha's prejudice against Shiva stemmed from his faith and materialistic outlook; as the mind-born son of Brahma, though he had astute intelligence, Daksha was prone to the vices of the ego. The *prajapati* was materialistic and lived a life of luxury and rituals, far away from the austerity of asceticism. Sati too, one can assume, grew up in a similar environment, yet tale after tale speaks of her individual yearning for the ascetic life from a very young age. It was her desire to break free from the trappings of the illusory world through her inner individualism that ultimately brought her, however briefly, the joy of a spiritual union with Shiva. This union, in turn, brought Shiva closer to a degree of materialism as a householder, and in doing so, Sati was the unifier of two opposing philosophical traditions.

Daksha and Shiva, representative of these opposing thoughts, were eventually compelled to form a truce due to the self-sacrifice of Sati, who ended the conflict. In the *Devi Bhagavata Purana*, Sati's sacrifice was seen as an extension of her ascetic inclinations. In the *Shiva Purana*, the fire in which she burnt was not *agni*; it was rather her own yogic fire, consuming her from within. Aware of the pain she would cause her husband, she promised to return to him and reunite the opposing forces of the universe—Purusha and Prakriti—in the form of Parvati, a more seasoned and stable version of herself. She had purpose even in death—each part of her in the form of a Shakti Peetha would establish dharma on earth. Her individual life and death were symbolic of the circle of life at large, wherein what is born must die, and death is what makes way for new life.

Parvati

सर्वमङ्गलमाङ्गल्ये शिवे सर्वार्थसाधिके।
शरण्ये त्र्यम्बके गौरि नारायणि नमोऽस्तुते

*Goddess Parvati is the auspiciousness in all that is auspicious.
She is the consort of Lord Shiva, who grants every desire of
one's heart.
I adore Devi Parvati, who loves all her children.
I bow to the great mother, who has given refuge to me.*

—*Durga Saptashati*, Saptashloki Durga, Verse 3

There is a certain beauty in the mythological tales of Devi Sati and Devi Parvati, wherein the failings of destiny are finally rectified and the story reaches its conclusion. While the former fell short of attaining her life's purpose, the latter, following the lessons represented by Devi Sati's manifestation, successfully achieved a lasting union with Shiva as Parvati, which Devi and the entire creation had so desired.

We now know the tragic end of Devi Sati's story marked by her wilful independence, self-determination and fierce passion. According to the *Shiva Purana*, as the human embodiment of Devi Adi Parashakti, it was Sati's destiny to find union with Shiva, bringing together Purusha and Prakriti. When she failed to do so, the entire creation was off-kilter, left unbalanced and in a sea of chaotic cosmic energies. Devi had to manifest in human form once again in an attempt to entice Shiva away from his penance, which was all the more severe following the grief and trauma of losing Sati. The task was not an easy one, and Devi Parashakti had to be born in an environment that would be supportive of her purpose—to parents who would help rather than hinder her path—and so she chose the mountain god King Himavan of the Himalayas and his beloved apsara wife, Menavati.

> In another reference occurring in the same Samhita, Ambika is mentioned as a sister of Rudra. 'This is your share, O Rudra! Enjoy it together with your sister Ambika.' This ambivalence of the female counterpart sometimes as sister and sometimes as wife of a male god considered to be the originator or creator of the world, is quite common in religious beliefs, especially when it is related to the first pair of the creation. The first pair is born together either of its own or brought into existence by some higher power and can variously be conceived either as brother-sister twins or as husband-wife, the progenitor of entire future creation, the jagatah pitarau—Parvati and Parmesvara of Kalidasa.[1]

The *Shiva Purana* describes King Himavan as an ardent worshipper of Lord Shiva. He too desired a daughter, and to attain this boon from Parashakti, he and his queen consort Menavati spent years in the cold, rocky terrain of the Himalayas, worshipping the goddess. After a long time spent in penance, the goddess, finally appeased by the couple's devotion, appeared before them, granting them the boon of a daughter. However, the girl was to be no ordinary being but Devi Shakti herself in human form. Uma Parvati, whose name literally means 'the daughter of the mountain', was destined to grow up and be the wife of

Shiva, and she was believed to be another incarnation or form of Sati. Parvati was one of Himavan's two daughters; Ganga, the older daughter, too had a significant association with Shiva and her story will be explored later in the book. In many ways, it seems to be a precursor to Parvati's story.

It is important to recognise here that as the daughter of Himavan, Devi Parvati shared many qualities with the forest goddess Aranyani from the Vedic texts or with Rudrani, Rudra's consort. I think this might have been a way of cementing the goddess' association with Himavan, or perhaps it was an attempt to unify and stitch together the earlier aspects of an elemental Vedic goddess with the Puranic Adi Shakti. In Vedic literature, Devi Parvati's name doesn't come up till much later in the Puranic period.

In the *Kena Upanishad*'s Verse 3.12, dating back to the mid-first millennium BCE, we hear of a goddess called Uma-Hemavati, a common name used for Parvati. How Parvati earned the name Uma-Parvati or Uma-Hemavati is once again a story similar to Devi Sati's; in fact, in many renditions of Devi texts, it is a shared myth featuring both Parvati and Sati, where the name is used for both interchangeably.

As the story goes, in order to marry Shiva, Parvati too had to undergo severe penance, much like Sati. But in the case of Parvati, Shiva was lost in deep meditation in the Himalayan caves. Hearing of his presence, Himavan sent his daughter Parvati to clean the Lord's dwelling place and provide him with fruits, clean water and all the hospitality befitting an honourable guest's stay in the Himalayan kingdom. Himavan knew his daughter's destiny and was providing a gentle nudge towards it. While caring with great devotion for the sage, who she did not yet know was Shiva, Parvati slowly but surely fell in love with him. As he was passing by, Kamadeva caught a glimpse of the couple, who were destined to be together. He decided to meddle and from his quiver of floral arrows, he shot one straight at the meditating Shiva.

Shiva, on opening his eyes, felt a pull towards the young and beautiful maiden who had been caring for him so diligently while he was meditating. He felt desire rise in his chest, but it carried a tinge of unexplainable exaggeration. The world around him seemed ever so bright and slightly fantastical, as though it were part of a great illusion. The suspicious Shiva felt certain that a divine being had meddled, and looking about Parvati, he caught sight of Kama with his bow of desire in hand, watching the couple from afar. The *Shiva Purana* describes the fierce rage that Shiva flew into, instantaneously incinerating the god of desire on that very spot, leaving Parvati quaking, who, through no fault of her own, had been subjected to a most horrid first meeting.

As a forlorn Parvati returned to her father's palace, she met with Sage Narada, who advised her in the ways of the ascetic yogic traditions to earn Shiva's love. It was here that Parvati took the first step towards the journey of a person's union with the Divine, which is represented through her own tapas to experience union with Shiva.

According to the Ramayana, Menavati, unable to see her daughter walk away from the comforts of the palace in the plain ochre robes of a yogini, cried, 'Uma! Uma!' This is how the goddess received her name Uma-Parvati or Uma-Hemavati. Despite her mother's cries, a determined Parvati, much like Sati, chose to undergo severe penance to attain her union with Shiva. Her determination and patience were so great that today, as much as she is a symbol of marital felicity, she is also undeniably an example of immense will in the yogic tradition. No one had yet mastered the tapas, or the yogic tradition, as quickly and adeptly as Parvati, and her *ojas* was so great that the gods began to worry again and gathered before Shiva. However, having lost and grieved Sati already, he was somewhat apprehensive of quickly jumping into another union.

Shiva thus tested Parvati, tempting her and offending her by dressing up as a sage and speaking ill of her beloved Shiva. There are, in fact, numerous regional renderings of this episode, which capture the traps laid by Shiva before Parvati, and how she succeeded each time with her devotion and determination. Finally, unable to listen to any more taunts and ill words about Shiva, Parvati decided to leave her meditation cave, remove herself from the presence of the loathsome sage (Shiva in disguise), and begin her tapas again. Just as she was leaving, Shiva took his own form again and asked the goddess to accept her place as his wife.

In both Parvati's and Sati's quests, there are many points of similarities, but, as I have mentioned before, there are also many points of differences, with Devi Sati's story providing many lessons. For instance, an episode narrated in the Puranas shows Devi Parvati using her diplomacy to bring her mother, the apsara Menavati, around to see Shiva as a viable groom. She managed to convince Shiva to transform into his pleasant avatar of Chandrashekhara, a householder, so that her mother might bid her off to her marital home with a light heart, not fearing the odd state and company that Lord Shiva was known to keep. This is perhaps an early example of how Parvati involved Mahadeva in the affairs of humans and the material world, where matters of superficial concern sometimes needed to be attended to for the sake of a good balance.

In the sacred literature of Gujarat, I am particularly drawn to the tale of Gauri, or Mahagauri, the fair one, and Shyama, the dark one. There are various stories about how the goddess earned the name Mahagauri, which all begin with an episode in which Shiva mocked Devi Parvati's dark complexion in jest. Annoyed by the remark, Devi performed intense tapas and requested Brahma to rid her of all her impurity and darkness, leaving her with the golden hue of the goddess Mahagauri. From the discarded dark form came Mahakali, or Shyama, the other side of Gauri.

As two opposing forms, Gauri became the placid and calm wife and Kali the fierce warrior and agent of destruction. Many people in Gujarat and Rajasthan in fact keep a Gauri *vrata* (or fast), considered to be most auspicious for earning Adi Shakti's blessings for a happy marriage, pregnancy and family life. The fast often occurs during the harvest season, which is why Devi Mahagauri is also associated with golden-yellow ripened corn.

Interestingly, the legend of Devi Parvati is also associated with one of the most important legends of the Dasa Mahavidyas. As the story goes:

> One day, Parvati went to bathe in the Mandakini River with her attendants, Jaya and Vijaya. After bathing, the great goddess' colour became black because she was sexually aroused. After some time, her two attendants asked her, 'Give us some food. We are hungry.' She replied, 'I shall give you food but please wait.' After a while, they again asked her. She again replied, 'Please wait, I am thinking about some matters.' Waiting a while, they implored her, 'You are the mother of the universe. A child asks for everything from her mother. [...] So that is why we are praying to you for food. You are known for your mercy, please give us food.' [...] 'We are overpowered with hunger, O Mother of the Universe. Give us food so we may be satisfied, O Merciful One, Bestower of Boons and Fulfiller of Desires.'
>
> Hearing this true statement, the merciful goddess smiled and severed her head with her fingernails.

As soon as she severed her head, it fell on the palm of her left hand. Three bloodstreams emerged from her throat; the left and right fell respectively into the mouths of her attendants who were flanking her while the centre one fell into her mouth. [...] From this act, Parvati came to be known as Chhinnamasta.[2]

It is as a mother perhaps that Devi Parvati's agency and independence shine the brightest for me. Kalidasa's poem 'Kumarasambhava' ('The Birth of Kumara') is a retelling of the birth story of Mahadeva and Parvati's firstborn son. None of Parvati's children had a natural birth. Kartikeya, according to Devi texts, was born through the dance of creation, forming a union between Shiva and Parvati. He was born from the seed of Mahadeva and the divine spiritual shakti of Parvati outside of Devi's womb. So intense were the cosmic energies rising from the divine couple that they could not be held by the cold waters of the Ganga or the stability of Prithvi, with each of these goddesses playing the role of surrogates for Kumara. He was eventually found by six apsaras in the forests by the Ganga's shores, where he was raised as the six-headed warrior Kartikeya. Parvati, having created him using her yogic fire, shared motherhood with Krittikas, the forest nymphs.

The story of Ganesha's birth similarly recounts the spiritual and ascetic powers of Parvati. She created a boy by collecting the dirt from her own body and moulding it into a doll, which was then animated to life. Driven by loneliness and the yearning for a child, Parvati used her agency, will and independence to create a child even in the absence of her husband Shiva. Getting Ganesha to then guard her bathing area and prevent Shiva from entering her innermost sanctum is a depiction of Parvati's individual will and agency.

When Shiva severed Ganesha's head, Parvati was so

enraged that her Mahakali form nearly destroyed the universe till Shiva replaced his head with that of an elephant and reanimated Ganesha, breathing new life into the boy. Shiva once again completed the union between Purusha and Prakriti by bringing Ganesha back to life through the yogic energies of both his father and mother. However, the first step towards creation was taken by Parvati and not Shiva.

It is always Parvati who draws Shiva into the ways of the world. In tantric literature, most of the teachings are shared in the form of a dialogue between Lord Shiva and Devi Parvati. She is the medium through which divine knowledge is passed on to humans. In this role of hers, she opens a doorway for the many aspects of Shiva himself: teacher, lover, husband, father and more. Their relationship also unfolds as that of a sweet and cherished couple having a lover's quarrel. For example, regarding Ganga's habitat in Shiva's world, there was an instance when Parvati became jealous. Hence, to clarify what Parvati meant to him, we can notice how in the *Skanda Purana*, Shiva, while speaking to Vishnu, resolves the issue by identifying Ganga with Parvati as the female aspect of the Divine:

> As Gauri (Parvati) is, so is the Ganga. Therefore, whoever worships Gauri properly also worships the Ganga. And as I am, so are you, O Visnu. And as you are, so am I. And as Uma (Parvati) is, so is the Ganga. The form is not different. And whoever says that there is some difference between Visnu and Rudra, between Sri and Gauri, or between the Ganga and Gauri is a very foolish person.[3]

Parvati becomes a transforming energy to his wild ascetic nature, bringing domesticity to her husband. It is in this balance that their divine union works. This dual character is inherent in the cosmos. Shiva, as the *brahman*, through ascetic practices, accumulates immense power that is so potent, unstable and wild that it is capable of mass destruction, while Devi Parvati embodies the creative energy that funnels this raw power, domesticating and stabilising it to create a universe of semblance and order.

Durga Mahishamardini

रोगानशेषानपहँसि तुष्टा, रुष्टा तु कामान् सकलानभीष्टान्।
त्वामाश्रितानां न विपन्नराणां, त्वामाश्रिता ह्याश्रयतां प्रयान्ति।।

*When you are pleased with our devotion,
You destroy all our (worldly) diseases;
but if you are displeased with us,
You destroy all our aspirations and wishes.
Those in your refuge can never go astray
and no misfortunes will befall them;
Your refuge is indeed the final refuge that one attains.*

—*Durga Saptashati*, Chapter 11, Verse 29

ॐ जयन्ती मङ्गला काली भद्रकाली कपालिनी।
दुर्गा क्षमा शिवा धात्री स्वाहा स्वधा नमोऽस्तु ते।।

*Salutations to Jayanti (who is ever-victorious),
Mangala (who is the bestower of auspiciousness),
Kali (who is beyond time),
Bhadrakali (who is the controller of death and life), and
Kapalini (who wears a garland of skulls),
Salutations to Durga (who is the Mother Goddess),
Kshama (who is an embodiment of forbearance),
Shiva (who is ever-auspicious),
Dhatri (who is the supporter of all sentient beings),
Swaha (who is the final receiver of the sacrificial
oblations to gods), and*

> *Svadha (who is the final receiver of the sacrificial oblations to manes).*
>
> —*Durga Saptashati*, Argala Stotram, Verse 1

*E*ver since I was a child, I have been hearing my father recite these two *shloka*s, particularly during Navaratri. The first shloka is dedicated to the all-powerful Durga, who is simply invincible. The second shloka would be uttered while tying the *mauli* (sacred red thread) around my right wrist until I was unmarried and around my left wrist now that I am married. This shloka is a preventive measure for any disease that may de-energise the devotee. Twice a year, as per the Hindu calendar, there are nine days dedicated to the worship of the mighty Durga, a manifestation of Shakti Herself.

The first round of Navaratri Puja is held in the month of Chaitra, as per the Hindu calendar, which, like most South Asian cultures, is based on the lunar system. It is the first month of the year. Navaratri means nine nights of praying to and worshipping the goddess. The Chaitra Navaratri concludes with Ram Navami, i.e., the birthday of Lord Rama. The second Navaratri, also known as the Ashvin Navaratri, culminates with Dussehra or Vijayadashami and has a direct connection with Lord Rama. On this day, Rama killed the greatest of asuras—Ravana, the demon king of Lanka.

I still love stories, and naturally, each and every story around the different avatars of Devi is as enticing as ever. One of my favourite goddesses is undoubtedly Durga. My first recollection of Durga is associated with the colourful calendar that would be hung in our kitchen, where my parents' house help always had a lamp burning in front of the goddess' image. Over the years, as I studied art history,

I saw various depictions of Durga in miniature paintings, in the kalamkari textiles, in the Bengali *patachitra* (scroll paintings), in the interiors of temples, and in the hundreds of pandals over the years of pandal-hopping during Durga Puja celebrations in India. However, my strongest memory, which is still the most evocative, is of the one who smiled at me from the calendar in my mother's kitchen.

With eyes gleaming like fire and translucent skin emanating overpowering energy, Goddess Durga is a terrifying sight to behold. She has 10 arms, a well-endowed body, voluptuous breasts and long dark tresses as she sits astride a lion, her preferred mode of transport (*vahana*). Each of her 10 arms carries a powerful weapon, ranging from a trishula to a chakra, from a *gada* to a *pasha*, and from a sword to a bow. With such powerful weapons at her command, which the mighty Durga uses with consummate skill, She is invincible. Durga is yet another manifestation of the eternal Shakti and Her emergence forms a unique story.

According to legend, Durga, who fought valiantly against several demons, was created out of the combined energies of the holy trinity of Brahma, Vishnu and Mahesh. All the gods of the heavens, or Indraloka, further supported her. In my calendar image, Durga was depicted sitting on her vahana with 10 arms, holding a different weapon in each hand such that each of the weapons was being given to her by a particular god. Her 10 arms also represent the 10 directions, in all of which she protects her devotees.

In one hand, she holds the conch gifted by Varuna, the god of the sea; in two of her hands, she holds the bow and arrow gifted by Vayu, the wind god; in another hand, she holds the thunderbolt of Indra, the king of the gods; in yet another hand, she holds the lotus, the symbol of steadfastness and spirituality; in another, she holds the discus (chakra) of Vishnu; in another, the longsword; and in another, Brahma's *kamandalu* holding the holy water; and in her forearms, she carries the powerful trident of Lord Shiva, which stars in the final act of killing Mahishasura.

Like Shiva, she is also *trayambake*, the three-eyed goddess. Her left eye represents desire as well as the peace and calmness of the moon. Her right eye is representative of the power of the sun, and her middle eye is the all-knowing eye of all knowledge, with the ability to turn to ash whatever is undesirable.

Naturally, in keeping with her powerful status, Durga's vahana is the lion, the all-powerful beast of the jungle who rules it with his physical strength as well as mental intelligence. Durga is often depicted either standing aloft the lion or sitting astride it in a way that shows control and power over the king of the jungle. Thus, another power is added to the might of the mighty goddess herself.

Yet another parallel legend goes like this: It is believed that when Durga came out of the waters of the Ganga as a spirit, she was given a physical form as a collaborative exercise between the devas. Her face was created by Shiva, torso by Indra, breasts by Chandra and teeth by Brahma. The lower part of her body was the work of Bhudevi; Varuna sculpted her thighs and knees; and Agni created her eyes. She thus became all-powerful as Durga, or Mahamaya, the mother of the universe who ensured the creation, preservation and destruction of evil; in short, she had amassed the collective energies of the Holy Trinity. So, now we come to the obvious question: why was Durga created from the eternal goddess Shakti?

She is not a benign, kind goddess like Lakshmi or Saraswati; she will kick you into action. Durga is fierce. She is mighty. She was created to slay the shapeshifter demon Mahishasura, to kill the demons Madhu and Kaitabha, to fight the evil present on earth, and to restore the good. As

Durgatinashini, she eliminated suffering. As she fought, she created tales of adventure and awe that continue to thrill her devotees and invoke deep faith in them.

These tales went on to be called the *Durga Saptashati* in the North, the *Devi Mahatmya* in South India, and the *Chandipath* in West Bengal. Compiled and penned by Ved Vyasa (the author of the Mahabharata), the *Durga Saptashati* is found in the *Markandeya Purana*. Consisting of 13 chapters, the book recounts Devi's tales of valour over the course of 700 stanzas. Devi defeated and killed through different avatars. She killed some demons through the *tamasic* avatar of Goddess Vishnu Maya, some through the *rajasic* avatar of Goddess Lakshmi, and yet others through the *sattvic* avatar of Goddess Saraswati. Yet the most interesting mythological tale concerning the celebration of the Navaratras centres on Shiva. In a popular version of the Shakta religion, Navaratri becomes associated with one of the Mahavidyas of the Dasa Mahavidyas. For example, a story shared by an aghori from Bakreshwar, a pilgrimage centre in Birbhum, explained that:

> Siva [...] was the hero, the god of the non-Aryans. In the opinion of the Aryans, the followers of the Siva were degraded, fallen... Siva used to live in Kailasa [and] did not live in other parts of the Himalayas, since the Himalayas were the heaven of the Aryans and under their control. But he married a girl from these Himalayas. She, the daughter of an Aryan ruler, having heard of his [Siva's] virtues, intensely propitiated him to be able to garland him [...] when Uma (another name of Sati, Parvati, Durga—the daughter of the Aryan ruler Daksa) married Siva, all the Aryan gods were mad with anger. How could Siva dare to marry the daughter of an Aryan ruler! They looked for an opportunity to teach him a lesson, or test his prowess. It was because of this that the Daksha Yajna ceremony was organised.

But when [at the ceremony] the Aryans got to know about Siva's divine supernatural powers, they lost their pride; they had to bow down to Siva. Siva then becomes Mahesvara [the highest among all the gods].[1]

In Sanskrit, 'durga' means 'fort'—a secure, protected space. As Durgatinashini, she is also the one who eliminates all suffering. Durga thus symbolises one who protects her devotees and is also a remover of all evils. There is a procedure that needs to be followed while engaging in prayer rituals. For example, while reciting the *Durga Saptashati*, there are two common practices which I am personally aware of and are as follows: One is Trayangam, where three prayers are recited before reading the *Saptashati*, and the other is Navangam, where nine prayers are recited before reading the *Saptashati*.

Trayangam is a procedure where one recites the *Devi Kavacham*, *Argala Stotram* and *Devi Keelakam*, along with the *Navakshari Mantram*. Thereon, the 13 chapters of the *Durga Saptashati* are recited.

Navangam is a procedure where the following nine prayers are recited prior to the reading of the main text: the *Devi Nyasa, Devi Avahana, Devi Namami, Argala Stotram, Keelaka Stotram, Devi Hrudaya, Dhala, Devi Dhyana* and *Devi Kavacha*.

The *Durga Saptashati* is also recited during Navaratri, with the chapters divided among the nine days. Each day, a new chapter tells the story of the killing of specific demons by the mighty Durga. The first day starts with chapter 1, which is about Madhu–Kaithabha Samhar; the second day involves chapters 2, 3 and 4 about Mahishasura Samhar; the next chapters 5 and 6, on the third day, are about Dhumralochan Vadh; then the fourth day is chapter 7 about Chanda–Munda Vadh. Chapter 8 is recited on the fifth day, which is about Raktabij Samhar; the sixth day is for chapters 9 and 10 about Shumbha–Nishumbha Vadh; the seventh day starts with chapter 11, Narayani Stuti; this is followed by chapter 12 on the eighth day, which is about the benefits of recital or Phala Shruti; then the ninth day commences with chapter 13, in which Devi blesses Raja Suratha and Vaishya (merchants); the exercise concludes with the *Devi Aparadha Kshama Stotram* recited on the tenth day (Vijayadashami/Dussehra).

These chapters of the *Durga Saptashati*, the story of Devi's glory, are recited during Chandi Homa as well, which is performed on the eighth day (*ashtami*) of Navaratri. The benefits of reading the *Durga Saptashati*, specifically the twelfth chapter, are revealed to the gods by Devi Herself, including how the practice removes all troubles, protects from evil spirits, and bestows wealth, grains and children.[2]

Navadurgas

हताधिकारास्त्रिदशास्ताभ्यां सर्वे निराकृताः।
महासुराभ्यां तां देवीं संस्मरन्त्यपराजिताम्।।

*All gods, robbed of their authority and driven away
by those two great asuras, remembered that invincible goddess.*

—*Durga Saptashati*, Chapter 5, Verse 5

The tales of Devi symbolise the power of good over evil. Perhaps to remind oneself of this eternal truth, people recite the *Durga Saptashati* at their homes during the nine days of Navaratri. While listening to the glories of the goddess, the devotee revels in the realisation of Her omnipotence. In addition to the numerous tales related to Durga is that of the Navadurgas, her nine forms (swarupas or rupas). Each of the nine rupas is worshipped individually every evening. In Hinduism, it is believed that these manifestations originate from either Goddess Parvati or Tridevi (personified by Saraswati, Lakshmi and Parvati). The nine swarupas of Goddess Durga are Shailaputri, Brahmacharini, Chandraghanta, Kushmanda, Skandamata, Katyayani, Kaalratri, Mahagauri and Siddhidhatri.

Shailaputri

The first of the Navadurgas, she gets her name from her father—shaila means 'mountain' in Sanskrit. After self-immolation as Goddess Sati, Goddess Parvati took birth as the daughter of Lord Himalaya. She is also Shailaputri, since she is viewed as the most flawless epitome of Durga and the mother of nature. In iconography, she is portrayed riding a bull and holding a trident, its three prongs representing the past, present and future, and a lotus, symbolising virtue and dedication.

Brahmacharini

After Shailaputri, Goddess Parvati took birth in the home of Prajapati Daksha. In this manifestation, the goddess was revered as Brahmacharini. She holds a *japamala* in her right hand and a kamandalu (water pot) in her left hand. Devotees seek marital bliss, harmony, success and elegance from her.

Chandraghanta

Goddess Chandraghanta is the married form of Goddess Parvati. In the wake of getting married to Lord Shiva, Goddess Mahagauri began adorning her forehead with a half-moon, because of which she came to be known as Goddess Chandraghanta, or the one who has a half-moon shaped like a bell. She is the third appearance of Durga, embodying harmony, serenity and success in everyday life. Chandraghanta is beguiling, has a splendid composition, and rides a lion. Like Durga, Chandraghanta has numerous arms (usually ten), each holding a weapon, and three eyes. She is all-seeing and ever-careful, prepared to fight evil from every direction on Mother Earth.

Kushmanda

Goddess Parvati travelled to the location where Suryadev

resided, and using her divine power, she created a blazing sphere of fire and light around herself. As Parvati emerged from this fiery orb, she radiated the eternal beauty of the universe. From that point forward, the goddess came to be known as Kushmanda. She is the goddess who has the force and ability to live within the sun; the gleam and brilliance of her body are the centre of the sun. Kushmanda is the fourth type of Mother Goddess, and her name signifies 'the maker of the universe', for she is the person who enlightened the dim universe. Like the different appearances of Durga, Kushmanda has numerous arms (around eight to 10), in which she holds weapons, a spark, a japamala and other sacred items. The spark is especially critical in that it signifies the shimmering light that she brings to the world. Kushmanda rides a lion, representing strength and boldness despite the adversary.

Skandamata

When the goddess turned into the mother of Lord Skanda (otherwise called Kartikeya), Mata Parvati came to be known as Goddess Skandamata. She is revered on the fifth day of Navaratri. Accentuating her unadulterated and heavenly nature, Skandamata is positioned on a lotus and she has four arms and three eyes. She holds the newborn child Skanda in her right arm and a lotus in the same direction, which is raised upwards. In one of her left hands, she holds a second lotus.

Katyayani

To annihilate the devil Mahishasura, Goddess Parvati appeared as Goddess Katyayani, who is a fierce avatar of the goddess. In this form, she is also known as the Warrior

Goddess. Katyayani is revered on the sixth day of Navaratri. Like Kaalratri, who is worshipped the next night, Katyayani is a fearsome sight, with wild hair and 18 arms, each gripping a weapon. She emits a brilliant light from her body that evil cannot ignore. Regardless of her appearance, she projects a feeling of quiet and internal harmony upon those who believe in her. Like Kushmanda, Katyayani rides a lion, always prepared to fight evil.

Kaalratri

When Goddess Parvati eliminated two evil asuras named Shumbha and Nishumbha, she came to be known as Goddess Kaalratri. She is another one of the Goddess' fierce and brutal forms. Kaalratri is otherwise known as Shubhankari, which means 'the one who does good'. She is dark-complexioned, with rumpled hair, four arms and three eyes. The breath from her mouth can reduce anyone to ashes. Like Kali, the goddess who obliterates evil, she is both respected and dreaded. In her left hand, she holds a *vajra* (mace) and a sickle sword, both of which she uses in various battles against evil. Her right hands, in contrast, gesture blessings and protection from darkness, easing all feelings of trepidation.

Mahagauri

According to legend, Goddess Mahagauri came to be known as such at 16 years old because of her limitless beauty. Her name alludes to the brilliant aura that is emitted by her body. Hindus believe that by giving proper respect to Mahagauri, all past, present and future sins will be washed away, resulting in a profound feeling of internal harmony. She wears white garments, has four arms, and rides a bull, quite possibly the holiest creature in Hinduism. Her upper right hand's posture alleviates fear, while her lower right hand holds a trident. Her upper left hand holds a *damaru* (a small drum), while the lower one bestows boons to her devotees.

Siddhidhatri

At the start of the universe, Lord Rudra revered Adi Parashakti for creation. However, she had no physical manifestation. The incomparable goddess of power, Adi Parashakti emerged as Siddhidhatri from the left side of Lord Shiva's body. She is the last form of Navadurga, celebrated on the last evening of Navaratri. Her name signifies 'the one who awards extraordinary powers'. Siddhidhatri grants astuteness and understanding to individuals who revere her. Similar to many of Durga's appearances, Siddhidhatri too rides a lion. She has four arms and carries a mace, a chakra (discus), a *shankha* (conch shell), and a lotus. The shankha represents one's life span, while the chakra represents the spirit of immortality.

∽

More recently, in the words of Stanley Kurtz, Goddess Durga has another attribute. He argues that the dynamics of Hindu child-rearing practices call for a radical reshaping of psychoanalytic concepts. The ideas of unity and multiplicity in Hindu traditions is uniquely represented by the legend of Durga due to her role in collective mothering. She is the symbol of tranquillity, serenity and purity. Contesting Freud's oedipal complex, Kurtz advocates for a more nuanced understanding of the Durga complex.[1]

Durga by herself is too multi-layered and a highly nuanced goddess who can at once be mighty, unforgiving and powerful, or, as Shantadurga in her temple in Goa, quiet. Further, as Durganashini, she is the destroyer of evil, bringing everlasting joy to her believers by putting an end to all their worldly sufferings. Perhaps this is why she is so popular.

Girija

जय जय गिरिवर राज किशोरी। जय महेश मुख चन्द चकोरी।
जय गजबदन षडाननमाता। जगत जननी दामिनि दुति गाता।।
नहिं तव आदि मध्य अवसाना। अमित प्रभाउ बेदु नहिं जाना।
भव भव विभव पराभव कारिनि। विश्व बिमोहनि स्वबस बिहारिनि।।

Hail to you, O daughter of the mountain king!
Be victorious, the one with the face of Lord Shiva and the moon!
Glory to you, O mother of Ganapati and Kartikeya;
O mother of the world!
Hail to you, O one with a body as bright as lightning!
You have no beginning, middle and end.
Even the Vedas do not know your unlimited influence.
O Mother! You create, sustain and destroy this world.
You are captivating the world and are the best.

—Devi Girija Strotram

As the only god and consort bearing a cosmic domestic family, Shiva and Parvati offer innumerable tales and forms that celebrate and venerate the role of the householder and domestic life. The forms of the god and goddess change as we move from one region to another; however, they are significant in that they show us the path to moksha (enlightenment) through the life of the householder. The tale of Goddess Girija is one such legend. Girija is an form of Devi Parvati and much of her myth comes from the *Girija Kalyana*, a text that is part of the *Shiva Purana*. As Sally Kempton says, 'Other names for Parvati are Gauri—the fair one, Minakshi—she with eyes like slender fishes, Shive—feminine form of Shiva, Girija—daughter of the mountain, Uma—maiden, Haimavati—she who belongs to the mountain king Himavat.'[1]

The story of Girija is part of Hampi's folklore and culture. We usually get to see different scenes and events from the story of Girija Kalyana in several murals and inscriptions depicting examples that are to be embodied in one's own life. I think it is a particularly fascinating aspect of Goddess Girija's mythology that her legends, tales and stories are not just a means of entertainment, reverence or veneration but are also about adopting the essence of her qualities in one's own life, embodying the philosophy woven through these myths.

Hampi has been mentioned as a sacred site in various Puranic texts such as the *Shiva Purana*, *Vaishnava Purana*, *Jaina Purana*, *Sthala Purana* and *Janapada Purana*. It has deep roots in Hindu philosophical tradition and mythology. The *Girija Kalyana*, which tells us tales of Devi Girija, is an excerpt from the *Shiva Purana* and has a significant association with the ancient city of Hampi. As the legend suggests, this is a story of penance and the ascetic path that was undertaken by Devi Girija, or Devi Parvati, to attain union with Shiva, marking all the obstacles and impediments that came her way and the sagaciousness with which she overcame them all. This divine wedding took place after Manmatha Vijaya, that is, when Kamadeva was reduced to ashes after he dared to disturb Shiva's penance with thoughts of lust and material pleasures.

We must understand why the above episode is referred to as 'Manmatha Vijaya'. It speaks about the significance of burning the desire for the physical world—the lust and pleasure that permeate material reality—in order for one to transcend the physical world and move closer towards a spiritual truth we know as the Supreme Reality. So, even though the episode of Manmatha's demise may seem somewhat unfair, it does hold a deeper meaning in the path to absolution.

In Hampi, these tales have long been sung and adapted into the local folklore, which have been passed down to the future generations by folk singers. But, of course, much of this sharing of knowledge has been oral—through songs, legends and tales—rather than through written texts, which morph according to the needs and beliefs of the society of the time. Their essence may remain the same, but how one imbibes them seems to evolve.

The famed 12th-century Kannada poet Harihara, observing the local traditions and culture in the city's temples, penned 'Girija Kalyana', which is a *champu-kavya*, a mix of prose and poetry. Since then, the local folks and artisans of the area have embraced the story and its message, allowing for its evolution, which continues to flourish even today, in the 21st century. It is truly interesting how we can trace the impressions left by people in their everyday life—be it in their lifestyle, culture or more—which are nothing but remnants of an ancient time that could have been long forgotten.

Yet, in South India, continuity can be noticed in the ritual of worshipping Devi Girija. For example, in Nanjangud, a small town on the banks of the river Kapila, records say that Devi Girija has been worshipped there for generations. Rulers may have come and gone, but the ritual ceremony and the divine powers of Devi Girija carry a syncretic traditional culture that symbolises the diverse cultural fabric of India. As Choodamani Nandagopal writes:

It is known from the records of the Shankaracharya Math of Sringeri that the ritual system followed was approved by the Math (monastery) and the priest family of Nanjangud belongs to this tradition. Mysore came under the rule of Islamic rulers like Haider Ali and Tipu Sultan; even then, it received munificent grants from these rulers. The emerald necklace donated by Tipu Sultan is specially used for decorating the bridegroom, Srikanthesvara, on the day of marriage. After the fall of Tipu Sultan, the British restored Krsnaraja Wodeyar III on the throne of Mysore who took considerable interest in streamlining the temple management and conducting of the customary rituals. He donated exclusive jewels for the Kalyanotsavam which adorn the divine bride and bridegroom on the occasion.[2]

The story goes that Parvati was once cursed by Shiva to take birth on earth and grow up as Daksha's daughter Girija. He would eventually come to claim her as Lord Virupaksha, but till then, she had to spend a certain amount of time on earth in human form. As the daughter of Daksha, she was also Dakshayini. Since her childhood, she had been in love with the idea of Shiva, with his stories and his legends, and as a result of this, she became an early devotee of the god.

Once, Sage Narada came to the court of Daksha. On seeing Devi Girija, he recognised her true form, bowed his head in veneration, and informed Daksha about the truth regarding his daughter. Narada told him that Shiva had also come to the earth as Virupaksha and was completing his austerities on Hemakuta Hill. He advised that Girija should go there and serve Shiva to win his favour. The *parvataraja* sent his daughter to Hemakuta Hill to do penance to win Shiva's favour; it was at the Pampa Sarovara where she would bathe in the water daily under the first light of the sun and then spend her entire day meditating, with her heart, mind and soul focused on Shiva. This is why today she is also called Pampamma or Pampambika.

During this time, the demon Tarakasura was causing great havoc in the three worlds and the devas and ganas went into hiding. Brahma, Indra and all other devatas turned to Vishnu who, through his own meditation, knew that it was only the son of Shiva and Girija who could end the terror of Tarakasura. Vishnu then called his son Manmatha and asked him to use his divine powers on Shiva and sow the seeds of love in his heart for Girija. The idea raised a strange apprehension in Manmatha, who politely objected to the task, fearing the consequences of angering Shiva. Vishnu, though fuelled by one's dharma, reminded Manmatha about how one had to often undertake the most unpleasant tasks for the sake of the well-being of the world at large.

Lord Manmatha prepared himself and entered the cave in which Shiva dwelled as Lord Virupaksha. He brought along Devi Girija and shot one floral arrow after another at Shiva from his sugarcane bow. Fragrant with the seeds of love, he was successful in breaking Shiva's penance. Furious at being disturbed, Shiva opened his third eye, annihilating Manmatha into nothing but a pile of ashes. Similar to the story of Kamadeva, Shiva barely noticed Girija and returned to his austerities, which of course broke the gentle heart of the goddess, who was guilt-ridden about the annihilation of Manmatha and distraught at Rati's pleas to bring her husband back.

Devi Girija promised Rati that she would win Shiva over through her tapas and then beg the Lord to restore Manmatha to life. Years passed in penance, and one day, Virupaksha appeared by the *sarovara* where Devi Parvati was diligently observing the toughest of austerities. Impressed with her efforts, God asked Devi what she wished for. In response, she wished first for the return of Manmatha to fulfil her vow to Rati. She then asked Shiva to marry her, as she was the human form of his divine consort. Warmed by her devotion and love, Lord Shiva granted both her wishes, and thus, Devi Rati returned to Vaikuntha with her husband Manmatha, while Girija and Virupaksha married with much pomp and aplomb and returned to Kailash.

The mythological marriage of Shiva and Girija is celebrated to this day in the form of Phala Pooje in Hampi. It signifies the union of the cosmic couple, which is known as the Girija Kalyana ritual. Nandagopal describes the ritual elaborately:

> The Kalyanotsava is conducted here in Asadhamasa corresponding to July/August for a period of eight days. Elaborate arrangements are made in the town and even the rituals are comparatively elaborate in nature. The household of the diksita, the principal priest, is considered as the paternal home of Devi and the saree and other mangala dravya to adorn the bride are offered in the name of Giriraja—the Himalayas. On the first day, the rituals commence by invoking the lord of obstacles, Vinayaka, followed with offering of oil and turmeric to women in the temple premises and inviting them to bring the *sumangali*s in the marriage rituals. The women feel it is the divine grace of Devi that they were given this special honour.[3]

Gajalakshmi

ॐ पद्मासनस्थिते देवी परब्रम्हस्वरूपिणी।
सर्व दुःख हरे देवी महालक्ष्मी नमोस्तूते

*My salutations to Devi Mahalakshmi
who is seated on a lotus,
is of the nature of supreme brahman,
and is the destroyer of all sorrows.*

—Mahalakshmi Ashtakam

Gajalakshmi literally translates to 'Lakshmi with elephants'. She is one of the most noteworthy manifestations of Lakshmi among the group of eight, or Ashtalakshmi. According to Hindu legend, Goddess Lakshmi was born from the foam of the ocean of milk when it was churned for amrita, the divine nectar, by Gods and demons. The myth of the churning of the ocean is mentioned in various holy texts, such as the *Vishnu Purana*, the Ramayana and the Mahabharata.

If the ancient narratives are to be believed, the manifestation of Lakshmi was crucial to restore balance to the universe, which was disturbed because of Indra, who had been cursed by Sage Durvasas, resulting in the waning of the former's divine powers. Indra had placed a precious garland presented by Durvasas on the head of his elephant Airavata. The latter threw this garland on the ground, which made Durvasas angry. Consequently, Durvasas cursed

Indra that all the celestial beings in his kingdom would be stripped of all strength, energy and fortune, which led them to be defeated by the demonic asuras in battles that followed this incident.

In order to restore the lost divine balance, Lord Vishnu instructed the gods to instead form an alliance with demons and churn the ocean of milk to bring to life Goddess Lakshmi, who had vanished into the oceans, as well as bring forth amrita, the elixir of eternal life. After receiving various gifts from the depths of the ocean, the golden Shri Lakshmi, adorned in pure white garments, emerged from the ocean. The sages were enthralled to see her and the celestial maidens danced and sang to offer their veneration. Elephants collected water from sacred rivers in golden vessels and ceremoniously poured it over Lakshmi to bathe her. The goddess was accompanied by Dhanvantari, the skilled physician of the gods. He held the pot of ambrosia, which was sought after by both gods and demons.

In terms of iconography, the goddess Lakshmi is often seated on a lotus, in the classic lotus position (*padmasana*), flanked on both sides by elephants. She has four arms; with both of her upper arms, she carries a lotus each, while her lower arms demonstrate the *abhyamudra* of protection and *varadamudra* of granting boons. The visual scene surrounding Lakshmi is representative of benevolence, prosperity, good luck and abundance. These Gajalakshmi motifs are extremely popular in both Hindu and Buddhist iconography.

The worship of the goddess has evolved over time but remains true to her fundamental qualities. Among the many symbols associated with her, Gajalakshmi is the most distinct. A sevenfold invocation of Shri Lakshmi ends with a prayer seeking her blessings for immortality and happiness, recognising her as a source of divine attributes, joy and universal well-being.

In Hindu iconography, most gods and goddesses have their specific vahanas. The elephant is associated with Lakshmi, Brihaspati, Shachi and Indra, and is believed to represent wisdom, divine knowledge and royal power. In one of the many myths, the earth is guided and protected by eight deities in the eight directions of the world, known as Ashta-Dikpalas, the guardians of the directions. Indra is one of them and his vahana is an elephant.

According to Hindu cosmology, the earth is supported by several mystical elephants in its prime directions. The elephant-headed Lord Ganesha is also known as Vighnaharta, the one who removes all obstacles. The interesting change in the iconography of Lakshmi came with the image of the elephants. As ArputhaRani Sengupta writes:

> Gaja-Laksmi appeared earliest in Buddhist sites from Gandhara to Sri Lanka. The icon of the goddess in terracotta is probably one of the most remarkable. Here, instead of elephants lustrating the goddess, she wears a mural crown surmounted by paired elephants. The voluptuous goddess represents the ideal of feminine beauty, her narrow waist, swelling hips and full breasts, and establishes an ideal that personifies her as the symbol of fecundity. In votive terracotta, the Tamluk *yakshi* sports fringed thigh bands with clasps designed as *triratna* with aegis worked originally in gold repoussé. She also wears a five-pronged headdress called *panchachuda*, with emblematic terminals.[1]

In the Dashavatara temple, Deogarh, ascribed to the Gupta period, there is a sculpture of an elephant raising its trunk in obeisance to a *naga*. It is worth mentioning here that Lakshmi is also worshipped as a serpent goddess, or

Nagalakshmi. According to Jackie Menzies' interpretation:

> Because Lakshmi is the goddess of wealth and prosperity, she often appears as the central deity in lintels, usually also being lustrated by two elephants (*gaja*) on either side. Since the elephant is a metaphor for rain-laden clouds, their bathing of Lakshmi symbolises the fertility rain brings to the earth. In this auspicious manifestation, Lakshmi is known as Gajalakshmi.[2]

The elephant has been an extremely important metaphor in Buddhist iconography and thought, right from the entry of the white elephant in Queen Mahamaya's dream which heralded the birth of Siddhartha Gautama, who later came to be known as Buddha, one of the Dashavataras (10 incarnations of Lord Vishnu). The widely accepted story of the conception of Buddha has been sculpted and painted by a number of artists throughout history. In one of the Gandhara reliefs depicting Queen Maya's white elephant dream, she is shown sleeping in her palace under full moon when she dreams of a white elephant that enters her womb from the right side, thus illustrating the story surrounding the birth of Buddha.

The Indian art critic Ananda K. Coomaraswamy, while discussing the iconic Basohli painting titled *Gajalakshmi* from the late 17th century, notes: 'Paintings are abundant, representing Laksmi risen from the ocean upon the flower of a lotus, and bathed by the two or four elephants of the quarters.'[3] The Pahari painting shows the goddess seated on a lotus, holding two lotus buds in her arms and flanked by two elephants bathing her with water carried in golden pots that they are holding with their trunks.

Kali

ॐ ह्रीं श्रीं क्लीं आद्या कालिके परमेश्वरी स्वा:

O Kali, my Mother, who is full of bliss.
In your delirious joy, you dance and clap your hands together!
You're the power that makes everything happen in your world.

—Kali Mantra

The mythos of Kali has always fascinated me simply because of the ferocious, terrifying and destructive nature of her persona that is accepted and celebrated in her worship. Kali or Mahakali is the goddess of death, time and destruction in Hinduism. Her name means 'she who is black' or 'she who is death'. She is the feminine form of the Sanskrit word *kala*, which means 'time', and its passing brings one closer to death.

Even her depiction is fearsome, as she is often described as black or blue in colour, partially or completely naked, and with a lolling tongue that is blood-red. She has multiple arms, each holding a weapon of destruction. She wears a skirt or a girdle of human arms, a necklace of severed heads adorns her neck, and in one of her hands, she holds a severed head dripping blood, signifying her mastery over death. There is nothing in this description that speaks of benevolence, gentility, love or protection in the way that perhaps the legend of Mahagauri or the previously discussed mythological tale of Parvati does.

Kali is extremely fierce, as though she exists in a world of black and white. Yet there are layers to this aspect of Devi, as considered in tantric texts as well as through the mythos of the *Devi Bhagavatam*—as Mother Goddess, she's relentless in her protection and unforgiving in her retribution.

Kali's origin can be traced back to the minor deities of the tribal villages of North and Northeast India and the mountain cultures of South Asia, which were slowly appropriated, transformed and imbibed by mainstream Hinduism. I believe this is where the untamed nature of Kali comes from, and it is particularly noteworthy that despite mingling with the Sanskrit tradition and Puranic literature, the mythology of Kali continues to retain its wild independence.

Kali makes her first appearance in the *Devi Mahatmya*, which is believed to have been written in the 5th or 6th century CE. In the *Devi Mahatmya*, the cult of Kali and her iconography commonly associate her with death but also with sexuality, violence and fiercely protective motherly love, which perhaps adds a paradoxical dimension to the goddess but also makes her one with a multitude of layers.

Kali, as the mother, is capable of singularly sustaining her devotees and worshippers—perhaps one could even say, her children. Take, for instance, her most popular iconography and depiction where she is portrayed as standing or dancing upon what seems to be the lifeless body of her husband, Shiva, who lies prostrate beneath her.

The goddess is often shown with her blood-red tongue hanging out, and this depiction harkens back to the tale of Durga slaying the demon Raktabija, whose name literally means 'blood seed', while Kali drank his blood. The demon had declared war in all three realms of the universe and had become a menace, torturing all of humanity and divinity alike. He had a boon that wherever his blood would fall, another Raktabija would grow on the spot. The gods called upon Durga to rid the world of the terror caused by Raktabija, but every time Durga would strike the demon, 10 more would stand in his place. Eventually, Durga summoned Kali, who lapped up the blood before it could fall on the ground. Thus, as Durga continued to strike Raktabija, Kali lapped up all the blood so that no new forms of Raktabija could form.

∞

The folklore of Gujarat and Rajasthan tells us about an alternative origin of Kali, where she was born from the dark skin that Mahagauri discarded after severe tapas, a result of Lord Shiva's jibe about the colour of her skin. From this darkness rose Kali, a form of Parvati, but one symbolic of the domestic goddess' feral warrior side.

When Mahakali put an end to Raktabija, so great was her hunger for blood that she refused to stop and continued to roam the earth, putting an end to all evil in her sight. Eventually, Mahadeva had to step in and lie in her path. The surprise and embarrassment of stepping on to the body of her husband, considered a grievous offence in this part of the world, resulted in Mahakali instantly transforming back to her benevolent form, Parvati.

It is perhaps this insatiable need for change, transformation and evolution that has made Kali an emblem of the New Age movements in the West. Since the late 20th century, many feminist scholars and writers in the United States, Europe and England have used Kali as a symbol of women's empowerment or adopted her mythos in their own philosophical schools and traditions. Kali's comfort with darker themes of womanhood, which are often shunned, such as sexuality, potent emotional states and torrential psychic experiences, have possibly spoken to women on both a theological and a physical plane.

To the Western world, the dark goddess Kali is one who protects our journey in unifying the mind, body and soul. She is the keeper of spiritual secrets, shining a light onto a rich and vast inner world. However, the mysteries of Kali surpass death and destruction despite her depiction being so black and white. The goddess is far more complex and her reach transcends the narrative of good and evil. Kali exists on the plane of relativity. Her untamed energy forces one to look at, accept and understand all sides of existence.

As Kinsley states through his scholarship, 'It is never Kali who tames Siva but Siva who must calm Kali.'[1] It is possibly the only instance where Devi doesn't exercise control, censure or balance over cosmic energy; here, she is allowed to be unbridled, creative and destructive in a pure form of potential. As John Hawley suggests:

> In a parallel tale, once she escapes the control of her aroused mate, Siva, she expands her form and relaxes her behaviour to the point where she dances a crazed dance on Siva's corpse. In these stories, she is, as Kinsley says, 'blood and death out of place'. In confronting her, we are not only horrified but potentially saved. A vision of Kali takes us beyond the constraints through which and within which we live. Kali releases.[2]

In the *Atharva Veda*, where Kali is first mentioned, she isn't described as a manifestation of the primordial goddess. She is rather a fierce black tongue, associated with Agni, the god of fire. It takes another four hundred years before Kali manifests in her own right, somewhere in the 6th century CE, in the *Devi Mahatmya* texts. Here, she is the battlefield goddess, a symbol of strength and victory, a patron of warriors, and emblematic of female power. Notably, Kali's association with Shiva is opposite to the role played by the benevolent Parvati.

Firstly, Kali derives her name from Shiva's Mahakaal form, which is inextricably tied to the god of destruction, much in the same way that Parvati is tied to Shiva. However, where Parvati tempers Shiva's ascetic energies and powers, soothing him into a state of balance and neutralising him, Kali instead challenges Mahakaal and propels him towards a state of destruction.

It was perhaps only in the 17th century, as a result of the efforts of Bengali tantric poets of eastern India (known as the Shakta tantric tradition), that the worship of Kali was given its devout makeover. She was no longer a terrifying symbol of a red-eyed, sacrifice-hungry crone. Kali was instead being described and depicted as a young, wild but beautiful mother. She was shown with a blue complexion, beautiful adornments, still naked to a degree, but with the gentlest of smiles playing on her features. She still held onto her weapons and the severed heads, which were fundamental to her imagery, but she was now the protective mother and not simply the battle-hungry warrior goddess. In Krishnananda Agamavagisha's own words:

> She is dark as soot, always living in the cremation ground. Her eyes are pink, her hair dishevelled, her body gaunt and fearful. In her left hand, she holds a cup filled with wine and meat, and in her right hand, she holds a freshly cut human head. She smiles and eats rotten meat. She is decked with ornaments, is naked and is absorbed in drinking. Having conceived the deity in this way, one should propitiate her in the cremation ground. The householder will worship her at home, at dead of night, having partaken of fish, meat, and wine and being naked.[3]

Despite the efforts of the Bengali tantric poets, in orthodox Hinduism Kali was still seen as a temperamental goddess, which I suppose is certainly one way of understanding her. She is unpredictable, which does make people wary, including some of those who are most devoted to her. However, it is perhaps in the tantric tradition that Kali finds her most patient worshippers.

In the tantric teachings that are built on a bedrock of magical stories and folkloric traditions, rituals and practices, Kali's worship closely resembles the form it took when she was a tribal goddess. One meaning of her name is 'the force of time', which takes her beyond the constraints of space and time, making her exist outside the limitations of the world or the physical, observable reality. This may be another reason why her worship, cult and traditions have remained more or less the same over centuries, passed down to generation after generation of devotees.

Interestingly, Kali became quite popular as a goddess in the eyes of Euro-American women as well. Rachel McDermott argues that Kali, in the eyes of the Euro-American women, came to be seen as an entity that derives her power 'from an embracing of opposites—maternal compassion and a distinctly female kind of rage'.[4] In May Sarton's 'The Invocation to Kali', we notice a verbal appeal of transformation:

> *Kali, be with us.*
> *Violence, destruction, receive our homage.*
> *Help us to bring darkness into the light,*
> *To lift out the pain, the anger,*
> *Where it can be seen for what it is—*
> *The balance-wheel for our vulnerable, aching love.*
> *Put the wild hunger where it belongs,*
> *Within the act of creation,*
> *Crude power that forges a balance*
> *Between hate and love.*[5]

For me, Kali is Maa Kali of the *Devi Bhagavatam*, the symbol of the Mother Goddess who is primordial, creative, nurturing and devouring in turn. She may ultimately be Maa Kali or the loving and benevolent mother, an aspect of hers revered by most Hindus today.

However, it is also important to recognise one final aspect of the goddess' tantric form, where meditating on her dual nature makes one simultaneously face the best in life and the reality of death. She can lead one to an understanding of the nature of existence where one aspect can't exist without the other. This is the ultimate form of salvation given to us only by Kali. This duality of Kali particularly shines in her imagery, where the red tongue, on one hand, speaks to her thirst for blood, while also speaking to the modesty of a wife recognising her mistake on the other hand. Her wild hair and bloodlust point to the metaphysical mysteries of life and death. Her three eyes make her omnipresent, and her voluptuous body is indicative of her sexual appetite as well as her ability to be a nurturing mother.

Finally, her stance and the mudras of each hand also point to dual practices; the right-handed tantric path, or Dakshinamarga, emphasises a pure, pious and benevolent tantric tradition, while the left-handed path, or the infamous Vamamarga, points to a degenerate and tormenting practice. The former is considered as a positive and creative form of practice; the latter is considered as destructive and violent. It is eventually our purpose to sever the human ego from our practice, which is represented by the severed head in her hand, to overcome this continuous cycle of life and birth.

Chamunda

ब्राह्मी माहेश्वरी चैव कौमारी वैष्णवी तथा।
वाराही च तथेन्द्राणी चामुण्डा सप्तमातर:॥

Salutations to the seven mothers, Goddesses Brahmani, Maheshwari, Kaumari, Vaishnavi, Varahi, Indrani and Chamunda.

—*Brihaspati Smriti*

Just as Devi Sati's story overlaps with that of Devi Parvati, the mythos of Kali too bears a resemblance to that of her tantric manifestation, Chamundeshwari. Devi Chamundeshwari, also called Chamunda, Chamundi and Raktandika, is a fearsome form of the divine mother Parvati, counted as one of the Sapta Matrikas—the seven forms of Adi Shakti or Parashakti.

To me, Chamunda holds the mystical secrets of the tantric tradition as one of the chief yoginis among the Chausath Yoginis, the 64 tantric goddesses. However, it is necessary to point out that in some traditions, there are 81 goddesses, led by the warrior form of Parvati.

Devi Chamunda earned her name by slaying the asuras Chanda and Munda. While she is more closely associated with Kali with respect to her attributes, her cosmic power stems from Parvati as an embodiment of her fierceness. Goddess Chamundeshwari subverts many of the beliefs of the Hindu tradition. She is most often portrayed as gracing places that are considered unholy, such as cremation grounds and burial sites. She is worshipped by ritual sacrifices of animals, and in ancient times, a cult of her worship also included human sacrifices. As the Shaivite and Vaishnavite influences grew, along with the arrival of the British in India, the tradition of human sacrifices stopped altogether and even animal sacrifices were significantly reduced.

In the *Devi Mahatmya*, there is a story of Chamunda's origin, according to which she emerged from one of the eyebrows of Goddess Kaushiki, another form of Durga. It was Chamunda's task to eliminate the demons Chanda and Munda, who were the generals of Shumbha and Nishumbha. Chamunda fought valiantly against the demons and their armies, and her fierce power ultimately led her to victory, giving her the name of Chamundeshwari.

In a later episode in the text, when Durga battled with Shumbha and Nishumbha, she created the Matrikas from her cosmic energies to assist her on the battlefield. According to this legend, Kali was the *matrika* who slayed Raktabija, the demon from whose blood a new demon version of himself was born. Kali, in this episode, was also given the name of Chamunda. Thus, in the *Devi Mahatmya*, Kali is Chamunda and the two goddesses are considered one and the same by the readers.

However, the story of Raktabija, as retold in the *Varaha Purana*, is slightly different. It perhaps provides another origin story for Goddess Chamunda. Here, the Matrikas appeared from the body of a central matrika, Narasimhi. Chamunda emerged from this lion-headed goddess' foot and was a representation of the folly or vice of tale-telling (*pasunya*). Notably, the two goddesses Kali and Chamunda are completely distinct from one another in the *Varaha Purana*, unlike in the *Devi Mahatmya*.

Yet another account of the goddess' origin tells us that

Chamunda arose from the frown on Devi Parvati's forehead when she witnessed the menace that the demons Chanda and Munda were creating. This tale firmly ties the goddess to the benevolent side of Devi as Parvati.

In all the tales of Goddess Chamunda, she is always associated in one form or another with the Matrikas. Chamunda is one of the Sapta Matrikas, or seven mothers, making an appearance in the Mahabharata, the *Devi Purana* and the *Vishnudharmottara Purana*. The Matrikas were fierce mother goddesses who were represented as both benevolent and truly fearsome, believed to have been abductors and eaters of children, and, in some tales, the embodiment of childhood pestilence, fever, starvation and disease. As she has been described in the *Agni Purana*:

> Om hrim Camunda! […] One whose terrific tongue is licking! […] One who has terrific laughter! […] One who is fond of blood, flesh and intoxicating drink! Kill. Om trample. Om cut. Om kill. Om chase. […] One who has sunken eyes! One having erect hairs! One having the face of an owl! One who holds a skull (in the hand)! Om. One who wears a garland of skulls! Burn. Om. Cook. Cook. Om. Seize. […] Pierce open. Om. Cut with the trident. Om. Kill with the mace. […] Om. Camunda. […] Kili Kili aum vicce hum phat oblations.[1]

In other words, Chamunda is as much a force of creation as one of destruction, pointing towards the mind's ability to create and destroy; we fan the flames of what we worship. The Matrikas were called upon to avoid these ills and they were appeased so as not to carry so many children with them before they were ever to reach the age of adulthood.

Chamunda is also an intrinsic aspect of worship in the tantric culture. For example, in Odisha, she is worshipped as either Bhairava or Chamunda. In keeping with the tantric concepts, there is no distinction between the two. Shakti, Maheshwara, Brahman, all denote the same being; masculine, feminine and neuter words are verbal and do not signify real distinctions. Instead, all three denote the one eternal Mahavidya, who is Sacchidananda.

> In the Yamala, Shiva says:—'Devi may, My Beloved, be thought of as female or male, or the Sacchidanandarupini may be thought of as Nishkala-Brahman. But in truth she is neither a female, male, neuter being, nor an inanimate thing. But like the term Kalpavalli (a word in feminine gender denoting tree), feminine terms are attributed to her.[2]

In the Elephanta and Ellora caves, we can see her sculptural depiction, derived from Puranic tales, as an all-powerful goddess enjoying the company of the other matrikas. She is, in some accounts, believed to be the leader of the group of goddesses. The other matrikas are considered as shaktis of the male gods, i.e., extensions of their actual creative power, whereas Chamunda exists in her own right, as the shakti of the Great Goddess herself, that is, Devi. In this form, she is the only goddess who is worshipped independent of any male counterpart, given the union of opposites existing inherently within her.

Poets invariably dwell on every lurid and gruesome detail of Chamunda's life, whether it be in Bhavabhuti's play *Malatimadhava* or in Somadeva's champu (a textual combination of prose and verse) called *Yashastilaka*. In the latter, Chamunda has been described as follows:

> Garlands of human skulls are her head-ornament. Corpses of children are her ear-ornament. The elbows of dead men are her earrings. Balls made from the bones of dead bodies from her necklaces. [...] Skeletons play

the part of toy-lotuses in her hands. Rivers of wine are the streams wherein she performs her evening ablutions. Charnel-fields are her pleasure grounds. The ashes of funeral pyres are her face-ornament. Raw hides constitute her robe. The intestines of dead bodies form her girdle. The bosoms of dead men are her dancing floor. She plays with the heads of goats as with balls. Her water-sports take place in lakes of blood. The blazing fires of cremation-grounds serve as her votive lamps at night. Human skulls are the vessels she eats from. Her greatest pleasure is when living creatures of all kinds are sacrificed at her altar.[3]

In the *Vishnudharmottara Purana*, we understand the Matrikas with regard to certain vices that tempt humans. The goddesses are representative of these vices and can show the path to overcoming them and moving towards a spiritual union with the Divine.

Chamunda as a matrika is considered among the chief yoginis, who are both manifestations of the matrikas and the daughters. Chamunda is further believed to have created seven yoginis from her own spiritual energies, forming a group of eight goddesses. These goddesses, I believe, are spiritual guides in the tantric tradition, with each battle they fight taking us away from our base inclinations to a higher spiritual (or mental) plane. On this plane exist the demons Shumbha and Nishumbha, that is, 'I' and 'mine'. It is the battle against the ego that the goddess represents, and Chanda and Munda are extroverted and introverted psychic energies of the ego respectively.

Further, the demon Dhumralochana is part of our distorted perception, and Raktabija, part of our contorted and complicated thought processes. As we battle on the mental plane against these demons, terrorised by fearful thoughts, by the illusions of the ego and more, Devi shields us and stands with us in the midst of this inner conflict. If we follow her example, we are taken from our limited sense of the self, which is a result of the ego mind, to the boundless infinite self that is recognised by the Divine.

Saraswati

या कुन्देन्दुतुषारहारधवला या शुभ्रवस्त्रावृता
या वीणावरदण्डमण्डितकरा या श्वेतपद्मासना।
या ब्रह्माच्युतशंकरप्रभृतिभिर्देव: सदा वंदिता
सा मां पातु सरस्वति भगवती नि:शेषजाड्यापहा

May Goddess Saraswati protect me.
She, who is fair like the jasmine, as radiant as the moon's rays,
and whose pure white garland is like frosty dew drops.
She, who is adorned in pure white attire,
on whose arm rests the veena,
and whose throne is a white lotus.
She, who is surrounded and respected by the Gods.
Please remove my weariness, sluggishness and ignorance.

—*Saraswati Stotram*

As a young schoolgirl, Devi Saraswati was perhaps the first goddess whom I was introduced to. Even today, Saraswati, the Hindu goddess of learning, wisdom, music and aesthetics, is called upon at the start of each new school year during the auspicious Saraswati Puja, held as part of the Basant Panchami celebrations that usher in the spring season.

Saraswati, also known as Bharati (eloquence) and Vedamata (the mother of the Vedas), continues to be an important goddess in our knowledge systems and institutions. However, her association with learning and wisdom dates back to the Vedic age. Devi Saraswati's first appearance occurred during the period of the *Rig Veda* as the Goddess Vac or Vacha. She was the goddess of speech, whose powers were parallel to the powers of creation, which speaks to the importance of words and language as descriptors of the world around us. Until we have a word for something, it doesn't truly exist, even if it is present in the physical dimension. The moment we find a word for it, it's as though it is born.

In later Puranic texts, Saraswati is identified as the mother of Sanskrit, one of the most ancient languages of the Indian subcontinent. There is an episode in which she rather appropriately gives Ganesha the gifts of pen and ink whilst commencing his education. This tradition continues in the Indian school system to this day, where pens, notebooks, and sometimes even books are kept at the Devi's altar at the start of each school year.

According to legend, Devi Saraswati is the shakti, or consort, of Brahma, the creator of the universe. However, there are some traditions, such as the Bengali Vaishnava tradition, which consider her as the wife of Vishnu. Regardless, she is widely known as the consort of Brahma, one of the gods in the Hindu trinity called Tridev. He is rarely worshipped by Hindus, possibly due to a curse laid upon him by Devi herself.

One day, Brahma was about to preside over an important holy ceremony. In the Hindu tradition, religious ceremonies are considered legitimate only when they are performed in the presence of both the husband and the wife. Devi Saraswati, it seemed, was taking her time to get ready, and Brahmadeva, unable to wait for his wife to arrive, created a new wife for the ceremony—Gayatri. With Devi Gayatri present, the ceremony could begin without any obstacles. When Saraswati finally arrived, she was far from pleased to see her husband with another woman as he participated in rituals that she was meant to partake in. In her anger, she cursed Brahma that he would never be worshipped by humanity. This is true to a large extent, since there are only a few places of worship for Brahma compared to the several temples dedicated to Shiva and Vishnu across the country.

As the consort of Brahma, Devi Saraswati has the power, or shakti, of creation. I think it is important here to return to her Vedic form as Goddess Vac, who was a creator but through language. Even in the Buddhist and Jain traditions, Devi Saraswati's role is hardly different and she continues to be worshipped as the goddess of learning.

In ancient India, one of the most sacred rivers around which civilisations grew and flourished was the river Saraswati. Indian mythology is full of tales where rivers are a sacred source, a means of purification and fertility, and the bringer of good fortune and blessings to those who bathe and cultivate with their water. This is certainly the case with the river Ganga. The river Saraswati no longer exists, but it is believed to be the origin of some of the most flourishing historical kingdoms and civilisations in the Indian subcontinent. It may be for this reason that 'saraswati' also means 'flowing' and 'watery', indicating the goddess' natural form as a river.

As per Hindu mythology's metaphoric association of fertility with the origin of civilisation, all creatures were born from the union of Brahma and Saraswati as the god and the goddess of creation. It was through them that the world was populated. They gave birth to Manu, the first man, as well as Rishi Saraswata, who was nourished by the wisdom and knowledge of his mother and carried forth the sacred knowledge of the Vedas.

Hindu sculptures depict the goddess in her youth, with glowing white skin and dressed in an all-white sari with a blue border. This white sari is symbolic of purity, and the goddess, who is mainly concerned with wisdom, is rarely shown decked in jewellery and other adornments. Her vehicle is the swan and she is sometimes shown seated on a lotus flower beside her husband. Today, her depictions increasingly feature a *veena* (an instrument of Indian classical music) in one of her hands, for she is also well-known as the goddess of music and is worshipped with much devotion by the *sangeet shastri*s of India.

Devi Saraswati forms the trinity of Hindu goddesses with Parvati and Lakshmi. As the consort of Vishnu, Lakshmi is the goddess of wealth, prosperity and beauty, a domain that is associated with the sustenance of the world. Parvati is the goddess of fertility and love, and her fierce forms representing death and destruction are associated with the path to enlightenment through ending the ego and building a balance between the spiritual and the material. Saraswati is then the goddess of artistry, wisdom and, as such, creation. She holds the creative powers through which the world was born. The three goddesses together represent the Shakti, the cosmic power that guides the universe.

The fact that Devi Saraswati's name is mentioned in the first of the four sacred Hindu texts, the *Rig Veda*, dating all the way back to the 1700–1100 BCE period, tells us of her continuing relevance in Hinduism. There is, in fact, a chapter in the Mahabharata that credits Devi Saraswati as the creator of the four Vedas, a reasonable assumption considering her position as the limitless fountain of universal and cosmic wisdom. As part of worshipping her, children are taught to write for the first time, musicians take in new students, and all matters of intellectual and artistic pursuits are celebrated.

Sharada

नमस्ते शारदे देवी काश्मीरपुरवासिनि।
त्वामहं प्रार्थये नित्यं विद्यादानं च देहि मे॥

Salutations to Devi Sharada, who resides in Kashmir,
To You, O Devi, I always pray for knowledge.
Please bestow on me the gift of that Knowledge,
which illumines everything from within.

—*Shri Sharada Stotram*

Devi Sharada, much like Devi Ushas, has her roots in the realm of knowledge and divine consciousness. However, where Ushas is the bringer of divine consciousness, Devi Sharada assists man in his quest for knowledge by being the guiding light. She is often called Guru Rupini, bestowing her grace by activating Jagadguru's storehouse of knowledge. She is thus the embodiment of all three shaktis—creation, sustenance and destruction—and the entire cycle of the universe. Adi Shankaracharya describes Devi Sharada as Brahmavidya, the goddess who represents the incommensurable Brahman itself.

> The name Sharada […] is quite familiar in the treatises on the history of Kashmir. […] Abdur Rahman originates the word Sharada as an abbreviation of Sharadaksharani, meaning 'letters sacred to Sharada or Saraswati', the Hindu goddess of learning. M.A. Stein,

referring to *Mahatmya*, describes other incarnations of the same deity as Narada, Vagdevi or Saraswati.[1]

In the *Devi Bhagavatam*, Sharada is considered to overlap with the primordial energy of Mahadevi, the divine feminine, in some ways. Here, she very well transcends the Trimurti as well as their corresponding shaktis, which makes her a stand-alone deity. Adi Shankaracharya thus compiled the *Lalita Sahasranama*, venerating Shri Sharada Parameshwari, the divine goddess, the primordial power.

> Stein (1900) also gave a detailed account of the 'Sharada Mahatmya'. It tells the myth that how a non-Brahman rishi, Muni Shandilya, son of Matanga, worshipped the goddess Sharada so hard that she appeared to him. This place is identified by Stein as 'Guś' (currently in Indian Occupied Kashmir). She promised him to show her real form, Shakti. [...] In the end, the goddess revealed herself in her triple form of Sharada, Narada or Saraswati and Vagdevi over the sacred place and invited him to her abode. He was then preparing for a ritual and took water from 'Mahasindhu'. Half of this water turned into honey and became a stream, the Madhumati Stream. Since then, bathing on the confluence of Sindhu (Neelum River Or Kishanganga) and Madhumati assures the complete remission of sins.[2]

I think an interesting way of understanding Devi Sharda is through that form of hers that is most popularly worshipped. In the Sharadamba temple, Sringeri, Karnataka, Devi Sharada is enshrined on the Shri Chakra Peetham. While a parrot is perched on her upper right hand, her lower right hand is in the *chinmudra* position that connects one to higher consciousness. In her upper left hand, she holds the *amrita-kalasha* that bestows immortality, and in her lower left hand is the book of supreme knowledge along with the japamala that signifies the beej mantras of the universe. Many believe that this sculpture of the deity was originally made of sandalwood and that the *murti-sthapana* was done by the great sage Adi Shankaracharya himself, sometime in the 14th century. As researchers Junaid Ahmad and Abdul Samad write about Sharada Peeth in Pakistan-occupied Kashmir (PoK):

> Sharada Temple is an archaeological complex [...] in Azad Jammu and Kashmir. Most scholars identified it conventionally as a Hindu Temple, one mentioned for Goddess Sharada.[3]

Within the shrine of the Sharadamba temple, there are several other Hindu deities who are associated with Devi Sharada and her form as the primordial goddess. The temple's *mahamandapam* has intricately carved stone pillars with images of deities like Durga, *dwarapalakas*, Raja Rajeshwari and devis, each of them sculpted as per the Shilpa Shastras. Additionally, there is an idol of Adi Shankaracharya. Each Friday, a procession of Sharada Maa, seated on a silver chariot, is carried out around the temple. The devotees can receive Maa's darshan and seek her blessings.

During the Navaratri festival, along with the procession of Sharada Maa, there are processions of Shakti Ganapati, Mahishasuramardini and Rajarajeshwari as well. At the front of the temple is a pillared hall featuring the artistic depictions of the goddess' legends and tales; many of these carvings boast of exquisite craftsmanship. The temple, in fact, is designed in such a way that it allows for the goddess to be visible to incoming devotees from far beyond the entrance.

The Sharadamba temple is built on the location where Adi Shankaracharya is believed to have established one of the Chaar Peethas. The temple follows all the traditions of Advaita Vedanta. The swamis, priests and gurus spend several hours a day in meditation, contemplation and sadhana. The site is known as a place of great spiritual power that invites sadhus to perform intense tapas and meditation as they sit still in one spot for hours and days, counting their *rudraksha* japamala. They may seem frightening with their *vibhuti*-smeared foreheads and ochre robes, but their faces hold a deep sense of peace and restfulness; sleep and other such bodily functions mean little to nothing to them.

The gurus in Sringeri Peetham believe that an individual must not only revere one's guru, listening to their words and teachings, but also imbibe the habits, way of life and conduct of their guru. Certain habits that are encouraged include the sattvic lifestyle of vegetarianism, cleanliness and discipline.

One worships God with bhakti *bhava* (the pure devotion of the heart). While knowledge and learning are crucial, so is keeping an honest heart filled with love. One should always conduct themselves with integrity, honesty and generosity, and they should be true to the teachings of the scriptures. Leading a simple life, loving and respecting people, and living up to the responsibility one has towards their family and community are the values that are ingrained here.

Vagadevi

सरस्वति नमस्तुभ्यं वरदे कामरूपिणि।
विध्यारम्भं करिष्यामि सिद्धिर्भवतु मे सदा॥

*Salutations to Devi Saraswati,
who bestows boons and is the fulfiller of wishes.
O Devi, when I begin my studies,
please always grant me the capacity of right understanding.*

—Saraswati Mantra

Vagadevi is another form of Devi Saraswati. In this form, she is the shakti behind speech, wisdom and learning. There is a unique symbolism in the way Vagadevi is depicted. In most of her iconography, she is shown with four hands, which represent the four aspects of a human being: mind, intellect, consciousness and ego. She is depicted as holding the scriptures in one hand. As the fountain of Indic knowledge, the goddess symbolises the wealth of sacred knowledge, as contained in the Vedas. In two of her other hands, she holds the violin and the veena, as if to say that music is both the play of love and life, cementing the Indian classical arts as a form of spiritual tradition in their own right. Most often, Vagadevi is shown dressed in all white, the colour being a symbol of purity or pure knowledge, and she rides a beautiful white swan.

It is believed that Vagadevi is the mother of the Sanskrit language, which became the language of learning in ancient

India, encompassing the scriptures, poems, sutras and Puranic texts. For the poets and dramatists of the Indian classical tradition, Vagadevi is the mother of all creative arts, although she is particularly worshipped for poetry, music and science. Before each new year, students visit her temple, bow their heads, and seek her blessings.

In the Brahmanas, Vac is vividly portrayed with a focus on her role in creation and rituals.[1] Representing speech, she is essential to sacrificial practices that rely on the chanting of mantras. One myth narrates how the gods retrieved Vac from the demons, either through strategy or enticement, after the world's creation. Once they secured her, the gods practised sacrificial rituals that sustained the universe, and these divine ceremonies would have been incomplete without Vac, who granted prosperity, vitality and immortality. Vac is also depicted as a creative force tied to the Vedas. One story describes her as infusing plants and trees with life by entering their sap, thereby giving life to nature all around. She is credited as the creator of the three Vedas, which symbolise the elements: the *Rig Veda* represents the earth, the *Yajur Veda* the air and the *Sama Veda* the sky. Prajapati, a central figure in the Brahmanas, is closely linked to Vac in the process of creation. He is portrayed as commencing creation by merging his mind and speech to impregnate himself. Scholar Daljeet writes:

> Metaphysically, the Goddess represents Shakti, the guided power, the transcendental source and support of all creatures and of entire creation. The *Rig Veda* calls the great Goddess 'Vak', the universal power. The *Rig Veda* further refers to her as Mahimata, the great mother, as the mother of gods; as Aditi, the universal nature and infinity; as Viraja, the universal mother, as cosmic cow oozing out of her teats ambrosial milk for the entire creation. She is said to be the daughter of

Primeval Ocean and carries Ambhrini as one of her many names, obviously to symbolize that she is both the unmanifest source and the manifest cosmos.[2]

In the Vedas, Vagadevi was recognised as the goddess of speech. It was much later that this goddess somehow morphed into Saraswati, for the distinction between the two is nearly non-existent. There is an inherent connection leading to their association with each other. The Vedic culture was largely a culture where the oral tradition was revered. Knowledge was passed down from the guru to the disciples through lessons that would take place beside rivers. Now, the river Saraswati, one of the oldest and most sacred rivers of India, was a site of learning. It is perhaps this association that gave birth to the notion of the goddess of learning being Devi Saraswati. In most post-Vedic references, we see that Vagadevi is usually addressed as Devi Saraswati.

It is speech that is believed to set human beings apart from other animals, making them capable of reasoning, and over time, Vagadevi came to be known for these higher faculties of the intellect. Her domain of power began to grow as mankind began to civilise itself using speech, culture, learning and wisdom. She began to also function as the goddess of intellectual advancement. Numerous epithets of the goddess speak to this association of hers with higher cognition, such as *smritishakti*, or the power of memory, *jnanashakti*, or the power of knowledge, and *kalpanashakti*, or the power of forming new ideas also called imagination. Thus, one can understand how popular this goddess would have been amongst the learning class, the Brahmins, and also among the creators, poets, musicians, shastris and writers in history.

According to the *Brahmavaivarta Purana*, Krishna is seen as the ultimate reality, or Purusha, in the first section. The second section mentions Prakriti, where his female counterpart takes on five forms, or shaktis, and one of these is Vagadevi. In this form, she is responsible for the creative function in relation to the other shaktis of the universe. She provides insight, knowledge and learning for the functioning of the world, making her purely sattvic and of a spiritual dimension.

In the *Brahmavaivarta Purana* and *Devi Bhagavatam*, we are told that Devi Saraswati's place exists on the tip of Krishna's tongue. As he creates the universe, there appears a beautiful young girl dressed in yellow and decked in beautiful jewels, carrying a veena and a book. Similarly, in older Vedic texts, it is believed that Vagadevi too rests on the tongue of Brahma, which indicates her importance in the process of creation through her association as a dynamic shakti to both Brahma and Vishnu, the gods of creation and sustenance.

In the *Rig Veda*, Vagadevi is said to impel everyone towards true and sweet speech and awaken happy and noble thoughts. Epithets such as *jihvagravasini* (she who dwells on the tip of the tongue), *kavijihvagravasini* (she who dwells on the tongues of poets), *sabdavasini* (she who dwells in sound), *vagisa* (the mistress of speech), and *mahavani* (she who possesses great speech) are often used for her.

> Vac plays a significant role in Vedic literature, not only in terms of being mentioned often but also from a theoretical point of view. Theologically it is suggested that she is coeternal with Prajapati. Although the *Brahmanas* are not consistent, sometimes stating that Vac was created by Prajapati, she does seem to have a theologically exalted position in these texts. There are also hints that it is through Vac, or in pairing with her, that Prajapati creates. This is different from the role of *Shakti* in later Hindu philosophic schools, in which the male counterpart of *Shakti* tends to be inactive.

Prajapati toils and desires the creation. Nevertheless, her role in the *Brahmanas* is suggestive of the nature of *Shakti* in later Hinduism. Her role vis-à-vis Prajapati is also suggestive of the theory of *shabda-brahman* (the absolute in the form of sound) and the *sphota* theory of creation (in which the world is created through sound).[3]

The predominant themes in Vagadevi's appearance are purity and transcendence. She is usually depicted to be pure white, like snow, or shining brilliantly, like innumerable moons. She is sometimes said to be smeared with sandalwood paste, another element signifying her transcendental purity; these themes are in keeping with her typical association with the *sattva guna*—the pure, spiritual thread of Prakriti. Vagadevi is rarely described as having a fearsome form and is usually portrayed as calm and peaceful.

Aranyani

आञ्जनगन्धिं सुरभिं बह्वन्नामकृषीवलाम्।
प्राहं मृगाणां मातरण्यानिमशंसिषम्॥

*I praise Aranyani, the mother of wild animals,
who is musk-scented, fragrant, fertile and uncultivated.*

—*Rig Veda,* Book 10, Hymn 146, Verse 6

Goddess Aranyani is the daughter of Lord Shiva and Devi Parvati. As Aranyani, the forest goddess, she is similar to Vana Devi. The goddess is described as being elusive, fond of quiet glades in the jungle, and fearless about remote and isolated places. In the *Rig Veda,* there is a hymn in the tenth mandala which asks Devi to explain how she wanders into these far-off places on the fringes of civilisation without any fear in the least.

It is believed that Devi Aranyani can be located following the sounds of her tinkling anklets, which are heard in the depths of forested areas although she is rarely, if ever, seen. Aranyani is also a dancer, and her ability to feed both humans and animals, without needing to till or plough any land, associates her with Devi Parvati, who is also Annapurna.

There is a certain poeticism in the tales of Aranyani, particularly that of her birth. One day, Parvati and Shiva were wandering in the forests and felt immediately taken with the place. Standing at the foot of a distinctly elegant tree, Parvati exclaimed to Shiva about the beauty of the forest, asking him which tree was particularly special to him. To this, Lord Shiva recounted a story about the Samudra Manthana: Upon losing his kingdom, Lord Indra had turned to Narayana for assistance in regaining it. Narayana advised that the devas should churn the great cosmic ocean with the asuras and cull out the nectar of life, i.e., amrita, rendering themselves immortal and winning back their kingdom.

The *kalpavriksha*, before which Shiva and Parvati were now standing, had come out of this churning of the ocean. This tree embodied the complete beauty of nature and was representative of its balanced perfection. Hearing these words from Shiva, Devi Parvati recalled that the kalpavriksha, also known as the *kalpapadama* and *kalpadruma* (or the Baobab tree), was significant among each region's flora for having medicinal and ecological value. The tree offered so much of itself towards the benefit of the human world that it was nothing short of a wish-fulfilling tree.

Lord Shiva then asked Devi Parvati to make her wish to the tree and observe how it was granted. A curious Devi, after meditating for a while, performed three *parikrama*s of the tree along with Lord Shiva, praying to be blessed with a girl who would have nine divine gifts of peace, purity, knowledge, energy, patience, respect, prosperity, success and happiness.

No sooner had Devi Parvati finished expressing her wish that a beautiful young girl emerged from the kalpavriksha before her and Lord Shiva. The girl had a snowy-white body clothed in roses, with flowers cascading down her hair. She had beautiful bow lips, a bright mouth and brilliant eyes. Her face radiated like the sun. She wore anklets, which produced enchanting music every time she moved. A stunning beauty, this young girl was glowing with vitality and youthful charm.

Both Shiva and Parvati looked at each other in surprise. Shiva told Parvati that they should name this *ashokasundari* (one who was created by the wish-fulfilling kalpavriksha) Aranyani, as Devi seemed to have wished for her own nine forms as Durga in the child.

∞

In Hindu mythology, the forests are worshipped as the manifestation of Goddess Aranyani, the goddess of the forests, animals and all life dwelling within the woods. The forest as a community is a model of our societal evolution. It is a source of life, a boon of creation venerated as both sacred and human.

Man participating in life in the forest has been explored in Aranyaka texts and has also been mentioned in various other Puranic texts. To this day, this approach to the forest's wisdom in achieving a spiritual balance is part of the beliefs and traditions of the tribal and peasant societies in Madhya Pradesh and Chhattisgarh. The forest thus becomes the highest expression of the earth's fertility and bounty and is symbolised as Aranyani. As G.C. Tripathi writes:

> In our Sanskrit literature (vide, e.g. Kumarasambhavam II.52), the two vanadevatas mentioned here are named as Malini and Vijaya! The vanadevatas find mention in Sakuntalam and Meghadutam as well. Like Diana who is a huntress moving around with a bow and a quiver, the Vanadurga has also a tough nature. In her mantra, she is addressed as purushi—a man-like lady. It is a very unusual word, formed with the addition of a feminine suffix to the word purusha or man. The mantra of Vanadevi is in fact a small prayer addressed to her in anustubh metre (a poetic meter in Sanskrit),

which may roughly be translated as follows: 'Wake up, O Man lady! Why are you sleeping? There is danger around me. Whether it is possible or impossible (I don't know) but Durga, noble lady, ward it off me! Hail thee!' The mantra is thus more a magical formula than a prayer, and the character of this sylvan Durga shows a mixture of the traits of Hinduistic Durga with those of a furious tribal goddess.[1]

Bhudevi

ॐ भूरसि भूमिरस्यदितिरसि विश्वधाया विश्वस्य भुवनस्य धर्त्री।
पृथिवीं यच्छ पृथिवीं दृंह पृथिवीं मा हिंसिः॥

*'Om…You are the object of sensory perception;
you are the Goddess who distributes the forms of the earth.
You are the creator of the Universe, the one
who sustains all existing things in the universe.
Sustain the earth, firmly establish the earth,
make the earth efficient in its motion.'*

—*Shukla Yajurveda*, Chapter 13, Verse 18

𝓑hudevi is the personification of Mother Earth and is mentioned as far back as the Vedic period. In the earliest of these texts, the goddess was known as Prithvi Devi and was believed to be the consort of Dyaus, the god of sky. In the *Rig Veda*, we have a canto describing how Dyaus fertilises Prithvi through rain, creating life. Furthermore, the fifth *mandala* of the *Rig Veda* is exclusively dedicated to Bhudevi, as follows:

बळित्था पर्वतानां खिद्रं बिभर्षि पृथिवि। प्र या भूमिं प्रवत्वति मह्ना जिनोषि महिनि॥
स्तोमासस्त्वा विचारिणि प्रति ष्टोभन्त्यक्तुभिः। प्र या वाजं न हेषन्तं पेरुमस्यर्जुनि॥
दृळ्हा चिद्या वनस्पतीन्क्ष्मया दर्धर्ष्योजसा। यत्ते अभ्रस्य विद्युतो दिवो वर्षन्ति वृष्टयः॥

*O Prithvi! You are the possessor of excellent qualities.
You are the greatness itself. You satisfy living beings through
your greatness.*

> *You are indeed the one who bears aloft the mountains.*
> *O Land! You are full of energy and you move in all the directions.*
> *You roar like a horse when you accept rain from the clouds.*
> *Your devotees sing your praise through the hymns that they chant.*
> *O Land! There are clouds in heaven and lightning streaks through them.*
> *It rains and it is your strength that sustains trees and herbs on the ground.*
>
> —*Rig Veda*, Book 5, Hymn 84, Verses 1–3

The *Atharva Veda*, Hymn 1 of Book XII, containing 63 verses, extols Prithvi, rightly speaking of her as the supreme female principle. Notably, Vishnu had early associations with Prithvi as a god responsible for sustaining creation. He is often shown as either protecting her or providing for her, and in some depictions, he is also shown as her consort. It was much later in the Puranic texts when Prithvi transformed into Bhudevi that the former's myths mingled with those of her new form. Bhudevi is a goddess who is fertile, maternal, creative, and both raw and powerful.

There is an account in the *Garuda Purana* where Vishnu's *viraya*, or energy, mingled with that of Lakshmi (who is associated with Bhudevi), creating a connection between the female and male principles of sustaining cosmic energies. In this account, Vishnu was thus a lover and protector of the earth, taking forms time and again to ensure dharma continues to exist on earth.

The earth, or *bhumi*, emerged from the depths of the ocean in the embodiment of a goddess: Lakshmi, Sri or Bhu. It was her plea that brought on the various incarnations of Vishnu. Today, she is also worshipped as a symbol of fertility in this form—the goddess of reproduction and nurturing, or the mother, so to speak. The *Matsya Purana*, for example, specifies the ecological condition of the planet when it sank:

> When the sun loses his lustre, the moon and the other planets vanish, when winds emit fire and smoke, when the sacrifices and *vasat* become weak and powerless, when the roads become void of birds and their beings, when the Rudras become void of their honour, when all the quarters are covered with darkness and when all the *Lokas* and regions disappear due to want of work, then when everything becomes peaceful the universe rests in Narayana.[1]

There is a long-standing relationship between Devi Lakshmi and the cosmic Prakriti, which perhaps gives us the best understanding of Bhudevi. On appearing on earth, Lakshmi came as three separate *guna*s—Sri of the *sattva* guna, Bhu of the *rajas* guna, and Durga of the *tamas* guna.

In Tantric Vaishnavism, there are verses extolling Bhudevi's greatness and her part as a consort to Vishnu alongside Sri or Lakshmi. In this form, Bhudevi becomes the medium through which the knowledge of Vishnu as a supreme cosmological figure is transmitted to the human world. It is she who engages him in the affairs of mankind, being a mediator between Vishnu and the devatas, Vishnu and *manav*, and so on. This places her firmly in the role of a mother nurturing her child and acting as a go-between for the father and the offspring.

Bhudevi, in her association with Sri Lakshmi, is also believed to have been formed through the nectar of creation, which—in her embodiment as a woman—gives her immense power, beauty and abundance. In the Pancharatra school of thought rooted in Vaishnavism, I think we see this significance given to Lakshmi or Bhudevi, where she is often worshipped with *soma*, the essence of plant and organic life. Her central place in philosophy is undeniable, not only as Vishnu's shakti, aiding the sustenance of the universe, but also in her own right as one of the prime goddesses.

In the Bhakti movement, Sri was worshipped by gurus, sages and saints, who wrote hymns, songs and poems about her loving relationship with Vishnu, which embodied the height of divine love and union. So inseparable were Vishnu and Sri that one symbolised the other and vice-versa. Bhudevi is thus the Mother Goddess to Vaishnava worshippers.

In the Samhitas, she is shown to have three forms depicted through nature or natural elements—the physical earth sustaining life, the universal and cosmic mother of all mankind, and matter itself that is formed through a cosmogenic creation. Creation occurs when Vishnu and Lakshmi (Bhudevi) enter the material world, the realm of humans, and partake in the experience of life. C. Sivaramamurti points out that Bhudevi's 'place beside Narayana is to the left near the conch while that of Lakshmi is to the right near the lotus'. He opines that 'there is a link between the conch and Bhudevi just as there is an affinity between Lakshmi and the lotus'.[2] The *Vishnudharmottara Purana* also notes the same.

As I have mentioned previously, there are certain schools of thought that refer to Vishnu as Srinivasa—in whom Sri abides. This is related to depictions where Bhudevi is usually depicted standing or sitting to the left of Lord Venkateswara (a form of Vishnu), which can particularly be seen in the Tirumala–Tirupati tradition, making Sri or Bhu a vital element in Vishnu's worship.

In the *Ashta Lakshmi Stotram* from the early 1970s, a prayer to the eight Lakshmis, we get a better understanding of the various manifestations of Sri. The manifestations of these goddesses are depicted in temples through eight decorative jars, known as *ghatasthapana*, a tradition that is specific to Devi. These jars are made out of clay and are similar to earthen pots; grain is planted inside them, symbolising the goddess of earth and fertility. This is perhaps the most direct connection between Sri and Bhudevi as well as an earlier form of her from the Vedic period—as Aditi.

In the symbolism of the jar, she is the abundant earth and a container of life and creation. She is the primordial power holding space for nourishment. When water is poured into the jar, it correlates with material prosperity and abundance. Notably, in Bhudevi's journey as an earth goddess is a deeper and more meaningful truth representative of our union with the ultimate spiritual source: Like all life forms on earth, we are born and temporarily endure life to ultimately return to the source of all creation, similar to the goddess herself.

Momai

ॐ ऐं ह्रीं क्लीं नमो नम: देवी दशामा नमो नम:।

Salutations to the Divine Mother, Dasha Maa (the Tenth), embodying wisdom, strength and divine energy.

—Dasha Maa Mantra

*D*evi Momai derives her name from Maha Mata, the Great Mother. This reflects her role as an ancient nurturing figure, embodying maternal strength and protection. Besides being known as Momai, she is also referred to as Dashama, Mammai, Mohmai, Untni Devi (the goddess of the dromedary) and Untadi Maa. She is especially revered in Kutch, where her chief temple is located in the village of Momaymora.

From the Vedic to the Puranic, the Mother Goddess is a recurring leitmotif in sacred Hindu thought, literature and iconography. She is transformed and assimilated into the tantric and the local village and cultic goddess too. Momai Mata is venerated for her power and benevolence, embodying health and prosperity. She is believed to bestow blessings upon her devotees, ensuring their well-being and success. The legend of Momai Mata's origin connects her to both the benevolent aspect of Durga and the fierce energy of Kali, highlighting her role as a worthy protector. Local folklore attributes miraculous powers to her, including the ability to cure illnesses, ward off evil spirits, and bless devotees with fertility and feminine strength.

Iconographically, when depicted in the form of a statue, she is shown with four arms, holding a sword, a bowl, a trident and a club, which symbolise her martial and nurturing qualities. However, in painted versions, she is frequently depicted with just two arms, carrying a trident and an incense burner. Her association with a black male goat, which sometimes appears beside her as a sacrificial animal, emphasises her protective role over her devotees.

In modern versions, Momai is seated on a dromedary, with four arms holding a trident, a red string, a lotus bloom and a sword. In some depictions, the string is replaced by a shield, reinforcing her role as a warrior goddess. She is presented in a surprisingly serene mountainous landscape, with snow-capped peaks and waterfalls, despite her origins in a semi-desert region. She symbolises power over diverse natural realms and her ability to bring peace and abundance to otherwise harsh environments.

A notable legend about Momai, recorded by Sigrid Westphal-Hellbusch and Heinz Westphal in their book, as recounted by Barot Shamalji of Porbandar, tells of her life in Satadipa near the Indus Delta.[1] A carpenter named Jalan, who emigrated from Satadipa around AD 1140, carried with him symbols of Momai, namely a swan and a peacock, representing her divine presence. Unfortunately, the peacock was attacked by local dogs, leading the Rabari community to fear the goddess' wrath. In response, they appealed to Devi Chamunda, who resurrected the peacock, symbolically ensuring Momai's ongoing protection. Since then, the Rabari people have revered Momai, who is represented not by an idol but by symbols—a feather whisk and white cowries. It is said that Momai possesses a thousand hands, represented by rows of cowries, which signify her vast protective reach.

Shakti puja, the worship of Devi, is the supreme embodiment of feminine energy and strength and holds profound significance during Navaratri. This festival celebrates the power of the goddess in her various forms, including Kali and Durga, revered as protectors and sources of unyielding strength. In certain areas, like in the state of Gujarat, Navaratri becomes a vibrant expression of devotion through various rituals and prayers, with dances such as the Garba, symbolising the triumph of good over evil and the enduring power of the Divine Feminine.

In Gujarat, the worship of the Mother Goddess is deeply woven into the region's cultural and religious fabric. Numerous local and cultic goddesses, such as Momai Mata, Bahuchara Mata, Shyamala Mata and Khodiyar Mata, are venerated, each embodying distinct qualities and powers. Amba Mata, considered the ultimate embodiment of sacred feminine power, symbolises divine strength, while Bahuchara Mata is associated with fertility, prosperity and governance. Shyamala Mata represents good fortune and business success, particularly among traders and the Jain community, while Khodiyar Mata is known for her protective qualities and widespread popularity among devotees. Amongst these deities, Devi Momai stands out as a traditional regional goddess, celebrated for her role in ensuring health and spiritual well-being.

Panchmahal, a region where Gujarati and Rajasthani cultural influences converge, is renowned for its rich tribal heritage. The area reflects a unique blend of architectural styles, textiles and folk traditions from both states, creating a distinct cultural identity. Located near the city of Godhra, Panchmahal is closely associated with the worship of Momai Mata. Rituals to honour her often include intricate jewellery and ornaments, reflecting the goddess' spiritual significance in the region.

In traditional representations of Momai, particularly in Gujarat's sacred textile art known as Mata-ni-Pachedi, her role as a powerful nurturing protector is emphasised. Mata-ni-Pachedi, or 'the cloth of the goddess', serves as both a spiritual canvas and a portable shrine. It is especially important within the Vaghari community, where it functions as a temporary sanctum for goddess worship, embodying divine power or shakti.

Devi Momai holds a special place with respect to these textiles, alongside regional goddesses like Hadkai Mata, symbolising strength, protection and resilience. Central to the Pachedi's panels are scenes that include Momai Mata surrounded by worshippers, animals and musicians, each element reinforcing her significance in the land and community. Her appearance in the Pachedi honours her deep bond with her devotees, depicting her as an ever-watchful guardian, accessible to her people regardless of location. These textiles ensure that Momai's presence and blessings remain portable, adaptable and deeply embedded in the lives of her followers.

Votive offerings for Momai Mora, particularly in Kutch, are unique and often include clay dromedaries. These clay figures reflect her bond with the dromedary, an animal that signifies endurance and resilience in Kutch's arid climate. In 1969, Haku Shah and others observed that the Rabari nomads, before leaving Kutch on their seasonal journeys to mainland Gujarat, would spend a night in Momai Mora's sanctuary and present her with a clay dromedary.[2] This offering is part of a ritual to secure her blessings for a safe journey, abundant harvest and good health. Annual offerings and celebrations honour Momai, where she is believed to protect livestock and heal the sick. In earlier times, the goddess was offered goats and water buffaloes as sacrifices, but never dromedaries, as these animals are sacred to her and represent her *chadiku* (mount). Momai's main weapon, the *trahur* (trident), along with her *dhal* (shield), emphasises her dual role as a protector and a warrior. She is believed to have been born from Brahma's mouth, an origin story captured in the Gujarati phrase *'Brahma na mukh ma thi peda thayeli'*, which places her existence in time immemorial, referred to as *mor vahi*.

The main sanctuary of Momai Mata is located in the village of Momaymora in Rapar taluka of Kutch, Gujarat. This temple complex, set on a small hill beside a sacred grove, contains a well and memorial stones. These are sites where weak and elderly animals, especially cows and dromedaries, are allowed to graze, reinforcing Momai's connection to the pastoral life of her devotees. The temple complex consists of a courtyard, residential quarters and a two-room temple. The first room houses a sculpture and a coloured image of Momai, while the second room contains images of Rama, Lakshmana and Sita, along with votive offerings and ritual objects. The courtyard also holds large, cubical memorial stones with intricate reliefs, representing the legacy of those who have sought her blessings.

Each year, during a festival held from September to October, people from different communities gather at Momaymora's sanctuary to sing, dance and honour the goddess. This celebration reflects her role as a unifying figure, respected by diverse groups beyond the Rabari. Through these ceremonies, Devi Momai is continually invoked as a guardian of the land and its people, embodying resilience, nurturing care and a fierce protectiveness that has endeared her to generations of devotees.

Tulsi

ॐ तुलसीदेव्यै च विद्महे
विष्णुप्रियायै च धीमहि
तन्नो वृन्दा प्रचोदयात्

*Dearest of Vishnu, Tulsi, I bow to you.
You give me supreme intelligence.
Oh Vrinda, enlighten my mind.*

—Tulsi Gayatri Mantra

Most Hindu households grow the sacred Tulsi plant, which represents Goddess Tulsi and is regarded as an avatar of Devi Lakshmi and the consort of Shri Vishnu. There are legends, especially in the *Shiva Purana*, that also draw parallels between Devi Tulsi and Vrinda, the wife of Jalandhara. Irrespective of the origin story we believe in, it is not possible to perform rituals of Vishnu worship without first paying one's respects to Devi Tulsi. Offering her leaves in the worship of Narayana—and even his avatars Krishna and Vithoba—is mandatory.

या दृष्टा निखिलाघसंघशमनी स्पृष्टा वपुः पावनी।
रोगाणामभिवंदिता निरसनी सिक्तांतकत्रासिनी।।
प्रत्यासत्ति विधायिनी भगवतः कृष्णस्य संरोपिता।
न्यस्ता तच्चरणे विमुक्तिफलदा तस्यै तुलस्यै नमः।।

> *My heartfelt tribute to you, Devi Tulsi,*
> *who absolves you of all your sins, who cleanses you,*
> *who heals all your malaises when you pray ardently,*
> *even the Lord of Death fears her; she will*
> *take you closer to Lord Krishna and*
> *set you on the path of salvation.*
>
> —*Padma Purana*, Book 5, Chapter 79, Verse 68

Traditionally, the Tulsi plant is reverentially placed in the centre of the courtyard of a Hindu house, called the Tulsi Vrindavan. In the *Devi Bhagavatam*, Devi Tulsi is referred to as being a manifestation of Lakshmi. As the story goes, once there was a king called Vrishadhvaja who was a devotee of Shiva and hence banned the worship of all other deities. Angered at the king's ignorance, Suryadeva cursed him that he would be abandoned by Devi Lakshmi. Upset by the curse upon his devotee, Shiva pursued Suryadeva, who fled to Vishnu, seeking shelter from the wrath of the god of destruction.

Meanwhile, many years passed on earth; Vrishadhvaja died, and so did his son. It was now his grandchildren Dharmadhvaja and Kushadhvaja who were worshipping Devi Lakshmi to gain her favour. She was happy with their efforts and blessed them with her benevolence, and was born to them as their daughter—Tulsi to Dharmadhvaja, and Vedavati to Kushadhvaja.

As time went by, Devi Tulsi gave up the comforts of the royal palace and went to Badrinath to perform penance to gain Lord Vishnu as her rightful husband. Brahmadeva, pleased with her tapas, appeared before her, telling her that she would have to marry the asura Shankhachuda before she could marry Narayana. Now, Asura Shankachuda himself had undergone a long and difficult tapas to please Lord Brahma. As a result of his prayers, he had been blessed with the boon of invincibility through the Vishnukavacha, the armour of Vishnu. As per this blessing, no one would be able to slay him or bring any harm to his body till he wore the *kavach*.

Shankhachuda and Devi Tulsi were married, and he practised his dharma. Even so, he often made mistakes for the sake of the betterment of the asuras. Sometimes, he would sin and use unfair means to gain victory for the asuras. After he won over the three worlds, driving the gods out of the Swargaloka, it was time to put an end to his unbridled thirst for power.

As a way to protect the universe, Lord Shiva decided to go to battle with Shankhachuda. As Tulsi Devi prayed for the protection and well-being of her husband, Lord Vishnu appeared before her in his divine form and reminded her of her true reality, urging her to return to her celestial abode. In anger and grief at having to betray her husband, Devi Tulsi cursed Lord Vishnu that he would turn to stone. Vishnu then turned into a stone and remained as such on the banks of the Gandaki. People believe that this stone was a *shaligrama* and that Devi Tulsi's decayed body became the river Gandaki in order to unite with Lord Vishnu, such that the strands of her hair became the Tulsi plant.

A similar legend tells us another story, except that here Devi Tulsi is Devi Vrinda, who was married to the asura Jalandhar known for creating havoc in all three worlds, having driven the devas out of the Swargaloka. His ambition had to be brought to an end, and it was Lord Vishnu who appeared before Vrinda, his most pious devotee. Vrinda, as it so happened, was performing penance through which Jalandhar would become immortal, and it was to prevent this from happening and maintain a balance in the world that Narayana had to intervene.

As part of the rituals of penance, Jalandhar and Vrinda

had to sit together and perform certain rituals as a married couple. Narayana, taking on the form of Jalandhar, sat beside Vrinda, destroying her chastity and the sanctity of the ritual. Realising the truth, a distraught Vrinda cursed Lord Vishnu to become a stone, and he turned into a shaligrama. Vrinda then immolated herself and became the Tulsi plant growing from the earth, gaining the status of the goddess who would always be worshipped alongside Vishnu. Since then, Tulsi has become an essential component of the act of worship itself. For example, in the Gautamiya tantra, the Haribhakti *vilasa* states:

तुलसी-दल-मात्रेण जलस्य चुलुकेन च।
विक्रीणीते स्वम् आत्मानं भक्तेभ्यो भक्त-वत्सल:॥

Shri Krishna is most affectionate towards his devotees.
Even if they offer him only one tulsi leaf
and a handful of water, he will be theirs.

It is believed even today that a person who waters and cares for the Tulsi plant gains moksha and the divine grace of Vishnu even if they don't directly worship him. Traditionally, the daily worship of the Tulsi plant is performed by the women of the household, specifically married women. Tuesdays and Fridays are considered particularly auspicious for worshipping the goddess.

Jyestha

ॐ रक्त ज्येष्टायै विध्महे
नील ज्येष्टायै धीमहि
तन्नो लक्ष्मी प्रचोदयात्:

*Jyestha Lakshmi, the elder sister of Lakshmi,
is just the opposite of Lakshmi. So we pray that Lakshmi
blesses us with wealth and abundance, and Jyestha leaves us
so that Lakshmi enters our house.*

—Jyestha Lakshmi Gayatri Mantra

There is an all-encompassing nature to worship in Hinduism. Our rich mythology makes space for the auspicious and the inauspicious, representing the duality of human nature. Devi Jyestha is an important goddess representing this duality. She is associated with Devi Lakshmi's older sister Alakshmi, the goddess of inauspicious things and misfortunes.

Devi Jyestha is a goddess who can be found in inauspicious places. In some ways, she is considered the patron devi of sinners and associated closely with wrongdoings. She represents the base nature of humanity, but this representation is the gateway to ascension towards spiritual enlightenment. Despite the secrets of her mysterious shakti, the worship of Devi Jyestha is naturally kept as far away from regular households as one can manage.

Devi Jyestha is mentioned as far back as 300 BCE,

alongside Mahadevi, the Mother Goddess. It is believed that the misfortune brought on by Devi Jyestha was placed at the altars of Devi Kali and Durga, who would then protect their devotees from these misfortunes. By the 7th and 8th centuries, Jyestha's worship had already peaked in South India, and subsequently, she became a lesser-known manifestation of Devi. As Julia Leslie explains in her book:

> Judging by the number of images still to be found today (often on the outskirts of a village), the goddess was once extremely popular in South India during the seventh and eighth centuries. She was certainly popular enough for the ninth-century Tamil Alvar, Tondaradippodi to comment on the number of foolish devotees she had kept from the truth but as the cult of the sakti rose, her following declined. Today, her image is rarely worshipped. It is either pushed into a corner where it receives little attention.[1]

Moving from the depiction of the goddess to her associations, one sees her holding on to emblems of inauspiciousness. She is the antithesis of Lakshmi, with a prominent nose that is similar to an elephant's trunk; her ink-coloured lower lip is left hanging low; and she has large, pendulous breasts descending to her navel. Nothing about this description can be considered gentle, graceful or elegant, which are often the adjectives used for Lakshmi. Devi Jyestha's hair is braided and piled on top of her head or wound in a style that is similar to *vasikabandha*.

In some depictions, Devi Jyestha is holding a broom, while her banner depicts the crow, a bird considered to be the harbinger of doom. The broom is symbolic of her bringing bad omens into the household by literally sweeping them in, and the crow, as already mentioned, is representative of negative aspects, and reminds us of the birds that usually gather around a corpse. Devi Jyestha's vahan is a donkey, another animal considered inauspicious, forever a beast of burden. In some texts, however, she is shown as being drawn in a chariot pulled by lions, with tigers following her.

There is an episode in the *Padma Purana* describing the Samudra Manthana where Devi Jyestha, in her form of Alakshmi, was seen rising from the sea before Devi Lakshmi. To some extent, it is agreed that her arrival was associated with the *halahala* poison being excreted by the ocean, which further ties into the lore of her being the inauspicious one. In contrast, Devi Lakshmi was born when the amrita was released. In other Puranic texts, Devi Jyestha is described as having emerged from the ocean wearing red garments when Lord Shiva swallowed the poison.

On seeing Devi Jyestha, the gods immediately turned away from her. She was obviously unwelcome and, as a result, was shunned and went on to dwell in inauspicious places. Perhaps this is why today she is worshipped in every household; people pray to be spared her wrath. As Leslie shows, according to the *Stri-dharma-paddhati*:

> ...we must turn to the section on meals and, within that, to the subsection on the wife's ritual offering before she eats. The wife's equivalent to her husband's pre-dinner ritual (bhojanavidhi) is prescribed as follows:
>
> Women should make an offering of food to the goddess Jyestha at the time of their own meal.
>
> The following two verses are attributed to Manu:
>
> If a woman does not make a daily food-offering to Jyestha, according to her resources, from the food she is about to eat, she will go to hell when she dies.
>
> Women who want sons, grandsons and wealth should propitiate Jyestha with a food-offering every day without fail.[2]

According to another tale from the *Linga Purana*, Lord Vishnu divided the material world into two extremities: good and bad. He created both Lakshmi and Jyestha to be aspects of this division; or rather, in some accounts, they emerged as a result of the churning of the cosmic ocean. Lakshmi ended up being the consort of Vishnu and when Jyestha complained of not having a groom of her own, she was married to Sage Dussaha.

The marriage of Jyestha and Dussaha also came with its tribulations. For all his patience, Dussaha eventually got tired of having his wife sour at the sight of anything auspicious. Dussaha spoke to Vishnu and Markandeya, who advised that the wise sage restrict the goddess' movement to places that were dark and believed to be inauspicious. Eventually, however, the sage abandoned his wife, for she was nothing but a bad omen.

A distraught Jyestha ultimately turned to Vishnu, who proclaimed that she would receive her offerings when she visited households as a result of their own *karma-phala*, the consequences of their actions. Thus, there is space in Hindu thought even for the inauspicious Devi Jyestha.

Kamadhenu

सर्वकामदुधे देवि सर्वतीर्थोंभिषेचिनि।
पावने सुरभि श्रेष्ठे देवी तुभ्यं नमोस्तुते॥

*Salutations to the great goddess,
the one who fulfils the wishes of her devotees.*

—Kamadhenu Mantra

Kamadhenu was the sacred cow that came out of the cosmic ocean when the devatas and asuras churned it for its many treasures. In Hindu mythology, Kamadhenu is considered divine and sacred and is worshipped as a goddess. In most Vedic texts, she holds a position of great esteem and is described as the mother of all cows, believed to have miraculous powers through which she could bestow upon those who prayed to her anything their heart desired.

In the Vedic period, life was sustained by agriculture, and the cow was truly a boon for mankind, providing nourishment and help with farming. Perhaps for this reason, Kamadhenu was associated with Bhudevi and the other earth goddesses. In a fascinating comparative study of Bhudevi and Gaia, Purnima Bakshi Kanwar states that:

> Bhudevi came in the guise of Surabhi the divine cow. Bhumi-sukta of the *Atharvaveda* gives a wondrous image of the earth as a sweet-smelling cow that offers sustenance from its golden udder.[1]

In the Vedic scriptures, Kamadhenu is also sometimes considered to be the mother of all bovines and the eleven Rudras. She is depicted as a cow of great beauty and strength, unique in her iconography, showing the head and breasts of a human female but the gleaming pure-white body of a cow. Some accounts describe her as having all the gods and deities within her body, which perhaps ties in with the importance of her role as the one providing sustenance and energy to the material world.

Kamadhenu is also known by other names such as Surabhi and Nandini. It is these names that perhaps give us some clues as to her form. Consider her original name, Kamadhenu—*kama* denotes desires and wishes, while *dhenu* means the giver of or the provider. She is a unique divine being who can fulfil all the desires and wishes of those who appeal to her. As Nandini, she is the most beloved daughter, who brings divine grace and sustenance to any household.

Since time immemorial, Devi Kamadhenu has been an integral part of the Indian tradition. She went with the devas after the Samudra Manthana to the Swargaloka but was later given to the Saptarishis. Rishi Jamadagni, followed by Rishi Vasishtha, came into possession of Kamadhenu afterwards. At every place, she gave plenty of milk and other fundamental necessities of life that ensured the rishis were taken care of and could focus on conducting rituals and sacrifices.

An alternate tale of origin for Devi Kamadhenu is that she arose from the breath of Prajapati Daksha, the creator of the human race and the mind-born son of Lord Brahma. In the Ramayana, she is said to be the daughter of Kashyapa and his wife Krodhavasha, who was one of the daughters of Prajapati Daksha. As per both these accounts, her lineage can be traced back to Daksha. The common link here, however, is her status as a divine gift or boon to mankind and her role as the mother of cows and buffaloes.

There is an interesting tale about Devi Kamadhenu. She was once living with Sage Jamadagni when the great king Kartavirya Arjuna came to visit with his people and army. Rishi Jamadagni was able to take care of the large retinue of the king because of the grace of Kamadhenu, but the surprise of such lavish hospitality made the king curious. When the king heard of the divine cow, in his arrogance, he stated that he wanted the divine creature for his own personal use and as part of his material wealth. He dragged her out and her calf was ripped away from her as he left.

Rishi Jamadagni's son Parashurama marched to the king's capital with his axe and fought single-handedly against the king's entire army who attacked him with their greatest might. Finally, the king came to the battlefield and as they duelled, Parashurama killed Kartavirya Arjuna himself, along with his arrogance and illusion, bringing back the sacred cow back to the ashram. Thus, it is said that Devi Kamadhenu freely gives her blessings but these are meant for the universal good and well-being rather than for hoarding as part of one's personal wealth and riches.

Interestingly, in other cultures across the world as well, we find instances where cows are worshipped. For example, in the Zoroastrian tradition, the name of the primordial bovine is Gavaevodata. While commenting on the formal changes in bovine worship, Kanwar points out how Kamadhenu came to be associated with a cosmic image or even the universe:

> The cow had enormous importance in the past, particularly in the cult of goddesses. In ancient Egypt the sacred cow was a symbol of abundant life. Later the sky itself was depicted as a great cow, her belly speckled

with stars, identified with the Goddess Hathor, who each dawn gave birth to the sun, the young bull-calf.[2]

Another similar story is related to the Ramayana. It tells us of the divine cow's presence in the ashram of Rishi Vasishtha when he threw a grand feast for King Vishwamitra and his entire army. Surprised at the hospitality, when the king heard of the divine cow, he too wanted to possess her. When the sage refused to part with the cow, King Vishwamitra tried to take her by force. Kamadhenu, knowing what was happening, produced an entire army of warriors to battle the king and his army, who were easily vanquished. As a result, a humiliated Vishwamitra gave up his kingdom and became an ascetic.

Devi Kamadhenu is believed to be so sacred that every part of her body is considered holy and revered in the Indian tradition. The internal body of the cow is sacred enough to be a place where even the gods can reside. She may not be usually worshipped in her goddess form but her significance can be felt across the Hindu tradition, where followers avoid inflicting any pain upon the cow. There are still some temples that place her in a site of veneration, particularly on the days of sacred pujas and occasions.

Kamakshi

क्लीं क्लीं कामाख्या क्लीं क्लीं नमः।

O Devi Kamakshi, we bow down to you!

—Kamakshi Beej Mantra

In the *Lalita Sahasranama,* a central text of Devi worship, Goddess Kamakshi is described as 'she whose eyes awaken desire' or 'she who has beautiful eyes'. It is believed that the goddess' eyes enchanted the hermit Shiva to participate in the affairs of the mortal world. In doing so, she became the bestower of prosperity, knowledge and fame, along with good progeny and an abundant life. Kamakshi embodies the autonomy and wild spirit of nature.

In South India, she is known as Kamakshi, and in the East as Kamakhya, and in both these incarnations, she is closely associated with Kamadeva, who played a role in bringing Shiva and Parvati together in a marital union. Kamakhya or Kamakshi is considered one of the most important goddesses and is a part of the legend of the 51 Shakti Peethas. Yet, interestingly, Dr Banikanta Kakati holds that:

> This mother cult of Kamakhya must have belonged to certain matriarchal tribes like the Khasis and the Garos. To win over their allegiance and support and facilitate the propagation of Aryan ideas and customs, royal patronage was extended to this local cult of Kamakhya.[1]

However, in the temples of South India, the association between the goddess and the god of desire is often celebrated and glorified to great heights, with much of her symbology evolving from that of the God of Love. She is shown as a beautiful woman who is seated on a lotus, dressed in a beautiful red sari, and decked in jewels made of gold and gems from the depths of the ocean and bright iridescent pearls. Her face carries the radiance of the rising sun. She is shown as having four arms: one carries a noose, the other an elephant goad, a parrot is perched on the upper left, while with her upper right arm she carries a bow made of sugarcane and arrows made of lotus stems.

The parrot, the lotus stem arrows and the sugarcane bow are all attributes of Kamadeva, further cementing the goddess' place in his mythos. In contrast, Kamakhya of the northeast is a symbol of a more primordial eternal feminine. Eminent scholar Birendranath Datta traces the mythical journey of Devi Kamakhya in his work:

> It is significant that Ka Meikha is the mythical grandmother on the paternal side, who has an important place in the bone burial ceremony of the traditional Khasi religion. The Sastric status of Kamakhya has been supported and buttressed by a number of Sanskrit works, prominent among them being the Kalika Purana (c. 10th–11th century), the Yogini Tantra (16th century) and the Hara-Gauri Samvada, believed to have been composed in these parts. Of these, the Kalika Purana, which is an important upa-purana, is the most valuable source of information.[2]

Devi Kamakshi is seated on the Shri Chakra. She is considered to be the representation of Shri Vidya in her epitome of beauty, grace and divine mysteries. In Kanchipuram is a beautiful temple abode built in honour of the goddess, known as the Kamakshi Amman temple. This is another Shakti Peetha, which is said to be among the most powerful sites of worship and energetic significance. In the tantric tradition, it is believed that this is where the navel of the world rests—where the *nadis* emerge and spread to the other parts of the body. These nadis are channels through which *prana* (spiritual energy) moves along the chakras from the kundalini all the way up to the *sahasrara-chakra*.

As a form of the goddess of creation, Devi Kamakshi is often worshipped through the *yoni* puja, the worship of the womb. This is an important and foundational part of the goddess' worship, where she is depicted as a cleft in the rock from where red fluid implied to be blood flows out annually. This occurrence usually takes place on the days following the first rains in the month of June. During this time, she is no longer kama, for kama evokes passion for pleasure at an individual level, while Kamakshi evokes it for the world at large, driving forward communities.

The worship of the mother, or the goddess as a mother, is an ancient tradition in India. While we live in a male-centric society, with the priest class dominated by men, the worship of the mother or the female form, along with her procreative abilities, has always coexisted. Life is created by women, creation is associated with women, and the red colour of blood flowing from a stone annually is also connected with the worship of the most sacred time for women.

In spiritual terms, I suppose we can say that the womb is representative of Prakriti, the natural world. In this world exist opposing forces—life and death, fear and love, sorrow and happiness, desires and detachment. Shiva, or Purusha, is the human imagination engaged with Prakriti to create life. It is important to recognise the regionally varying practices of worship that evolved and adapted themselves to the various forms and manifestations of the goddess.

Kinsley, who has done an in-depth study on the Dasa Mahavidyas, describes the Kamakhya temple in Kamarupa, Assam, as having rich and varied imagery.[3] In various sacred texts, this place is highly revered as a Shakta centre, as it is believed to be the spot where Sati's yoni fell on earth, marking it as her primal or original seat, known as *adi pitha*. The stone yonis in the main temple symbolise figures like Kamala, Sodasi, Matangi and the Mahavidyas. Kamakhya herself is sometimes viewed as an embodiment of Sodasi. The reverence extends further as the nearby shrines honour the remaining Mahavidyas and other goddesses.

In Kanchipuram, the culture is pure and sattvic, with the devotees being vegetarian and only a few temples still conducting animal sacrifice. Sacrifice is more common in the worship of Durga and Kali, the more fearsome representations of Devi. However, due to societal norms in place since the British Raj in India, this practice has been on the decline. Devi's blood, as linked to the womb or yoni worship, also connects her with her sisters Lakshmi and Saraswati. Most popular in the southern parts of India, she is largely extolled as a goddess of families, fertility and domesticity.

As legend goes, after the incineration of Kamadeva at the hands of Shiva for disturbing his deep penance, Shiva's *guna*s moulded the ashes of Kama in the shape of a man and begged the Lord to bring him back to life. Shiva glanced at Kama and breathed life into him, bringing him back in the form of Bhandasura, a demon who was given the boon that he would never die at the hands of one who was born of a sexual union. As a product of Shiva's anger, Bhanda had immense rajas guna within him and he chased after and troubled the gods and the devatas.

Bhanda soon took over Indradeva's city and his army.

When this led to a war, the devatas sought Shiva and begged for refuge. He instead directed them to Devi. When Bhanda came looking for the devatas to the city of Kanchi with the intent to end their existence, Indra performed a yajna to invoke Devi, and from the fire of the *havan kund* arose Shri Chakra and the beautiful Devi Kamakshi. In the cave where the devatas were hiding out, she stomped her feet on the ground, causing a great big earthquake that made Bhanda stumble and fall. She eventually killed him after fighting a long-drawn battle and buried him in the city of Kanchi, erecting a victory stone at the site of the burial. It is so believed that the gods erected a temple on that exact spot at Kanchi in her honour, and it is there that the goddess is forevermore worshipped as the mother, the protectress and the benevolent one.

Lajja Gauri

ॐ ह्रीं श्रीं महागौर्यै दुर्गायै नमः।

I offer my salutations to Goddess Mahagauri and Durga, who embody supreme beauty, purity, and strength.

—Devi Mahagauri Mantra

*T*he Indian tradition of art since the third millennium BC has produced a great variety of mythological hybrid beings, which today have become fixtures in the country's art history. Devi Lajja Gauri belongs to this tradition and is directly associated with the lotus and the *purna kumbha*, or the brimming pot, and may have had roots in the Indus or Chalcolithic culture of India. While trying to search for the meaning behind the forms of Lajja Gauri, Carol R. Bolon found that:

> Like Hindu mythology, the image of Lajja Gauri communicates simultaneously on many levels. On the human level, the image of Lajja Gauri acts as a temporal reference point, that is, the female giving birth, an auspicious occurrence: she is the embodiment of human fertility. On the divine level Lajja Gauri is the embodiment of the idea of fertility, of generation, of life-force. On the cosmic level the image suggests universal laws and processes of generation of all life. Mythic narratives about Lajja Gauri exist as well. Most

of these seek to explain her headless state, and these may only be modern, the inventions of villagers who have become alienated from the original intent and meaning of the image. Some others, however, may preserve a thread of her original meaning.[1]

In her iconography, Devi Lajja Gauri is almost always shown lying on her back, her toes tense, and her legs splayed out as though she were giving birth. However, there is rarely any indication that she is pregnant. For some, this posture of the goddess is emblematic of sexual freedom, seemingly suggestive. She is a goddess who is shown to be sexually receptive.

I suppose it is important then to consider the iconography of the entire pantheon of Indian goddesses where, notably, it is almost impossible to find a goddess showing signs of pregnancy or the process of childbirth for that matter. The birth of a child from a goddess is usually veiled in a metaphor and the tale of an actual childbirth resembling the human experience is completely absent. As J. Kedareswari writes:

> A large stone image of Lajja-Gauri yielded from the Vellal village, Kurnool district, from a dilapidated temple on the banks of the river Bhavanisi in the Srisailam submersible areas measuring 31" × 29" × 9" also proves the popularity and cultic significance of Lajja-Gauri. Similarly, a smaller image measuring 10 × 12 cm yielded from the excavations at Keesaragutta datable to the fifth century CE, signifies the worship of Lajja-Gauri even at home, which shows the union of Vaisnavism and Saivism as we find the mother Goddess holding the linga in the right hand and the head of a lion representing Narasimha in the left hand.[2]

In Devi's depiction, we can also notice the variations in the size of her sculptures made to represent a fertility goddess. Strangely enough, she is often shown headless, with her vagina the prime focus of her depiction. These figures first appeared around the beginning of the Christian era. There are some theories as to why the goddess is shown as a headless, mysterious figure, with some scholars attributing it to a feminine coyness towards nudity which made the goddess feel ashamed to display herself with such abandon. There is no denying the goddess' popularity as an aspirational figure to the human need to procreate. She is present in numerous temples and other monuments across Southeast Asia.

In the Nuapada district of Odisha, there are two plaques of Lajja Gauri, measuring 10 to 12 centimetres in height and made of limestone, a popular material found in the region. The plaques date back to approximately the 8th century AD, and they show the goddess as squatting on the ground, her legs stretched out in the traditional position of childbirth. Her pendulous breasts, the bare navel and the vividly displayed vagina point to her fertility as well as her brilliant youth. Where one would expect to see her head, we instead have lotus leaves, with the stem shaping her neck, and a lotus in full bloom where the goddess' head should be. The upper part of her body, depicting nature in all its glory, perhaps shows her association with agricultural communities and their land's fertility and fruitfulness.

Among the Bhiyans of Odisha, an indigenous community that is largely dependent on hunting–gathering for their survival, we find a similar goddess. The tradition of the goddess could very well have been carried forward, or perhaps she comes from their beliefs and lore. Similarly, in the Bastar region of Madhya Pradesh, there is a depiction of a woman goddess with outstretched legs carved in a *gotul*, a tribal youth dormitory belonging to the Muria tribe. The posture also conveys desire, sensuality, the creative power and the essence of the female form. Her sexuality is associated with the fertility of the woman and is a source of agricultural fertility that refutes eroticisation.

In her book, Bolon highlights the importance of distinguishing between the sacred, luminous depictions of Lajja Gauri and figures designed solely for sensual appeal.[3] The deeper spiritual meaning of the image of the goddess might get lost without making this distinction. Although her portrayal includes sensual aspects, Lajja Gauri's symbolism extends beyond physical allure, conveying a profound spiritual essence beneath an outwardly provocative form. This expressive style is typical in Indian art, as seen in the *maithuna* figures on the walls of the Khajuraho temple, where intimate scenes symbolise the ecstatic experience of divine union.

The image of Lajja Gauri continues to be enigmatic. In a Harappan seal, we see a woman with her legs stretched out and a plant growing from her vagina. This is a far more direct and obvious symbol of fertility and is perhaps the earliest precursor of the goddess who came to be Lajja Gauri. This symbol has stayed in the Indian art canon for centuries since, and while the goddess may not be part of the main pantheon of goddesses—rather remaining a minor, tribal goddess—her image, iconography, affiliation to Shakti and the primordial essence remain shrouded in mystery.

Manasa

जरत्कारु जगद्गौरी मनसा सिद्धयोगिनी।
वैष्णवी नागभगिनी शैवी नागेश्वरी तथा।।

*Jaratkaru, the World Mother or Jagadgauri,
is a perfected yogini by mind (Manasa Siddhayogini).
She is Vaishnavi, the sister of the Nagas,
and she is also Shiva's consort, the Queen of the Nagas.*

—*Manasa Devi Dvadashanama Stotram*

The tales and legends of Hindu mythology often reflect an interesting cultural overlap with those of parallel cultures such as the Greco-Roman myths or the Mesopotamian epics. This is perhaps a result of trading relations and the eventual expansion of these civilisations. One of the most obvious among these is the mythos of Devi Manasa, the goddess of snakes, which is rather popular in West Bengal.

Goddess Manasa in Bengal is worshipped for protection, for it is believed that the goddess has immense power to ward off snakes, as she is the mother of snakes. According to *Brahmavaivartta Purana* and *Devi Bhagavatam*, Goddess Manasa has twelve different names: Jaratkaru, Jagadgauri, Manasa, Siddhayogini, Vaisnavi, Nagabhagini, Saivi, Nagesvari, Jaratkarupriya, Astikamata, Visahari and Mahajnayuta. Those who utter these twelve names during the worship of goddess Manasa need not be afraid of any kind of snake. In Mahabharata, she is mentioned as the dear sister of Vasuki, the king of snakes.[1]

Devi Manasa is a central character of the 'Manasamangal Kavya', a verse poem recounting the legend of the goddess composed in the Bengali language sometime in the medieval era. The association of the goddess with snakes is an aspect shared by various gods and goddesses of other civilisations such as in ancient Mesopotamia, Egypt, Greece, Phoenicia and further out in Scandinavia and other Western European countries.

In the depiction of her forms across the globe, the most famous is the Sumerian sculpture dating back to 3500 BCE to 3000 BCE, which presents the figure of two snakes twisting around one another. To the pharaohs of Egypt, the snake was part of their royal emblem. Geb, the Egyptian god of the earth, is often depicted as having the head of a snake and was, by extension, the presiding deity of snakes. Even closer home, in the Indus Valley civilisation, Harappan seals have been discovered that bear the image of snakes, e.g., the Pashupati seal. Each of these accounts indicates the presence of Manasa, the goddess of snakes, in one form or another, as a deity of significant power and dominion.

In India, Goddess Manasa is worshipped by all Hindus, free from the trappings of caste, community and social hierarchies. Her worship is most popular in the months of Ashadha and Shravana, which bear the Indian monsoon. This is perhaps because it also happens to be the time when snakes come out, and most devotees pray to the goddess for her protection against snake bites. Interestingly, Goddess Manasa is also seen as being associated with wealth and the welfare of children. It is believed in many villages of rural India that beneath the spot on which a snake rests lies a great treasure.

The traditional Yama-Pata is an adaptation of the Coksudan-Pata for the liberation of the soul while the Manasa-Pata straddles tribal mythology aimed at enlightenment and glorification of the snake goddess Manasa. The ritual recitation accompanied by the unwinding of vignettes painted to illustrate the story is part of the Manasa cult. The following story and painted illustrations of Goddess Manasa and Behula–Lakhindar are by Gurupada Citrakara who hails from Nayagram in the Midnapur district of West Bengal.

Victory! O Victorious One, who takes away the poison. Your bed is made of serpents; your throne is made of vipers. The snake which is the seat of the goddess is enchanted by good words.

The boat is shaken with fury
The ropes are pulled,
Who is the fool to abuse Mother Manasa?[2]

Even though Devi Manasa has always existed in some form or another, she is barely mentioned in the ancient Puranas. She appears for the first time in the later Puranas such as the *Brahmavaivarta Purana* and the *Devi bhagavatam*. The Puranic texts and the 'Manasamangal Kavya' present different origin stories for the goddess.

In the Puranas, Devi Manasa emerged as a result of Rishi Kashyapa's meditation while composing the mantra for the removal of snake venom. It is believed that Kashyapa was in the midst of reciting the mantra during the *Brahmamuhurta* and that was when the goddess appeared. As she was born from the mind of Sage Kashyapa, she was known as Manasa, or 'mind-born'. In the *Brahmavaivarta Purana* as well as the *Devi Bhagavatam*, Devi Manasa was the wife of Sage Jaratkaru. This union was the result of a thousand years of penance at Mount Kailash, after which Rishi Kashyapa gave away his daughter as a bride to Sage Jaratkaru.

There is another tale in the Puranas about Devi Manasa, who woke her husband to offer prayers at dusk to the gods. Angered by this disturbance, Rishi Jaratkaru vowed to forsake his wife. A distraught Manasa called upon all the gods for assistance: Vishnu, Mahadeva and Rishi Kashyapa. However, not one of them could bring Rishi Jaratkaru to change his mind. As a final effort at appeasement, they told the rishi, if nothing else, to have a child with Manasa to lessen her sorrow. The result of this union was the mind-born child Astika. In all Puranic texts, Devi's depiction is that of a devoted daughter and wife to Rishi Kashyapa and Rishi Jaratkaru, respectively.

Alternatively, in the 'Manasamangal Kavya', Devi Manasa is the daughter of Lord Shiva and also goes by the name of Siddhayogini. There is much debate and many opposing opinions regarding Devi Manasa's origin and the origin of her name. To some, she is a variation of the Kannada goddess Manchamma, while others say she is another form of Mudama, a regional goddess from Mysore who transformed into Manasa when she reached Bengal.

I think it is interesting how there is little evidence of the existence of Manchamma; there is limited documentation and even fewer images. She is purely a goddess existing in the realm of local lore, stories and legends. The goddess who is actually an invisible snake lady is worshipped once a year. No idols are used in her worship. Devi Mudama, on the other hand, is perhaps more similar to Manasa. She is represented in her sculpture form as a half-woman–half-snake being, usually worshipped by the lower caste people of Mysore.

In the *Shiva Purana*, Devi Manasa is believed to be the daughter of Lord Shiva. In fact, it is this confusion in terms of parentage—whether she is the daughter of Shiva or Kashyapa—that has relegated her to the status of a minor goddess. As the daughter of Shiva, she has inherited his destructive fury, which is wielded towards those who rise against her devotees or refuse to acknowledge her stature as a goddess.

In most depictions of Devi Manasa, either in stone, bronze or terracotta, we find certain shared features. Her iconography shows her bearing either two or four arms, wearing a crown on her head designed to hold seven snake hoods. Manasa is shown sitting beside her husband Sage Jaratkaru and her brother King Vasuki, with her son Astika in her lap. There is an image of Devi Manasa at the Varendra Research Museum in Bangladesh, where she is shown sitting in a yogic posture. This stems from both her father figures, Kashyapa and Shiva. She is holding a japamala in her lower right hand, a snake in her upper right hand, a manuscript in her lower left hand and a *ghat (bowl)* in her upper left hand.

The earliest image of the goddess was found in the form of a Mangalkot sculpture in Bogra, Bangladesh, perhaps pointing to an ancient tradition of worshipping the goddess. Coomaraswamy and Sister Nivedita say the following:

> This legend of [Chand Sadagar and] Manasa Devi, the goddess of snakes, who must be as old as the Mykenean stratum in Asiatic culture, reflects the conflict between the religion of Shiva and that of female local deities in Bengal. Afterwards Manasa or Padma was recognized as a form of *Shakti* [...], and her worship accepted by Shaivas. She is a phase of the mother-divinity who for so many worshippers is nearer and dearer than the far-off and impersonal Shiva...[3]

In fact, there has been a discovery of over 48 images and figures of Devi Manasa, which have come out of North Bengal alone. Most of these stone images are believed to have appeared in the pre-Islamic period, as after the advent of Islam, the imagery of Manasa also evolved. There was then a less mythological framework surrounding the legends of the goddess, and her stories were rooted in the human world, featuring more human episodes, such as that with Chand Sadagar, the king who refused to worship Manasa as a goddess. In Bengali folklore, it is Devi Manasa who stops Lord Shiva from ingesting the halahala during the Samudra Manthana.

Matangi

ॐ शुक्रप्रियायै विद्महे श्रीकामेश्वर्यै धीमहि तन्न: श्यामा प्रचोदयात्।

*Let us meditate on the beloved of Venus.
We contemplate Shri Kameshwari (the goddess of desire and love).
May that Shyama (dark-complexioned goddess) inspire and guide us.*

—Matangi Gayatri Mantra

Devi Matangi is the ninth goddess among the 10 Mahavidyas. As the Hindu goddess of inner thought and wisdom, she rules over the domains of speech and supernatural powers. As one of the 10 Mahavidyas, there are many layers to the spiritual import of this goddess; to me, she is first and foremost one of the primary gatekeepers of spiritual knowledge.

Matangi is described as the Dark One—a form of Saraswati who was incarnated as the daughter of Matanga, a sage hailing from the Chandal caste who resisted the caste system and its bounds and regulations to become a Brahmin through the path of karma. This was unheard of and an extremely rare occurrence in those times. She is a manifestation of Sati, the first incarnate wife of Lord Shiva who stepped into Daksha's yajna fire, sacrificing her life to protect the honour of her husband, which is why she is also an embodiment of Kali.

Devi Matangi's iconography depicts her as a goddess with a dark emerald complexion and a mark on her forehead shaped like the disc of a moon, which is why she's considered as the three-eyed goddess. She also wears a crown decorated with jewels. Her eyes are drawn in blissful intoxication. She is forever young, suspended at the youthful age of sixteen, with the divine beauty of full breasts and a slim waist. In her four hands, she has a noose, a mace, a sword and a hook.

> The first myth dealing with Matangi's origin is found in the *Saktisamgama-tantra* and concerns the appearance of Uccista-matangini, one of Matangi's most common forms. Once upon a time, Visnu and Laksmi went to visit Siva and Parvati. Visnu and Laksmi gave Siva and Parvati fine foods, and some pieces dropped to the ground. From these remnants arose a maiden endowed with fair qualities. She asked for leftover food (uccista). The four deities offered her their leftovers as *prasada* (food made sacred by having been tasted by deities). Siva then said to the attractive maiden: 'Those who repeat your mantra and worship you, their activities will be fruitful. They will be able to control their enemies and obtain the objects of their desires.' From then on this maiden became known as Uccista-matangini. She is the bestower of all boons.[1]

A fascinating aspect of Devi Matangi is that she destroys demons by first winning them over with her beauty and dispels the darkness for those living in an illusory world. She is often shown seated on a corpse, holding a skull and a bowl of blood, with long billowing hair. She plays sweet songs on her jewel-encrusted veena—which is not too different from the instrument of Devi Saraswati, and through her music, she fulfils every desire of her devotees. Matangi is almost always surrounded by birds, green and red parrots in particular, who are representative of a guru.

In fact, Matangi is rather closely associated with Devi Tripura Sundari; she is the advisor to the goddess. She has an especially close relationship with the South Indian temple city of Madurai, where she is venerated as Goddess Meenakshi Amman. Her varied associations establish Matangi as an integral goddess in the Hindu pantheon. Her *dhyana* and siddhi are as diverse as her forms; she is worshipped as both a white goddess—purity and sattvic guna—and a dark goddess—fierce and warrior-like. She is the tantric Saraswati, or Madurai's benevolent Meenakshi, but she is also Shyamala and Kali.

As an outlier goddess, especially one who often exists beyond the mainstream and is rather removed from the daily worship of Devi, Matangi facilitates the process by which unstruck divine sounds are manifested in our world in the form of speech and in their refinement, i.e., literature and music. It is believed that if one meditates upon Devi, she provides them with incredible knowledge, spiritual insight and inspiration.

In the tantra system, Matangi's crescent-shaped moon on the forehead is a reminder for the devotee that hers is a path of sacrifice in order to attain siddhis. The veena is her mastery over the music of the universe and inspires man to harmonise their life to this sweet sound, avoiding the jarring extremities driven by the ego. The parrots of Matangi are emblems of karma, the fundamental law of the universe that we cannot escape the consequences of our actions. Kinsley also argues that she is a protector of women's dignity. In elaborate instructions for a ritual, it is clearly stated that:

> In the *Tantrasara* we are told that at night, in a cremation ground or at a crossroads, the *sadhaka* should offer

fish, meat, cooked rice, milk, and incense to Matangi to acquire poetic talent and victory over enemies and to become a second Brhaspati (the gods' priest-guru). We are also told in the same text that to achieve the highest knowledge of the scriptures, Matarigi should be offered *uccista,* cat meat, and goat meat. In the *Purascaryarnava,* Karna-matangi is invoked in the hope that she will whisper in the *sadhaka's* ear the truth about some question posed by the *sadhaka.* We are told elsewhere that those who recite Matangi's mantra one hundred thousand times, offer ten thousand flowers in the sacrificial fire, and worship her yantra will get great wealth, will be able to control an angry king and his children, will be immune to the troubles caused by evil spirits, and will themselves become like deities. In this case, to ensure the success of their *sadhana,* worshippers are cautioned to refrain at all times from criticizing women and treating them like goddesses.[2]

Meenakshi

ॐ जटा जूट समायुक्तमर्धेन्दु कृत लक्षणाम्।
लोचनत्रय संयुक्तां पद्मेन्दुसद्यशाननाम्॥

I meditate upon the one adorned with matted hair,
marked by a crescent moon.
She is endowed with three eyes and has a face
as radiant as the lotus and the moon.

—Maa Durga Dhyaan Mantra

I think one of the most fascinating aspects of Hindu mythology is its translation from region to region. This certainly finds its way in the tales, stories and legends of the gods and deities, but it can also be found in a more intrinsic form through their aspects and the associations to their shakti.

Devi Meenakshi is perhaps a prime example of this form of translation. She is worshipped in the southern part of the Indian subcontinent as an avatar of Parvati, the wife of Shiva. The Meenakshi Amman Temple in Madurai, Tamil Nadu, is perhaps the most significant site of worship, where she is venerated alongside her husband Lord Shiva, who is in his Sundareshwara form.

Meenakshi Kalyanam, which is the wedding of Devi Meenakshi and Lord Sundareshwara, is celebrated annually at the temple. The goddess and the god are believed to have ruled over the city of Madurai for a long time in their human avatars. There is a belief that on the day of his wedding celebrations, the Lord performs miracles. This probably stems from the episode of the wedding. As Nandagopal writes:

> Another important text is the Sivalilarnava of Nilakantha Diksita of seventeenth century, in which there are detailed descriptions of the rituals of Minaksi Kalyana, such as kanyadana, sambandha mala (exchange of garlands between the bride and the bridegroom), lajahoma, asvarohana and agnipradaksina. The author is silent about the saptapadi and mangalya dharana. He describes the tradition of nalang (the reception), unjal (swing) and finally offering hospitality to the gods who have come to participate in the marriage ceremony.[1]

What really sets apart the mythos of Devi Meenakshi are the stories that tie her to the region, rooting her as a devi of the city of Madurai, for it is this city with which she has the strongest association. Madurai was a dominant power in South India and was part of the Pandyan Dynasty sometime in the 4th century BCE. The city of Madurai served as the capital of the Pandyan rulers. As an interesting side note, in the Mahabharata, the Pandyans are mentioned as the supporters of the Pandavas.

The legendary Pandyan king Malayadhwaja Pandya, who backed the Pandavas, and his wife Kanchanamalai were having trouble conceiving an heir. The king prayed to the gods and goddesses for the boon of a child. Shiva, showing mercy on the couple, granted him the fruit of his tapas in a rather unexpected way. The king was making a sacrifice in hopes of begetting a child when from the sacrificial fire emerged a young girl of three years of age.

The child looked like an ordinary one, but she had three breasts. It was believed that she would lose her third breast when she met the man who was to be her husband. She was a beautiful child; her eyes were enchanting and shaped like a fish, earning her the name Meenakshi, which in the Tamil language means 'fish-eyed'. Interestingly, in the case of representation, Goddess Meenakshi is also associated with Goddess Sri because of the presence of her chakra. As Kinsley observes, at the renowned Meenakshi temple in Madurai, coins featuring a human-like representation of Meenakshi on one side, with the Sri Chakra on the other side, are sold.[2] The temple also offers images depicting Meenakshi standing above the Sri Chakra.

The king, ecstatic about having a child at last, left no stone unturned in the education of his daughter. She learned to become a fine warrior, engaging in martial arts and archery and fighting with a sword. When she came of age, her father invited the bravest of warriors, kings and princes from the neighbouring kingdom to Madurai, as he wanted to see his daughter married. As was the tradition, a Pandyan daughter could not ascend the throne; it was thus necessary to find her a suitable husband who could take over the reins of the kingdom and, by extension, the dynasty.

The suitors brought with them many precious gifts, trying to win over the princess, but Meenakshi had already made up her mind that she would marry only he who was her equal in combat. Each suitor who was challenged to the task eventually suffered defeat, and so Meenakshi remained unmarried. Her father, unhappy with the turn of events but unable to go against his beloved daughter's wishes, eventually relented, and Meenakshi, breaking the Pandyan tradition, ascended the throne in her own right.

As a queen, Meenakshi conducted many military campaigns and in one of these campaigns, she travelled up north to Mount Kailash, where she met her equal in the martial arts. This was none other than Lord Shiva, who was standing before the goddess in his Sundareshwara form and knew who she was. He was only waiting for the goddess to recognise him. As Meenakshi's third breast disappeared, she realised that she was before the man who was meant to be her husband. Not only had Shiva fulfilled the prophecy, he had also met her condition. The two eventually returned to Madurai, where they were married. In another version of the myth, Henry Whitehead writes:

> In Madura during the time of the Pandya dynasty, there was a wicked irreligious king called Pandian. In his pride and presumption he closed the temple of Minachiamman, the renowned local goddess. She was enraged at this and, in order to take vengeance, became incarnate as a new-born infant. King Pandian, who greatly desired to have a child, one day found the deity incarnate as a little girl, lying in the palace, with a very curious bracelet on her arm, which was the exact copy of one belonging to his wife. He wished to adopt the child, but the astrologers warned him that she would bring evil upon his house, so he had her put in a basket and cast into the river. A merchant picked the basket out, brought her up as his own daughter, and called her Kannahai. Shortly before this, it happened that the god Siva also became incarnate, as another merchant living at Kaveripampatinam, a village at the mouth of the river Kaveri. Hearing of the girl's mysterious origin, he went and married her. After some years he became very poor, and, in spite of his wife's remonstrances, took her strange bracelet to Madura to sell it. It happened that King Pandian's wife had lost her bracelet, which exactly resembled this one, a few days before this. So the merchant was arrested on the charge of stealing it, brought before the king and put to death. In a few days, his wife, Kannahai, went to

Madura, heard what had happened, took the form of Thurgai, the demon-killing goddess, and slew Pandian. Since then she has been worshipped by the people. The slaughter of Pandian created in her a desire for bloodshed, and she is now a deity whom it is thought prudent to propitiate.[3]

Devi Meenakshi is an emblem of agency, independence and strength; an inspiration to all her female devotees to not be restricted by the gender norms placed upon them by society.

The union of Meenakshi with Shiva is represented in a unique style in the South Indian Pandyan dynasty artwork.[4] It is unclear if the legend is based on historical events. However, the iconography of the goddess is apparent. She is shown in a human form with two arms as well as a divine form with four arms. Interestingly, in the Meenakshi Sundareshwarar Temple, the presiding deity is her consort Sundareshwarar, that is, Shiva.

Mumba

या देवी सर्वभूतेषु विष्णुमायेति शब्दिता।
नमस्तस्यै नमस्तस्यै नमस्तस्यै नमो नमः॥

*Salutations again and again to Devi,
who resides in the name of Vishnu's maya in all beings.*

—*Durga Saptashati*, Chapter 5, Verse 5

The tale of Mumba Devi is one of trial and perseverance. The world needed the form of Mahakali to be born out of Parvati, but the volatile form of Kali required concentrated powers to control the inevitable destruction that she might wreak. Lord Shiva, in a bid to support his wife, suggested that Devi Parvati should take birth on earth as a fisherwoman. It was the way of the fisherfolk to cultivate concentration, perseverance and patience to achieve their goal of catching enough fish to not only fill their own family's stomach but also be a viable income stream for the community. Thus, Devi Parvati was born as Matsya, later known as Mumba, in a fishing village.

> The largest pagoda in Bombay is in the Black Town, about a mile and a half from the fort. It is dedicated to Momba Devee, or the Bombay goddess, who, by her images and attributes, seems to be Parvati, the wife of Siva.[1]

As Mumba, Parvati dedicated herself to learning all the

perseverance and concentration that was required of a fisherwoman, under the guidance of her community, as this was a way of life for them if they were to at all become worthy earners. When Mumba finally mastered the many techniques of possessing great powers of concentration, it was time for her to return to her heavenly abode and back to her form as Parvati. The purpose of her life in this incarnation was complete. In order to propel the completion of this manifestation of Devi Parvati as Mumba Devi, Shiva arrived in the fishing community in the form of a fisherman seeking the hand of Mumba Devi in marriage, recognising her divine form.

As soon as the humble community of fisherfolk learned of the divine nature of their beloved Mumba and the graciousness of the divine couple in recognising their skill and, by extension, their place in the world, they begged the goddess and the god to stay with them forever. Mumba Devi, touched by the love and devotion shown to her by the community from the time of her birth to her youth, agreed to stay with them forever as the *grama devata*, the local village goddess. Thus, she is known as Aai (Marathi for 'mother') to the folks of the fishing community of Maharashtra. As scholars Marika Vicziany and Jayant Bapat write:

> The temple of Mumbadevi is only one of the thousands of temples that are scattered throughout the city, and the temples are only one manifestation of the religious life of Mumbai's citizens. Both the temples and the religious life of Mumbai are poorly researched and understood, with myths taking the place of established fact. In that mythology, the Kolis [Mumbai's aboriginal fishing community] have a special relationship with Mumbadevi.[2]

The legend of Goddess Mumba stems from the *Sthala Purana*.

As historian and scholar K. Raghunath writes:

> It is stated therein that in times of yore, there lived in this region a very powerful and mighty giant bearing the name of Mumbarak, and the island derives its name from him. By means of austerities he pleased Brahmadev and prayed to be favoured with a blessing that he would be incapable of meeting with death at anybody's hands, and that he would ever prove successful.
>
> According to another version, it can also be supposed that the Emperor Mumbarak may have given the island his own name and called it Mumbapur or Mumbarak. He was a hater of the Hindu religion. For this reason the Hindus gave him the appellation of giants and after his death composed the above account of his, which is now read and venerated as a Purana.[3]

On receiving Brahma's blessings, Mumbarak set out to harass both the gods and the people on earth, who immediately turned to Vishnu for guidance and a solution. Lord Vishnu, understanding the gravity of Mumbarak's actions, turned to his own *aradhya*, Shiva, and together they each extracted a portion of lustre from their own bodies to give form to a devi who would destroy the giant. The goddess was fierce, aggressive, and the embodiment of righteous anger. Beating down the demon, she asked him to seek a blessing on his deathbed. The demon, recognising the divinity of the goddess, asked for mercy and begged that he be known forevermore as an extension of her name and that she be celebrated on earth by his name. Granting the demon this boon, the goddess adopted the name Mumba Devi from thereon.

Renuka

श्री गणेशाय नमः। श्री रेणुकायै नमः।
गिरिपृष्ठे समासीनं शङ्करं लोकशङ्करम्।
प्रणतः परिपप्रच्छ संशयस्थः षडाननः॥

Salutations to Lord Ganesha and Goddess Renuka.
Seated on the mountain peak is Shankara,
the benefactor of the world.
Prostrating, the doubting six-faced Kartikeya questioned him.

—*Shri Renuka Sahasranama Stotram*

The legend of Devi Renuka is one the most accessible to mankind, for she was believed to be the daughter of the King of Vidarbha, a small kingdom in Maharashtra, and hence a demigod. The legend tells us that she was an incarnation of Goddess Parvati.

King Prasenjit of the Ikshvaku dynasty was known for his supremacy but he continued to be childless despite his three beautiful wives. He performed many rituals to beget a child, and after numerous trials, from the flames of the sacred fire, was born a beautiful daughter as bright and brilliant as Devi Durga. Since the goddess was not born from a womb, she was known as Ayonija, while the king called her Renuka. Having been born from fire, she was also called Agnija, and it was noted that even as a young child, she was spiritually precocious and learned all the arts and skills befitting a princess.

Once Devi Renuka was of a marriageable age, Rishi Agastya suggested that she marry Rishi Jamadagni. However, Jamadagni seemed reluctant to marry the princess, for after all she was of noble birth and he was doubtful if she would really be able to settle into the difficult and plain life of the hermitage while minding the strictest of austerities. A determined Renuka moved to the hermitage and proved that she could live and thrive just as well in the wilderness of the forested hermitage as she could in the beautiful corridors of the palace.

Rishi Jamadagni eventually accepted her and they were married in the presence of all the devatas and devis, the Saptarshis and the wise sages. As a wedding gift, Indra gave them the sacred cow Kamadhenu, who could offer whatever they needed and asked for. As K.L. Kamat writes:

> The cult of Yellamma is rooted in mythology. In the narrative Yellamma is Renuka, the obedient wife of the brahmana sage Jamadagni. The nymphs and the celestial Citraratha were once engaged in erotic sport in the river Malaprabha, which distracted Renuka who had gone to fetch water for the sage. Aroused by their love-play Renuka joined them in the river. Jamadagni who saw her swimming naked in the river was enraged and commanded his five sons to kill her. Four of his sons refused but the youngest son Parasurama immediately killed his brothers for their disobedience and set out to seek justice for his father. However, the moment Parasurama beheaded Renuka he recognised Goddess Yellamma in disguise and begged for forgiveness. He installed Yellamma's head for worship and requested that his brothers be restored to life. The brothers came back to life, but as eunuchs because of their cowardice.
>
> In another version Renuka was distracted by youths engaged in water sports and returned home

late, which made sage Jamadagni suspect her chastity. He ordered his sons to punish their mother but four of them refused. The sage cursed them to become eunuchs and got Renuka beheaded by his fifth son, Parasurama. To everybody's astonishment Renuka's head multiplied by tens and hundreds and travelled to different regions. This miracle made four of her eunuch sons and others to become her devotees who worship her head ever since. It is generally believed that the primary function of a myth is to provide a justification for a ritual. Several scholars are of the opinion that myths provide accounts of social customs and values. The votaries of Yellamma re-enact dramatic events in the life of Renuka biannually during the full moon. The women would strip naked to perform Nagna Puja once a year in the full-moon day of Magha, and young girls would walk naked to the local Yellamma temple where they would be initiated as devadasi. The Nagna Puja was banned in the mid-1980s ostensibly to maintain propriety.[1]

In South India, Goddess Yellamma is worshipped for her abundant strength. She is known by many names: Jogamma, Holiyyamma, Renuka and more. The historical sources in the Deccan tell us of a long tradition of Devdasis,[2] which was perhaps established sometime in the 10th century AD. Now, it is not entirely clear but there are various myths from the Yellamma tradition portraying it as the root of the Devdasis.

The most widely believed tale tells us that Princess Renuka, now the wife of Jamadagni, would always bring water from the river Malaprabha for the rishi's daily worship and rituals. On one such occasion, when she was on her way to the river, she witnessed a group of youthful boys engaged in water sports, being in their element enjoying themselves as embodiments of virility. This delayed her return, which led to Jamadagni suspecting his wife's chastity. He ordered his sons to punish their mother and to release her from her human desires, but they naturally refused. The rishi, angered by their loyalty to their mother, cursed them to become eunuchs and had his wife beheaded by his fifth son, Parashurama. Unexpectedly, Renuka's head instead multiplied by tens and hundreds and travelled to different regions of the state, and to this date, the worship of her head is considered sacred.

The worship of Goddess Yellamma is extremely popular amongst members of the lower caste, who are often poor and illiterate. These individuals take a lifelong vow to serve the goddess along with their families and children. They dedicate their entire existence to the devotion of the goddess, completely surrendering themselves, which is unseen in contemporary times. It is through the efforts of these individuals that the cult of the goddess still remains alive, even though it is slightly disembodied.

In an elaborate ceremony, the Jogatthis and Jogappas are initiated into the service of Devi. The new initiates, after bathing, are taken to the head priest with their community members. The priest tells them the ways in which they have to serve Yellamma; they have to visit the shrine on full-moon nights at least twice a year, reiterating their devotion towards the goddess. During these visits, they are often expected to be completely nude or in semi-nudity.

Some of the Jogatthis and Jogappas are also known for covering themselves up with neem foliage and other such bounties of nature. These rituals have, over the course of time, particularly in the last decade, become highly publicised events. It has become a meeting place for teenagers, who are just beginning to understand their bodies and are driven by their curiosity, turning the sacred event into a spectacle sport to view nude and semi-nude bodies. Alain Danielou provides extremely interesting information, which states:

> In Yoga, this story is given a particular meaning: Renu or Renuka means 'semen'. Her five sons are the five centers of the body. The smallest is the center of extreme-purity (*visuddha cakra*), behind the forehead, here represented by Parasu-Rama. The mind is the abode of lust, symbolized by the forest where Citraratha and his heavenly damsels dwell. Once the mind has stimulated the power of sex, the yogi cannot recover his mastery over himself, the brilliance of his inner light, until he has burned up lust by bringing the power of his seed up to the fifth center.[3]

Nonetheless, it is a fascinating experience to bear witness to or participate in any way in these rituals and traditions of worship of Devi Renuka. Many of her devotees are recognisable by the turmeric and *kumkum* smeared on their foreheads. They are adorned in simple clothes, wearing crowns and jewellery made of cowries. Many don't prefer wearing jewellery at all, looking instead for a symbolic union with the divine goddess by forsaking all material symbols of the world and losing oneself in the transcendental world created by her.

Sandhya

गायत्री नाम पूर्वाह्ण सावित्री मध्यमे दिने।
सरस्वती च सायाहे सैव सन्ध्या त्रिषु स्मृता॥

Gayatri is remembered in the morning, Savitri at midday, and Saraswati in the evening; thus, the same Goddess is remembered all three times of the day.

—Sandhyavandanam

An integral aspect of Hinduism is the manner in which its tales, legends and stories of gods and goddesses serve as lessons in living an ideal life, perhaps even pointing the way towards enlightenment and breaking away from the circle of life, death and rebirth. Legends across all civilisations are the means by which we transmit the ethics, values and morals of our communities from one generation to the next.

In Hinduism, such a transformation takes on a multi-layered meaning to reflect the diversity and the varied richness of life. An example of this multitudinous existence is perhaps the tale of Sandhya and Kama, two divine siblings, both born from the mind of Brahma. Eminent scholar Wendy Doniger traces the term Sandhya philologically in her book:

> This consideration not only distinguishes the Sanskrit term from its Greek and Latin cognates but gives

greater force and meaning to the female who is 'just' an image. Samjna may even be a riddle term for Sandhya, another name for the Dawn; the shadow woman is then evening twilight, and the sun has two wives. The parallels between Samjna and Sandhya are striking, for each is the wife of the sun, ambivalent and incestuous. Each also designates a linguistic symbol: just as 'Samjna' means 'sign' or 'image', so 'Sandhya' becomes the term for the 'twilight speech' of later Hindi poetry, a speech marked by riddles, inversions and paradoxes.[1]

As the legend goes, Lord Brahma was once holding divine court with all the devatas of Indraloka. In the midst of their discussion, a beautiful maiden sprung from Brahma's heart, followed by a handsome and youthful man, holding a sugarcane bow and floral arrows. The young man bowed before Brahma, asking him as his divine father to inform him of his purpose. Brahma, taken by the immense beauty of the youth, heady with the fragrance of the arrows in his quiver, charged him with spreading love and romance among all creatures, thus expanding the world's population.

The youth was named Kama or Manmatha ('the enchanter'), who could with little to no effort bewitch anyone he so chose to. Brahma further declared that no one, not even himself, would be averse to the effects of Kamadeva's arrows. Till then, no one had said anything about the girl who was standing at the centre of the divine court: the beautiful Sandhya. Kama himself felt attracted to his sister. Filled with a false sense of pride because of Brahma's boon, he decided to check its efficacy.

He shot an arrow in the midst of the court that had an immediate effect on all who were present, including Lord Brahma and Devi Sandhya. Watching the chaos that had ensued in court, Dharma, the god of righteousness, ashamed to witness this impropriety, evoked Shiva to right the wrongs that were evidently occurring.

When Lord Shiva appeared, he rebuked Lord Brahma for transforming the sacred court into one of erotic pleasure. On the other hand, the helpless Devi Sandhya fell at Shiva's feet. Moved by her repentance, the Lord transmitted the mystic secrets of transcendental knowledge to the goddess, making her a goddess of divine knowledge in turn.

Devi Sandhya, having received darshan from the great ascetic Lord Shiva, was naturally inclined to performing austerities, penance and deep tapas from the very beginning. She also felt a certain amount of guilt and responsibility for having stirred such intense feelings of passion and lust in her own immediate family. Unable to bear the shame, she vowed to burn herself with her own energetic fire and cleanse her soul to remove the taint of the incident. For years on end, Devi Sandhya thus performed penance to appease Lord Shiva. He appeared before the goddess when her tapas finally came to an end and offered to grant her three boons.

After much consideration, Devi first asked for all human beings to be made conscious of sexuality and sexual desire only after they attained puberty. Her second boon was to be known as the greatest devotee, the one who performs the toughest of austerities and penances to attain salvation. Lastly, she prayed to get a good husband and to be forever protected from the lustful gaze of other men, so much so that if a man ever glanced at her with lust, he would turn into a eunuch.

Lord Shiva granted her all three boons and asked her to go to the banks of the river Chandrabhaga. Rishi Medhatithi was performing a yajna there to absolve Chandradev from the curse he had received from Daksha for ignoring all his other wives and being attentive to only Rohini, who was also Daksha's daughter. In the havan kund of the yajna,

Devi Sandhya would be able to fulfil her vow to rid herself of what she thought of as a tainted body and come back to the world in a new incarnation. If she thought of the man she wanted as her husband before she jumped into the sacred fire, then she would receive her boon of becoming his wife in her next incarnation.

Further complicating the myth from the perspective of the woman question, Doniger mentions a short passage from the *Harivamsa Purana*, describing Devi Sandhya's thoughts about the nature of women's subordination to men:

> She became very worried, and thought, 'To hell with this behaviour of women.' She kept blaming herself and her own womanhood: 'No one should remain a woman, ever; to hell with this life with no independence. In her childhood, youth and old age she is in danger from her father, husband and sons, respectively. It was stupid of me to abandon my husband's house; I did the wrong thing. Even though I have not been recognized, I have suffered now in my father's house, and there she is, the female of-the-same-kind, with all her desires fulfilled. I have lost my husband's house because of my naive stupidity, and it is no better here in my father's house.'[2]

During the yajna, Sandhya felt herself drawn to one of the Brahmins at the ceremony because of his radiance, purity and compassion. She thought of him and jumped into the fire. As her body burned, her essence travelled up to the heavens to be absorbed by Lord Shiva. Suryadeva then took her body and divided it into three parts, Pratah-Sandhya, Madhyanha-Sandhya and Shyam-Sandhya, and she is forevermore associated with him through these three aspects of hers.

As the yajna drew to an end, Sandhya emerged once more in a new form from the havan kund—a beautiful maiden glowing with youth, radiance and beauty. She seemed to be made of gold and everyone gasped at the appearance of this divine maid. Rishi Medhatithi adopted her as his own daughter and named her Arundhati, who became a disciple of Rishi Vasishtha, learning spirituality and gaining transcendental knowledge from him. She loved him as her guru but also as a man, and from the young age of five, she had determined to have him as her husband. As this was part of her preordained destiny, after much tapas, she went on to live as an emblem of chastity after her union with Rishi Vasishtha. It is extremely invigorating to see how diverse these myths became due to the movement of time.

> The *Markandeya* prefaces one of its retellings of the story of Samjna [Sandhya] with a brief but stunning sequence:
> Samjna was the daughter of Tvastri and the wife of Martanda, the Sun. He produced in her Manu, called Manu Vaivasvata, since he was Vivasvant's son. But when the sun looked at her, Samjna used to shut her eyes, and so the sun got angry and spoke sharply to Samjna: 'Since you always restrain (*samyamam*) your eyes when you see me, therefore you will bring forth a twin (*yama*) who will restrain (*samyamanam*) creatures.' Then the goddess became agitated by terror, and her gaze flickered; and when he saw that her gaze darted about, he said to her again, 'Since now your gaze darts about when you see me, therefore you will bring forth a daughter who will be a river that darts about.' And so because of her husband's curse Yama and Yamuna were born in her. [74.1–7]³

Shitala

जय-जय माता शीतला, तुमहिं धरै जो ध्यान।
होय विमल शीतल हृदय, विकसै बुद्धि बलज्ञान।।

*Victory to Mother Shitala! Whoever meditates on you
gains a pure and cool heart,
along with wisdom, strength and knowledge.*

—Shitala Mata Doha

*D*evi Shitala Mata is among the most popular aspects of Mahadevi, the primordial goddess, beloved by many households in India as the goddess who heals. Shitala, meaning 'the one who cools', is associated with curing diseases such as smallpox, chickenpox, measles, and so on.

If we look into the tradition of Devi Shitala, she was popularised early on as a village goddess and her worship was tied to community worship and gatherings. One of the primary reasons why Devi Shitala is so popular among the rural and semi-rural populace is because of the lack of availability of and accessibility to healthcare, with her remaining as the goddess who heals. In fact, it was believed that smallpox, chickenpox and measles were caused as a result of the goddess' anger and that praying to her would bless one with a cure.

In the Bengali vernacular text *Shitala Mangalkavya*, the goddess' role is described as that of the village mother, further crystallising her association with a rural and semi-rural populace. Devi Shitala is believed to especially look after mothers and children, but she can still be a protective and a destructive force. The legend of the goddess in these parts is perhaps similar to the make-up of a children's tale.

Devi Shitala's mount is Jvarasura, who is a fever demon. Many rural folks even believe that she is accompanied by Ghentu-debata, the god of skin diseases; Olaichandi, the goddess of cholera; and Raktabati, the goddess of blood infections. All these gods and goddesses reside in their abode in the neem trees. In most villages, a shrine to Shitala Mata is found underneath a neem tree.

The above legend does bear the need for some unpacking. It is interesting that their abode is said to be the sacred neem, which is known for its many medicinal properties and is beneficial for one's health and longevity. In fact, the leaves of the tree are known for its cooling properties and used as an ayurvedic cure; for example, bathing with water in which neem leaves are soaked overnight is an excellent home remedy for relief from itching in the case of measles and the pox.

According to the myths around her, when Devi Shitala first arose from the sacrificial fire, Brahma granted her the boon that humans would always worship her as long as she carried the seeds of a particular lentil with herself. The goddess, along with her companion Jvarasura, travelled to visit the gods in their realm, and somehow, along the way, the lentils transformed into smallpox germs, wreaking havoc on anyone who came into contact with her.

The gods asked Devi to have mercy on them and to take her germ-infested lentils to earth. Devi agreed and descended to earth along with her mount Jvarasura. Her first stop was the kingdom of King Birat, a devotee of Shiva. King Birat refused to give supremacy to Devi Shitala over his beloved Shiva, and an annoyed goddess threatened to infect his people. The king refused to be swayed by the goddess' threat and she brought upon his people and his kingdom a plague of 75 different kinds of pox. The disease was so rampant that it resulted in waves of death, until King Birat finally relented and Devi Shitala healed his people. It is a notable fact that she also happens to be the *kuladevi*, or the clan deity, for many families in North India.

The depiction of the goddess' form is very unlike her. She is shown as a young woman, carrying in her hands a silver broom, a winnowing fan, a small bowl and a pot of water. These items are the means of curing diseases, and the broom is considered as an implement to sweep away the germs. After she collects the germs, she sprinkles water from her pot, which holds the sacred water from the river Ganges with all its healing properties, and purifies the house. In some of her depictions, she is also shown as holding neem leaves.

According to the *Shitala Mangalkavya*, the goddess is not worshipped on any specific annual date, even though Krishnashtami is widely believed to be the day one worships Devi Shitala. Her presence is not meant simply to occasion the explanation of diseases or for offering prayers for a respite from them; to me, this is an oversimplification of her mythology. She is more a goddess who is representative of our overall well-being, a composite auspiciousness that can drive one towards spiritual enlightenment through a healthy body and mind.

Santoshi

ॐ श्री संतोषी महामाया गजानंदम दायिनी।
शुक्रवार प्रिये देवी नारायणी नमोस्तुते।।

Salutations to Goddess Santoshi, the bestower of joy, Beloved of Fridays, O Devi Narayani, I bow to you.

—Santoshi Maa Mahamantra

Among the many forms of Devi, while some have descended from our ancestors and have further morphed and been moulded by the Hindu sociocultural structures and community values, others have a more modern origin, as can be observed in the recent popular iterations of the goddess. Devi Santoshi is one among the latter, having emerged as a goddess among the masses only in the 1960s. Santoshi Maa, as she is venerated, means 'the mother of satisfaction', and women—especially in North India—propagate her worship through a fast held for 16 consecutive Fridays to win the goddess' favour. With regard to what Lise McKean writes:

> …in fashioning her as they do, the patrons of Bharat Mata have specific social and political objectives in mind. Like Santoshi Ma, she is a relatively new goddess, although of a very different kind; and again like Santoshi Ma, she earns her quick accessibility by building on connections her patrons seek to forge with

other, older forms of the Goddess in India. This is evident in the massing of images of other goddesses and heroines (*satis*) in the impressive Bharat Mata temple recently completed in Hardwar, a great pilgrimage centre on the Ganges, north of Delhi. McKean not only provides a vivid description of this building—half temple, half museum—but also offers a close analysis of the motives of those who have constructed it, especially as revealed in guidebooks distributed at the temple itself.[1]

With Santoshi Maa's puja *vidhi*, or the rituals of worship, we see a rather interesting form of indoctrination that has been passed down largely through word of mouth. The literature preaching the goddess' mantras and shlokas and the vrata, or ritualistic fasting, was shared much later. By the time her prayers were scripted, she was already popular in most households, boosted by the Hindu calendar art, which disseminated her imagery and iconography widely and at little cost. Thus, in a most organic manner, Santoshi Maa found her way into the Hindu pantheon and has remained popular ever since.

We have another fascinating example of the popularisation of Devi Santoshi through mainstream media. In the year 1975, a Bollywood movie called *Jai Santoshi Maa* ('Hail Goddess Santoshi') was released. The movie presented a story about Devi's ardent devotee Satyavati, a young maiden from the 18th century. She is believed to be the worthiest of the goddess' worshippers and through her grace, she was married to a good man, but with him came her in-laws who created problems and mishaps for Satyavati.

Much of the movie is filled with trials and tribulations for the poor Satyavati, which can be said to be a test of her devotion and of Santoshi Maa's power to offer her protection and guidance. Some parts of the movie show the goddess taking a human form to protect her devotee. Eventually, tired and exasperated by all the trials and tribulations that she must suffer at the hands of the world, Satyavati attempts to end her life, but she is stopped by Sage Narada, who tells her about observing a fast for Santoshi Maa. Satyavati devotedly keeps the fast for 16 consecutive Fridays, at the end of which her misfortunes turn into fortunes.

The movie is perhaps the most interesting format by which Devi's worship was propagated amongst the mainstream audience and people belonging to Hindu households. It propelled the newly anointed goddess to the heights of devotional fervour, simply because of the relatable tale of Satyavati, a tired and long-suffering housewife. In a single sweep, the goddess entered the pan-Indian Hindu pantheon and her imagery and iconography were adopted in Hindu temples. In the movie, the goddess is believed to be the daughter of Lord Ganesha. However, this is not mentioned in the scriptures and thus it is uncertain as to whether this is true or a popularised notion, a neo-myth, if you will, created for the goddess. Hawley, on a similar note, writes:

> As her film brought her to life, however, Santoshi Ma quickly became one of the most important and widely worshipped goddesses in India, taking her place in poster-art form in the altar rooms of millions of Hindu homes. People throughout India, especially women, kept (and still keep) a vow of fasting for sixteen consecutive Fridays. On those days they made special offerings to Santoshi Ma, hoping to be blessed with a wish fulfilled. Then, and at other times too, they read her story and sang her songs. The annual calendar of Hindu festivals also responded to her advent. In late summer there is a celebration of brother–sister solidarity, *rakhi* or *rakshabandhana*, which the film

identified as the moment of and reason for Santoshi Ma's birth. Not unexpectedly, then, her image began to appear on the bright paper medallions that decorate the threads (*rakhis*) sisters tie onto the wrists of their brothers and other male relatives and friends on that day. Everywhere, Santoshi Ma images and shrines were added to temples, and in some cases, as had already happened in Jodhpur, she took over the place of the presiding deity in temples that had previously been dedicated to other goddesses.[2]

The creation of Santoshi Maa's mythology is also a notable study in myth-building. The movie was often screened alongside Hindu ceremonies, religious rituals and festivities. It was very much a community event, a reason to gather together as one would in a *satsang* or sacred *sabha*. Many of the members of the audience arrived barefoot, as these viewings were held in temples, and slowly over time, small shrines and temples began cropping up in the country dedicated to Santoshi Maa.

In a short period of time, the movie became a cult success, and even years after its release, there were special Friday matinee screenings in line with Santoshi Maa's sacred day. This was a modern version of listening to her *vrata katha*, and watching the movie found its way into the worship of the goddess. The success of this 'modern celluloid goddess' produced significant research on and scholarly interest in Santoshi Maa.

According to art historian Michael Brand, Santoshi Maa emerged in the sixties, when there were five well-established temples dedicated to her in North India.[3] Her iconography was also slowly crystallising in this period through calendar art and other 'low' forms of art that were widely available to the public. Further, according to Hawley, it was the wife of the director of *Jai Santoshi Maa* who pressed her husband to 'spread the goddess' message'.[4] In fact, it is an interesting origin story that makes one wonder what would have been the nature of the goddess' worship in the absence of her celluloid form? Would she have been as widespread and popular in Hindu culture as she is today?

In Santoshi Maa, devotees recognised the pre-existing aspects and characterisations of Devi's cult. This made her all the more relatable to them, making her similar to the goddesses they had known and grown up with. Even her iconography borrows from older Hindu goddesses, such as her seated and standing postures on top of a blooming lotus. The weapons attributed to her—the sword and the trident—immediately bring to mind the power and assurance of Durga.

According to sociologist Veena Das, even the episode of Santoshi Maa and Satyavati from the movie bears a striking resemblance to the tales of Sati Anasuya, who humbled the pride of three jealous goddesses—Saraswati, Lakshmi and Parvati—as the ardent devotee of Goddess Manasa, who herself as a younger goddess fought long and hard for recognition.[5] Following the resemblances Santoshi Maa shares with Sri, Hawley writes:

> ...the worship of Sri, either alone, in tandem with Vishnu, or in her new 'eight forms', has never been more widespread. It is difficult to say exactly what is responsible for this new upsurge of interest in the worship of the most familiar form of the Goddess in South India. The new momentum would seem to have something to do with the rise of goddesses such as Santoshi Ma and Vaishno Devi elsewhere on the sub-continent. Closer to home, in Tamil Nadu itself, it may well be connected to what seems to be a general rise in the popularity of manifestations of the Goddess, as exemplified by a rejuvenation of the

cults of Karumariamman and others. But whatever is powering this new interest in goddesses of various kinds, the devotees of Sri clearly feel that she deserves this attention—because, as one might say, she has it all. And not only does she have it, but she gives it away to all who worship her: good fortune in this life, and liberation in the next.[6]

As for the rituals of worship and fasting, these evolved after the release of the movie. It is believed that the fast is to be observed for sixteen Fridays or until the devotee's wish is fulfilled. After praying to Santoshi Maa, she is offered flowers, incense and a bowl of raw sugar and roasted chickpeas, i.e., *gur-chana*; the goddess is not supposed to be given any sour or bitter foods. The devotees begin these rituals early in the morning and themselves avoid eating bitter and sour foods. Once the wish is fulfilled, a devotee must perform an *udyapana*, or a conclusion ceremony to the vrata, as part of which eight *kanya*s, or young girls, are to be served food.

Vana Devi

Can I take a pot of water off you?'
the woman duly asks the river.
Before he climbs the tree to pluck a fruit, the man asks,
'Can I take a fruit off you?

—An old tribal saying

In one of the shlokas in the *Brihat Samhita*, Varahamihira says, 'At night, only after worshipping the tree with milk porridge, sweets, rice, curds, semi-ground sesame seeds, eatables of various kinds, wine, flowers, incenses and perfumes, gods, manes, demons, goblins, serpents, asuras, Shiva's hosts or Shiva ganas, Ganesha and others should be worshipped.' Thereafter, touching the tree, one should recite the following hymns:

अर्चार्थममुकस्य त्वं देवस्य परिकल्पितः।
नमस्ते वृक्ष पूजेयं विधिवत्सम्प्रगृह्यताम्॥
यानीह भूतानि वसन्ति तानि बलिं गृहीत्वा विधिवत्प्रयुक्तम्।
अन्यत्र वासं परिकल्प्यन्तु क्षमन्तु तान्यद्य नमोऽस्तु तेभ्यः॥

Oh, Tree! You have been conceived for the worship
of this particular deity. This worship, offered by me
in accordance with the traditions, may kindly be
accepted by you. May all those beings that dwell
in this tree accept the offerings made

> *according to rituals, and then depart to another tree for residing. May they forgive us now.*
>
> —*Brihat Samhita*, Chapter 58, Verses 10–11

The Indian classical texts—the Puranas, the Mahapuranas, the Adikavya Ramayana and the Mahabharata—have always fascinated me, particularly in my explorations of Indian aesthetics and cultural heritage. The Puranic texts, i.e., the *Bhagavata Purana*, the *Devi Bhagavata Purana*, and the *Shiva Purana*, are storehouses of Indian myth and storytelling. However, I feel more in control by reading and studying historical sources. The latter bring in strong chronological facts, which produce an intellectual gravitas—the key to rationally structured writing.

However, keeping aside the importance of historical data, I will not devalue the received wisdom of the indigenous people of the land. The myths and legends are the backbones of tribal and folk societies, for their faith drives their way of life. The hearsay and orality of their tradition are to be as respected as the written word.

While understanding the concept of Vana Devi, I go back to the Uttara Kanda of the *Valmiki Ramayana*, which is the older version of the epic. Tulsidas' Ramayana does not include the Uttara Kanda. He completes the Ramayana with the *rajyabhishek* (coronation) of Rama.

After becoming pregnant, Sita decided to leave Ayodhya to ensure that her husband Rama could keep up with his *rajadharma*, as dharma (righteousness) was the guiding force of his life. Throughout his mortal life, Rama maintained his commitment to Ayodhya and rajadharma which, for him, were even above his personal joys. So when an ordinary citizen in his kingdom cast aspersions on his commitment and duty towards his kingdom, Rama, putting aside his deep love for Sita, asked her to leave the kingdom.

After leaving Ayodhya, it is believed that Sita found shelter and protection at the ashram of the great Sage Valmiki in the present-day town of Bithoor, which is at a distance of around 20 km from Kanpur. In order to help her keep her identity secret, the sage gave her the name of Vana Devi, and even today, devotees worship Vana Devi as a manifestation of Sita, who is actually another expression of Goddess Lakshmi, who, in turn, is yet another form of Shakti. However, as Vana Devi, there are some overlaps in the worship of Sita, as she is also known as Vana Durga. For many years, Sita lived incognito as Vana Devi and that is how she was addressed even as the mother of Luv and Kush, until the time was right for Sita to reveal her identity. Thus, in the Uttara Kanda of the Ramayana, Sita and Vana Devi are interchangeable.

In classical literature, Vana Devi is the goddess of the forests. In southern India, she is known as Vana Durga. The Sanskrit word for 'forest', or *vana*, is *aranya*. There are different kinds of forests: *tapovan* is a forest where sages and ascetics pray and perform yajnas. The jungle sanctuaries are known as *mahavana*, while the sacred groves are called *shrivana*s.

In the sacred forests within the Indian subcontinent, some people often hear the gentle tinkling of anklets at midnight. These forests are the abodes of the female energy in the form of the primordial Devi or Shakti. These female spirits, which can be both fierce and benign, guard the forests. In Bengal, the forest guardian is known as Bonbibi. It is believed that the most fearless of them all is Aryani, the goddess of the forest.

Aryani is also the guardian deity of the flora and fauna residing within the forest. There is a beautiful temple of Aryani Devi in Arrah, Bihar. In fact, most temples have an intimate relationship with forests; some powerful temples are associated with their very own sacred tree, which is called a *sthala vrikasha*. Many gods are also associated with certain trees, flowers, fruits and other forms of flora—for example, Shiva with the Datura tree and Devi with the hibiscus flower.

In understanding the numerous forms of the *nirakara* (or formless) Shakti or the *saguna* (or physical manifestation) Devi, many interwoven myths and legends and their regional interpretations come into play. Both sacred and secular literature are full of stories about the many representations of Vana Devi or Aryani in different parts of the sacred geography of India. There is yet another story that places the temple of Vana Devi in Mau, Uttar Pradesh, while one more speaks of a Vana Devi Temple in Visakhapatnam. In Goa, there are two temples devoted to Vana Devi: one is Dhakti Vana Devi and the other is Vhodli Vana Devi.

In tribal literature, there is a legend about how the peace in the forest is destroyed after Vana Devi, who had transformed herself into a young attractive woman, fell in love with a young hunter who saved her life. The flip side of this story is that it enraged the forest and Devi was cursed and bitten by a poisonous snake. Thus, Vana Devi is a leitmotif in the pictorial displays of almost all tribal communities of India, whether it is the Saura community of Odisha, the Gonds of Madhya Pradesh, who are known for their Warli paintings (Maharashtra) and *dhokra* and bell metal artefacts (Bastar, Chhattisgarh), the Cheriyal scroll paintings from Cheriyal (Telangana), the Kalamkari paintings from Andhra Pradesh, or the Madhubani paintings from Bihar.

The Gond Pradhans are a community who paint several themes from their local environment, local gods and goddesses, the Mahua tree and their Bada Dev. They have strong ritual beliefs and customs; along with Vana Devi, they also believe in Goddess Kali, who is known by the local names of Marahi Devi and Phulvari Devi.

In the month of Paush, the Hindu women of Goa take part in a ritual folk dance dedicated to Vana Devi, called Dhalo, with great enthusiasm over five nights, including the *malani purnima*, which normally falls on a Wednesday. As *jal* (water), *jangal* (forests) and *jameen* (land) are an inalienable part of the tribal communities, their ecosystem is very much a part of their everyday life. Thus, they are naturally the best environmentalist warriors and Vana Devi is their icon and the queen of their forests, who keeps them safe and maintains the balance within the dynamic and often dangerous forests, where serpents, scorpions and tigers are always looking for prey. It is by propitiating and pleasing Vana Devi that the tribal communities not only feel one with nature but also learn to respect nature and the bounty of the forest.

The biologically diverse forests that the tribal communities inhabit provide them with everything they need, from food to shelter to clothing. Everyone invokes Vana Devi to bless them with good health and prosperity for their families. In fact, Vana Devi is a popular and common theme in the *bhitti chitra*, or the mud wall paintings with which the women decorate their homes, which serves as a wonderful way of propitiating the goddess and remembering her all the time. Vana Devi is thus omnipresent in the house and an icon of worship.

Aditi

देवानां युगे प्रथमेऽसत: सदजायत।
तदाशा अन्वजायन्त तदुत्तानपदस्परि।।
भूर्जज्ञ उत्तानपदो भुव आशा अजायन्त।
अदितेर्दक्षो अजायत दक्षाद्वदिति: परि।।
अदितिर्ह्यजनिष्ट दक्ष या दुहिता तव।
तां देवा अन्वजायन्त भद्रा अमृतबन्धव:।।

*We shall very clearly state the story of the birth of the gods.
Before the birth of the gods, being came into existence from non-being.
From the creation-tree (uttanapada), came forth the earth (bhu),
and the upper worlds (bhuvah) came forth from desire.
Aditi gave birth to Daksha, and Aditi was born of Daksha again,
O Daksa! Aditi is your daughter! All the Gods took birth later.*

—*Rig Veda*, Book 10, Chapter 72, Verses 3–5

Goddess Aditi is a primeval goddess who is referred to in the Vedas as the mother of gods, an association which extends to the Puranic texts, where she is considered the mother of Vishnu in his dwarf avatar as well as in his incarnation as Krishna. In the Vedas, Aditi is an elemental goddess. She supports the sky and sustains all existence by nourishing the earth. I think it is important here to consider the powers and shakti that were credited to the devis of the Vedic period. These feminine powers were the sources of sustenance, creation, wisdom, destruction and more. The role of the mother as the goddess was also multifaceted, for she was seen as both benevolent and fierce at the same time. She was known as the 'boundless one', and was the personification of the infinite. In certain sacred texts, she is also considered to be the mother of the group of celestial deities known as the Adityas. As given in the *Rig Veda*:

अदितिर्द्यौरदितिरन्तरिक्षमदितिर्माता स पिता स पुत्र:।
विश्वे देवा अदिति: पञ्च जना अदितिर्जातमदितिर्जनित्वम्॥

Aditi is the heaven, Aditi is the atmosphere,
Aditi is the Mother and the Father and Child.
Aditi is all Gods, Aditi the five-classification of humanity,
Aditi is all that has been born and shall be born.

—*Rig Veda*, Book 1, Chapter 89, Verse 10

In this sense, Goddess Aditi bears a remarkable similarity to Goddess Saraswati and perhaps can be considered as a precursor to her. In certain Vedic texts, she is closely associated with space, or *akasha*, and with mystic speech, or *vac*, the sort that gives form to ideas, which is an attribute of Saraswati. I suppose we can look at her as a feminine version of Brahma, the god of creation, because she moulds the primal substance of the universe to create what we see in the world. In the *Rig Veda* alone, her name has been mentioned 80 times, which bestows much significance upon her as a divine goddess.

There is a verse in the Vedic scriptures which explains the circle of life as an unbreakable cycle of birth and death. It says, 'Daksha sprang from Aditi and Aditi from Daksha.' This is seen by many scholars as a reference to the eternal cycle of life and death. In the *Shiva Purana*, Goddess Aditi is one of the daughters of Prajapati Daksha and Panchajani. She is a sister to Devi Sati. According to the text, Daksha married his daughters, including Aditi, to Rishi Kashyapa.

When Rishi Kashyapa was residing in his ashram with his wife Aditi and Diti, he was pleased with Aditi's devotion to him and promised her a boon. Aditi asked for an ideal son, and accordingly, Indra was born. Aditi went on to give birth to other sons, who were collectively known as the Adityas. In other texts, Aditi has 33 sons with Rishi Kashyapa, and 12 among these are whom we know as the Adityas. As R. Nagaswamy writes:

> It is known that Vedas give the foremost place to the human mother as a goddess, even preceding the father. There is a well-known passage in the Vedas in which the teacher tells the student, at the time of the completion of his studies, some basic tenets to be observed in worldly life, and in that the worship of God is advocated. The first sermon is 'worship thy mother as god' (*matr devo bhava*) and then only it speaks of 'worship of father as god' (*pitr devo bhava*). *Matr devo bhava, pitr devo bhava, acarya devo bhava, atithi devo bhava* is the Vedic dictum which shows the importance given to the mother as a god by the Vedic Indians.[1]

As I have already stated, the *Rig Veda* sees Aditi as an important figure. Her motherly protectiveness is seen to extend to her devotees and worshippers—she is often prayed to in order to guard and protect those who turn to her. She is the goddess who can provide safety, security and, in some cases, abundance. Similarly, as in the Rajasuya rite, where water (Goddess Apah) is also worshipped beside Indra and Mitra (Varuna), in the same context, we find another prayer where Goddess Aditi's name appears along with Visvedevas, Mitra–Varuna and Dyavaprthvi. Interestingly, in this hymn, we find Aditi being addressed as Vishvarupi, who encompasses the entire universe.

Annapurna

अन्नपूर्णे सदापूर्णे शंकर प्राण वल्लभे।
ज्ञान वैराग्य सिध्यर्थं भिक्षां देहि च पार्वति॥
माता च पार्वति देवी पिता देवो महेश्वर:।
बान्धवा: शिव भक्ताश्च स्वदेशो भुवनत्रयम्॥

*Oh Annapurna, who is forever complete,
more beloved to Lord Shiva than life.
Oh Parvati, give me the alms of Your grace
to awaken within me spiritual knowledge,
inner freedom, prosperity, and spiritual attainment.
My mother is Goddess Parvati,
my father is the Supreme Lord Maheshwara.
My relatives are the devotees of Lord Shiva,
wherever they are in the three worlds.*

—*Annapurna Stotram*

*D*evi Annapurna is the goddess of abundance and nourishment and is as important as Lakshmi in most Indian households. Her name is a combination of two words: *anna* ('food') and *purna* ('fulfilment'). She is an avatar of the benevolent Parvati, the wife of Lord Shiva and the goddess of domesticity. As the goddess of nourishment, Devi Annapurna never allows her devotees to live without food, an idea of nourishment that extends beyond bodily hunger and includes nourishment of the soul and the mind.

In popular culture, eminent film-maker Ritwik Ghatak

metaphorically invoked the goddess in his movie *Meghe Dhaka Taara* (1960). Nita, the female protagonist, recognises Goddess Annapurna as the nourishing force and provider for her impoverished family. She yearns throughout her life to get a glimpse of the abode of Shiva. At long last, she sees it when the moment of her final union with the absolute arrives, as Shiva, in the form of Mahakala, embraces her as she dies.

Maa Annapurna is believed to be the goddess of Kashi (now Varanasi in Uttar Pradesh). Kashi is the city of Kashinath (or Lord Shiva) and his consort there is Devi Annapurna. According to legend, the god and goddess used to spend many nights playing the game of dice in their city. Once they began playing the game, they would be so deeply engrossed that they would indulge in betting on who would be the winner and who the loser, which resulted in the match gaining an edge of fierce intensity. Once, Lord Shiva lost his trident during the game, and as he tried to win it back, he bet his snake and lost again. He continued to play and bet more of his possessions until he had nothing left but a begging bowl.

A rather humiliated Lord Shiva went into the Deodar forest near the city to seek respite when he ran into Lord Vishnu. On learning of his plight, Lord Vishnu suggested that he play the game again and that with his support, he would win back everything he had lost. Lord Shiva, trusting his dearest Vishnu, went back for another game, and this time he won. Now Devi Parvati, suspicious of her husband's sudden turn of luck, called him out for cheating, not knowing exactly how he was doing it but feeling certain that he was. The two got into an argument and continued quarrelling until Lord Vishnu intervened and admitted to his part in the story, claiming that the dice was an illusion and that it was moving according to his will. To this, Lord

Shiva said that everything material was an illusion, for that was the way of the world; even the food we ate was only *maya*. However, these were not the right words with which to placate an already incensed Devi Parvati, who was cheated out of her rightful victory.

Food is not an illusion—just ask a hungry man unable to feed himself for a week! Calling food an illusion was nothing short of challenging Parvati's domain and calling her an illusion. In order to prove her point and her importance in the world, she disappeared, saying that she would see just how well the world survived without food, which was, after all, only an illusion!

Now with Devi Annapurna's disappearance, the entire natural world came to a standstill. Seasons no longer changed, lands became barren, and it was next to impossible to try and grow any kind of crops. There was a severe drought, which led to a food shortage, widespread hunger and absolute chaos and suffering in the human world. Even the gods were affected, as were the asuras, who prayed to Goddess Annapurna to end their suffering. Devi Annapurna, unable to see her children crying and perishing out of hunger, once again appeared in the world in the city of Kashi and started distributing food, thereby ending the drought and food shortage and imparting a lesson as to her significance.

Lord Shiva, who naturally realised his mistake, recognised how he was incomplete as Kashinath without his shakti and appeared before Goddess Annapurna with his begging bowl. Food could not be dismissed as an illusion, as it was necessary to nourish not only the body but also one's soul. Kashi, or Varanasi, is thus called the city of lights; Devi Annapurna resides here, providing nourishment in the form of enlightenment, truly releasing us from maya. If one cooks food with the spirit of holiness, it is believed to be *prasadam* for Annapurna.

In Bengal, Annapurna is also known as Annada Mangal, or the one who provides the anna (food). In the literary tradition of the Mangalkavyas, *Annada Mangal* is considered to be one of the greatest works of Bengali literature, invoking Devi Annapurna eloquently. As the literary historian Asitkumar Bandyopadhyay writes:

> *Annada Mangal* is considerably the best work of the eighteenth century in the history of the prominent texts of Bengali literature. Although the writer primarily wanted to describe how at the behest of Devi Annapurna's worship, King Krishnachandra and his forefather Bhavananda Majumdar became the King. Yet, the poet has also described in detail the mythical aspect of the story behind Devi Annapurna.[1]

In most Hindu households, Devi Annapurna is honoured with a red hibiscus flower placed on the stove before the day's cooking begins. In *Annapurna Sahasranama*, she is known by 108 names. Each name depicts her as completely perfect: the goddess of food and nourishment, and the shakti of Shiva. She is Devi beyond all illusions, and as such, she's the supreme goddess of the universe who takes away our fear and provides us with her protection whenever she is evoked with Annapurna stotras.

नित्यानन्दकरी वराभयकरी सौन्दर्यरत्नाकरी
निर्धूताखिलघोरपावनकरी प्रत्यक्षमाहेश्वरी।
प्रालेयाचलवंशपावनकरी काशीपुराधीश्वरी भिक्षां देहि
कृपावलम्बनकरी मातान्नपूर्णेश्वरी

Salutations to Mother Annapurna, who always gives joy to Her devotees, along with boons, and ensures they're fearless; who purifies all the poisons and sufferings in their minds; who sanctified the lineage of the mountain king;

who is the goddess of Kashi, O Mother Annapurna,
please grant us the alms of Your grace.

Today, Devi Annapurna is worshipped in all households and restaurants across India. Her story teaches us that neither Purusha nor Prakriti can exist in the absence of the other, for they are both equally responsible for human survival.

Gayatri

ॐ भूर्भुव: स्व: तत्सवितुर्वरेण्यं।
भर्गो देवस्य धीमहि धियो यो न: प्रचोदयात्

The Earth, the Sky and the Heavens.
May we meditate on the divine radiance of that revered Sun.
May it inspire and illumine our minds.

—Gayatri Mantra

The goddess is perhaps the earliest form of initiation into religion for a child in a Hindu household—specifically, Devi Gayatri, who is considered Vedamata in the Hindu pantheon. Gayatri has often been seen as interchangeable with, or the same as, Goddess Saraswati. She is worshipped as part of the Trimurti of the Tridevis: Gayatri (knowledge), Lakshmi (wealth) and Kali (shakti). As Mahadevi, who is rather closely associated with Saraswati, Devi Gayatri is also venerated as the Mother Goddess, the progenitor of all the devas and the entire universe, or *srishti*. This is best explained in the words of Sunita Pant Bansal, who writes:

> According to the sacred texts, Gayatri is Brahma, Gayatri is Vishnu, Gayatri is Shiva, Gayatri is the Vedas. Gayatri is a metre of the Rig-Veda consisting of 24 syllables. This metre has been used in a number of Rig Vedic *mantras*. The syllables are arranged differently for different *mantras*, the most common being a triplet of

eight syllables each. The Gayatri *mantra* composed in this triplet form is the most famous and sacred of all mantras. It is a prayer in honour of the Sun, also called Savitur. According to the Skanda Purana, nothing in the Vedas is superior to Gayatri.[1]

Our first introduction to Devi Gayatri is often through the Gayatri mantra, which is believed to be the crown jewel among the treasures of Indian theological knowledge passed down orally from generation to generation. For one to be initiated into this most sacred of all mantras is by itself the greatest of privileges. It is believed that the sound of the Gayatri mantra, whether chanted, invoked, or simply focused upon in the mind, has the power to activate divine grace.

As one of the foundational mantras within the Hindu sacred texts, the Gayatri mantra was first recorded in the Vedas, namely the *Rig Veda* (in Book 3, Chapter 62, Verse 10), a text that is believed to have been compiled around 2,500 to 3,500 years ago. It is certainly in this Sanskrit text that the Gayatri mantra is believed to have made its first appearance, but given the largely oral tradition of ancient Hindu scriptures, it is possible that the mantra was already widely prevalent at this time. It is thus indisputable that the sacred chant is one of the most revered chants in Hindu mythology, considered to be second only to the sound of Om, the sound of the universe.

Certain scholars believe that the content or the knowledge held in the other three Vedas—the *Sama Veda*, *Yajur Veda* and *Atharva Veda*—stems from the *Rig Veda*. Thus, by extension, the Gayatri mantra also finds its presence in all the Vedas. Another goddess invoked by this mantra is Savitri, who represents complete and absolute purity as the essence of the supreme consciousness. Invoking this supreme consciousness with the Gayatri mantra helps us to loosen the clutches of maya (illusion) and brings us and our existence one step closer to the Divine.

The iconography of Devi Gayatri is notable in her many associations with the other gods and goddesses of the Hindu pantheon and indicative of her continued presence in the philosophical systems that have been evolving since ancient times. She is shown as having five heads as well as 10 eyes looking in all directions including the earth and the sky. She has 10 arms, each of which holds a weapon of Shri Vishnu, or Narayana, clearly pointing to her role vis-à-vis his many earthly incarnations. She is accompanied by her vahan—a white swan—and with one of her primary arms, she is also shown holding a book to portray her position as the goddess of knowledge and education. She brushes away ignorance and half-baked knowledge and showers us with the ability to accumulate and understand earthly (material) and divine (spiritual) knowledge. As an incarnation of Saraswati, Devi Gayatri is also a consort of Lord Brahma, symbolising his shakti of creation, and has herself become the patroness of the arts.

> She is another consort of Lord Brahma. According to one interpretation, the goddess Gayatri is the luminous emanation of the infinite power of the Original One in three aspects in the three parts of the day; as Gayatri in the morning, as Savitri at noon and as Saraswati in the evening. As the goddess of learning she is sometimes said to be the daughter of Brahma, the original creator emanating from his mind (*manasakanya*). In the worship of Durga in autumn, Lakshmi and Saraswati accompany her as her two daughters.[2]

In her iconography, as Brahma's consort, she is shown as a poetess and a musician. She is depicted as seated on a lotus beside him. She still has five faces representing the *pancha pranas* or *panch vayus* (the five lives): *prana, apana, vyana, udana* and *samana*. She also represents the *pancha tattva*s of which this entire universe is made: earth, water, air, fire and sky. In her 10 hands, she is shown carrying the In her 10 hands, she is shown carrying the shankha (conch), chakra (discus), *kamal* (lotus), *kasha* (whip), *ankusha* (a sharpened weapon with a pointed hook), *ujjwala* (a utensil), rudraksha *mala* (a garland made of rudraksha), and *gada* (mace), with two hands in varadamudra (symbolising the dispensing of boons) and abhayamudra (symbolising protection).

Early bronze images of Gayatri appear in Himachal Pradesh, where she was revered as the consort of Sadashiva. Some of these forms are terrific in nature. One of the bronze images of Gayatri, dating back to 10th century CE, was obtained from the Champa region and is now preserved in a museum in Delhi. It appears with five faces and 10 hands, holding a sword, a lotus, a trident, a disc and a skull, with varadamdura on the left, and a goad, a noose, a manuscript and the jar of ambrosia, with abhayamudra on the right.[3]

Gayatri, Savitri and Saraswati together are the presiding deities for the Gayatri mantra, which is chanted three times a day by Hindus. They are the goddesses of all knowledge, material and spiritual. Devi Gayatri is thus invoked during the morning prayers and is the beholder of the rules and traditions contained in the Vedas, including the ritual fires. Every householder, or *grihastaya*, is expected to keep alight the five sacred fires, starting with *garhapatya* and including *ahavaniya*, *dakshinagni*, *sawta* and *aavasadha*, for the success and performance of the daily Vedic rituals.

As the patron goddess of poets, she presides over the knowledge of rhyme and metre regulating poetry, preventing its formation in a whimsical fashion that is devoid of any structure. The Gayatri mantra, one of the primary sacred chants of Hinduism, contains 24 syllables and follows the

Vedic metre. Chanting the mantra is said to remove the greatest of sins, as per the *Bhagavad Gita*.

Hindus believe that the mantra provides us with a certain clarity of perspective, freeing us from delusion and assisting us in realising the presence of God. In this sense, the Gayatri mantra represents the Supreme Lord; it is the Supreme Truth. Traditionally, it is meant for spiritual advancement, and chanting the mantra takes us to the transcendental plane. The Gayatri mantra, and thus Devi Gayatri as its shakti, is the sound of the Brahman, or the Supreme Creator, and holds a significant place in the Vedic pantheon.

Katyayani

ॐ कात्यायनि महामाये महायोगिन्यधीस्वरि।
नंदगोपसुतं देवि पतिं मे कुरु ते नमः

*Katyayani, Great Goddess, Great Yogini, supreme ruler.
O Divine One, make the son of Nanda (Krishna) my husband.
Salutations to you!*

—Maa Katyayani Mantra

Devi Katyayani is venerated on the sixth day of Navaratri, the Hindu festival of Devi worship. She is one of the nine deeply revered forms of Mahadevi and is known as the destroyer of evil. She has an interesting iconography featuring four hands. One hand holds a sword to destroy the illusion of the material world; in two hands, she holds lotus flowers to symbolise being just, honest and virtuous, even when facing unjust situations; and her fourth hand is always in the abhayamudra, blessing her devotees to lead a life that puts one on the path to ultimate salvation. In the following translation of the *Devi Mahatmya*, Sage Medhas describes Devi to kings and merchants:

> O best of men, human beings have a craving for offspring, out of greed expecting them [loved ones] to reciprocate; do you not see this? Just in this fashion do they fall into the pit of delusion, the maelstrom of egoism, giving (apparent) solidity to life in this world

[samsara] through the power of Mahamaya [...] This blessed Goddess Mahamaya, having forcibly seized the minds, even of men of knowledge, leads them to delusion. [...] She is [also] the supreme, eternal knowledge [vidya] that becomes the cause of release [mukti] from bondage to mundane life.[1]

There are many legends around the birth or origin of Devi Katyayani, as is seen in the mythos of Devi. However, the most popular and well-accepted myth is of her being the daughter of Rishi Katyayana, who, after years of worshipping Mahadevi, was granted the boon of a daughter in the form of Goddess Katyayani. The reason Devi Adi Shakti was created was because Mahishasura was wreaking havoc in all three realms with his evil deeds. The divine beings turned to Lord Vishnu, seeking a solution to this menace. However, Mahishasura had a boon that he would be killed by no living man or animal, which he took to mean a boon of immortality.

For Mahishasura, a woman was not and could never be a viable threat, for he had suppressed and disempowered women through his reign of terror, thinking of them as helpless beings able to do little beyond the domestic realm. Lord Vishnu, along with Shiva, Brahma and all other devatas, prayed to Adi Shakti to take human form and defeat the evil that was Mahishasura. Thus, Devi Katyayani took birth as a little girl to Sage Katyayana. Her birth was meant to fulfil the purpose of putting an end to Mahishasura's evil, and also the evil of the repressive and exploitative way of life on earth, especially with regard to women. Interestingly, Adi Shakti (Mahamaya) is a feminine energy that is ultimately not dualistic but a singular one, which always returns to the form of Mahamaya.

> The sacred verses, the offerings (yajna), the sacrifices (kratu), the penances (vrata), the past, the future and

all that the Vedas declare, have been produced from the imperishable Brahman. Brahman projects the universe through the power of Its maya. Again, in that universe Brahman as the jiva is entangled through maya. Know, then, that prakriti is maya and that Great God is the Lord of maya. The whole universe is filled with objects which are parts of His being.[2]

The Puranic stories about the goddess' birth give us beautiful descriptions of her divine beauty, grace and warrior-like ferocity. It is said that she had shining bright eyes; in her shakti form, she had 18 hands and shone like the light from a thousand suns. All the gods had gifted her their weapons to kill the demon Mahishasura. Shiva gave his trident, Vishnu his Sudarshana Chakra, Varuna gave the conch shell that emitted a terrific war cry, Agni gave the dart, Vayu the bow, and Surya his quiver of arrows. Indra bestowed on the goddess the bolt of thunder, Kubera the mace, Brahma his japamala and kamandalu, while Kala gave the sword and shield. Vishwakarma, the divine architect of the heavens, tied the gifts of the gods together by giving Devi a hatchet and numerous other weapons. Mounted on her vahana, the lion, Goddess Katyayani embarked on the final battle.

Mahishasura was living in the Vindhya mountains. He was the son of Rambha, the lord of the asuras. In his youth, he fell in love with Princess Mahishi, who, repulsed by his overt gestures, cursed him to transform into a wild water ox. Mahishasura thus had the ability to turn into a wild ox demon and his name was associated in equal parts with Rambha and Princess Mahishi.

When Devi Katyayani finally approached Mahishasura in the Vindhya mountains, a fierce battle took place between the goddess and the demon. He brought the entire might of the asura army against Devi and in the end, the goddess beheaded the demon with a swift strike, bringing an end to him and his symbolic rampant ego that was driven by blind ambition. The killing of the demon Mahishasura is celebrated all across India even today, especially during the nine days of Navaratri culminating in Durga Puja. This episode of Devi as the slayer of the demon is venerated in her most famed *strotam*, Mahishasuramardini, which is sung to celebrate the glory of the goddess as a protector, a benefactor, a devoted mother, a ruler, and the supreme power of the universe. The following excerpt from *The Laws of Manu* suggests Manu's vision for the social order:

> For when this world was without a king and people ran about in all directions out of fear, the Lord emitted a king in order to guard this entire (realm), taking lasting elements from Indra, the Wind, Yama, the Sun, Fire, Varuna, the Moon, and (Kubera) the Lord of Wealth. Because a king is made from particles of these lords of the gods, therefore he surpasses all living beings in brilliant energy [tejas], and, like the sun, he burns eyes and hearts, and no one on earth is able even to look at him. [...] In order to make justice succeed, he takes all forms again and again, taking into consideration realistically what it is to be done, (his) power, and the time and place. The lotus goddess of Good Fortune resides in his favour, victory in his aggression, and death in his anger; for he is made of the brilliant energy of all (the gods).[3]

I think what is truly interesting about Devi Katyayani is that she is not considered just a warrior goddess in Hindu mythology. It is not one-dimensional; rather, she is also worshipped as a goddess of love and devotion. A story from the *Bhagavata Purana* takes us back to the Dvapara Yuga, to the shores of Gokul, where eligible beautiful *gopi*s would fast in honour of the goddess through the entire month of

Margashirsha. They would devotedly offer prayers to Devi to secure Shri Krishna as their beloved and consort.

The puja *vidhi* done by the gopis and the various rituals for this most sacred of fasts were quite detailed. The women made a clay idol of Goddess Katyayani from the mud collected from the banks of the Yamuna and they worshipped that idol with purity and devotion in their hearts. They offered her idol *dhoop, bati* and the red flower beloved to Devi and fasted in Her name, deeply wishing to be one with their Kanha. It is this ritual of fasting that is followed to this day, wherein young girls fast and pray to Devi Katyayani in order to be married according to their wishes.

Ganga

देवि सुरेश्वरि भगवति गंगे त्रिभुवनतारिणि तरल तरंगे।
शंकर मौलिविहारिणि विमले मम मति रास्तां तव पद कमले।।

*O Devi Bhagavati Ganga, the Goddess of the Devas,
You liberate the three worlds with your merciful waves,
You who dwells atop the head of Shankara,
May my devotion remain firmly established on your lotus feet.*

—*Ganga Stotram*

One of the most revered rivers of India, the Ganga has its own myth. Several stories surround the origin of this holiest of holy rivers. Ganga is another manifestation of the Eternal Goddess.

इमं मे गङ्गे यमुने सरस्वति शुतुद्रि स्तोमं सचता परुष्ण्या।
असिक्न्या मरुद्वृधे वितस्तयार्जीकीये शृणुह्या सुषोमया।।

*O Ganga, Yamuna, Saraswati, Shutudri (Sutlej),
along with Parushni (Ravi), hear my praise together.
With Asikni, Marudvridha, Vitasta and the Arjikiya,
and with Sushoma, listen to my invocation.*

—*Rig Veda*, Book 10, Chapter 75, Verse 5

Ganga is praised as the embodiment of purity and abundance and described as melodic, fortunate and the source of nourishment, akin to a cow that gives plentiful milk. While the *Rig Veda* briefly mentions the Ganga, the

Puranas elaborate on her attributes. The Ganga is often depicted as a four-armed deity riding a crocodile or seated among crocodiles. In some representations, her four arms hold a jar of amrita, japamala, lotus and gestures of blessing. Alternatively, she may be shown holding a *kalasha* and a lotus, with her other hands making gestures of granting boons and averting fears.

A dip in the chilling waters of the Ganga is believed to be a form of penance, washing away the sins and wrong deeds one has committed in their life, a spiritual rebirth so to speak, and through which one can attain moksha or enlightenment. In India, among the Hindus, it is customary to immerse in the Ganga waters the ashes of a deceased person's body after their cremation; it is how the departed souls find their way to the Divine Supreme. There is, in fact, a rather interesting tale about the origin of Ganga as a river and the purpose of her descent to earth.

Narayana, the preserver of the world, is believed to have descended to earth in 10 incarnations, known as Dashavatara, to restore the cosmic order. One of these incarnations is the Vamana rupa, or the form of a dwarf, which Narayana adopted to bring an end to the terrorising siege by the asura Bali, who had through his tapas acquired immense power that made him strong enough to defeat the devatas, and this was a threat not only to the gods but also to mankind.

Narayana appeared in his Vamana avatar before the *virata* rupa of Bali (a larger-than-life bull) and tricked him into a deal. Vamana Narayana asked Bali to give him enough land to cover three steps. The asura, known for his generosity, agreed to this request, not knowing that it was Lord Vishnu who stood before him. Vishnu, as the dwarf Vamana, covered the whole planet in his first step and in his second step, crossed the heavens, where Lord Brahma washed his feet with water from his kamandalu, which led to the birth of the Ganga. In his third and final step, Vamana Narayana rested his foot on the asura Bali's chest, pushing him into the Patala Loka (the underworld).

Another tale speaks of Rishi Durvasas, known for his fiery temper and mercurial nature. One day, Rishi Durvasas, a form of Lord Shiva, came across Devi Ganga when he was out on a stroll. At the very moment that Devi greeted the sage, a gust of wind blew away his cloth covering, which caused the goddess to laugh mirthfully. Rishi Durvasas, offended at Devi's girlish reaction, cursed her. She would be reincarnated as a river to help humans purify their bodies and souls. The concept of the purification of the soul has since been associated with the river. It has been considered a metaphor for self-rectification since the Vedic era. It is interesting to note that mythology contains important philosophical metaphors that make complex concepts lucid and impactful. For example, in the *Brahmavaivarta Purana*, Vishnu says to Ganga, 'O Ganga, you will also flow through Bharata and you will remove the sins of sinful people.'[1]

The most popular tale is that of Bhagirath giving Devi Ganga the name Bhagirathi. As the tale goes, King Sagara, an ancestor of Lord Rama, was a strong leader. He had two wives, Sumati and Keshini. From Sumati, he had begotten sixty thousand sons and with Keshini, he had one son. One day, the king decided to perform the Ashvamedha yajna, which frightened Lord Indra, for there was no one strong enough to stand up to the king as a contender.

Indradeva instead stole the horse before it could be sacrificed by King Sagara and hid it behind a tree where Rishi Kapila was meditating. The rishi, who was a descendant of Manu and a great-grandson of Lord Brahma, found himself facing the sixty thousand sons of King Sagara, who were accusing him of stealing their father's yajna horse.

Appalled and angered at the insult, Rishi Kapila burned them all to ashes using the ascetic fire from his third eye.

When Ansuman, the son of King Sagara and Queen Keshini, learned of the fate of his brothers, he went to the rishi's ashram, begged for his forgiveness, and requested him to suggest a way to liberate his brothers' souls. The rishi, having had some time to calm down, advised the prince to meditate and call upon Lord Brahma to release Ganga from his kamandalu, for it was only that holy water which could purify the soul of his brothers.

Ansuman meditated on Lord Brahma but failed to please him in his lifetime. The seven generations that followed him also worshipped Lord Brahma, until King Bhagirath, from the seventh generation, finally managed to sort out a way with his boundless determination and devotion. Bhagiratha's worship pleased Lord Brahma, who told him to pray to Lord Shiva, for he was the only one who could hold the tremendous force of Ganga in his hair, and keep her from destroying the earth with her force. As Eck writes:

> Above all, it is mercy and compassion that flow out from the foot of Visnu or from the hair of Siva in the form of this mothering river. It nourishes the land and all its creatures, living and dying. The hymns repeatedly affirm that this river is intended as a vehicle of mercy:
>
> This Ganga was sent out for the salvation of the world by Sambhu, Lord of lords, filled with the sweet wind of compassion.
>
> Sankara having squeezed out the essence of *yoga* and the Upanisads, created this excellent river because of his mercy for all creatures.[2]

Bhagirath worshipped Shiva for many long years until the god was finally pleased. When Lord Brahma released Devi

Ganga from his kamandalu, she fell on the earth with a tremendous force that was blocked by Lord Shiva's jatas (locks), releasing only a small, manageable stream of the river. Bhagirath followed the route of the Ganga and finally immersed the ashes of his forefathers in her water, which granted them moksha. This tradition has continued among the Hindus of India as they often use the sacred Ganga water to purify their being and immerse the ashes of their family's and loved ones' bodies.

Hariti

भूतमातेति संहृष्टे ग्रामेग्रामे पुरेपुरे।
गायन्नृत्यन्हसँल्लोक: सर्वत: परिधावति।।

With joy, the people in every village and every town, singing, dancing, and laughing, run all around, calling upon Bhutamata (Mother of all beings).

—*Bhavishya Purana*, Part 4, Chapter 136

More than the form of a goddess, Hariti is female divinity itself. A *yakshani* who is part of the Buddhist tradition, she is believed to have been residing in the city of Rajgir when Buddha visited there. The Vinaya Pitaka of the Sarvastivada school and the Samyukta Ratnapitaka Sutra of the Chinese Sutrapitaka tell us her story: she was the wife of Panchika, a *yaksha* general from the Gandhara region. She bore him five hundred children and, as a result, came to be known as Bhutamata, the mother of demons, as these children formed the race of the asuras.

To feed herself and her children, she adopted the practice of cannibalism and stole other people's children. This theft of children led to pandemonium and fear among those dwelling in the city, who turned to Buddha for protection from this evil. To teach the yakshani a lesson, Buddha arrived at her dwelling with a beggar's bowl in hand. Hariti was not at home and Buddha quickly hid her youngest and most beloved child, Pingala, inside his bowl. On returning home, Hariti could not find Pingala anywhere and was overwhelmed with grief. Ultimately, she turned to Buddha and requested him to find the boy. Buddha agreed to do so as long as she gave up her cannibalism and followed his precepts, to which Hariti agreed. Finally, Buddha returned Pingala to her.

Hariti bears a striking resemblance to the Greek goddess Tyche, whose story could have been transmitted to East Asia through the influence of Greco-Buddhism. In Greek art, Tyche is often portrayed with children, holding symbols of abundance, such as the cornucopia and the ship's rudder, along with the wheel of fortune symbolising control over destiny. Tyche may even stand upon the wheel, overseeing the course of fate. Tyche is revered as a protector of children and feared for punishing negligent parents and disobedient offspring. In Chinese and Japanese Buddhism, Hariti is not only revered as a guardian deity but also feared in local folklore as a malevolent force bringing misery to families.

Having made an unbreakable vow, Hariti now turned to Buddha to find a solution for feeding herself and her five hundred children. The latter sent monks from his monastery to her dwelling each day to deliver abundant food for her and all her children. To pay this generosity back, Hariti became the custodian of the Buddhist monastery, and there are actual records of Hiuen Tsang's (or Xuanzang's) visit to ancient India where he has noted the appearance of Hariti in almost all the monasteries he visited between India and Nepal.

After her conversion to Buddhism, Hariti drastically changed her ways and Buddha himself ordained her as an *upasika*. From a devouring demoness, she became a protector and a deity. In her iconography, she is often shown with a baby in her arms and three or five children standing around her knees. It didn't take long for a cult of Hariti to form; so unique was her story that it provided hope for even the most lost and deprived souls. Hiuen Tsang records that a stupa was built in honour of Hariti in Peshawar by King Ashoka, where people still offer sacrifices to obtain her blessings. However, Hariti did not enter mainstream Devi worship; she is rather a part of an important cultic practice.

> Another figure from the Buddhist narrative closely associated with the travails of childbearing is Angulimala, a murderer who embraces the dharma. In contemporary Theravada Buddhism, Angulimala is revered as a saint and is a symbol of spiritual transformation. His story is taken as evidence of Buddha's great power as a teacher and of the moral salvation that Buddha's dharma offers. Still, though he becomes an arhat and Hariti does not, the two are similar in important and striking ways. Both spill a lot of innocent human blood before meeting Buddha, both are finally tamed by wisdom (not might), and both become protectors of pregnant women and very young children after their transformation. Thus, the Angulimala legend potentially broadens the claim that South Asian Buddhist narratives portray ritual treatments of fertility as distasteful yet tolerable through complex characterizations.[1]

Dr J.N. Banerjea has drawn parallels between Hariti and Rakshasi Jara of Magadha.[2] As the story goes, King Brihadratha of Magadha was considered a foolish king. Not wanting such a man to rule over the grand empire of Magadha, Sage Chanda Kaushika cast a spell upon him. He sent him a mango that was believed to have been charmed with the greatest of blessings for progeny. The king gave the mango to his two favourite queens, who ate it in equal portions, birthing two halves of a child. Rakshasi Jara, who knew about Chanda Kaushika's plan, brought the two halves of the boy together, bringing him to life, who was forevermore known as Jarasandha.

Jara had the power to assume many forms and she was worshipped in the royal home as well as by the common public. This unanimous acceptance of her led to her becoming a *griha-devi*, or the goddess of the household, as mentioned in the Mahabharata. Her youthful beauty and her images, where she is surrounded by her children, are described in the Mahabharata as decorating the walls of the palace. It is believed, writes J.N. Banerjea in *Development of Hindu Iconography*, that whoever draws her figure is always blessed with prosperity and abundance and those who don't, experience poverty and hardship.[3] In another instance, we find a lot of intercultural similarities interwoven between the myths and their narratives. As Langenberg writes:

> Although Hariti is seen primarily as a 'Buddhist' goddess, this sectarian label is probably misleading. Indo-Grecian and Kusana-era seals and coins show, for instance, tutelary couples variously identified with any number of Brahmana, Iranian, or Buddhist Hariti/Pancika-like deities. In the Gandharan context, this tutelary couple (found also at Mathura) is not primarily a signifier of sectarian affiliation but rather serves a functional role as the bringer of fertility and wealth.[4]

Prakriti

कार्यकारणकर्तृत्वे हेतुः प्रकृतिरुच्यते।
पुरुषः सुखदुःखानां भोक्तृत्वे हेतुरुच्यते॥

*In the realm of action and causation,
nature is considered the cause;
in the experience of pleasure and pain,
the individual is considered the cause.*

—*Bhagavad Gita*, Chapter 13, Verse 21

Prakriti is perhaps the most ancient manifestation of Devi. While much of the Hindu pantheon of gods and goddesses, from Shiva and Parvati to Vishnu and Lakshmi to Krishna and Radha, entails an incarnation or association with the fundamental divine essence of the universe, Prakriti is a part of the dual-natured and eternal fundamental principle of existence.

The principle of Purusha and Prakriti exists in all of creation, even in you and me, where one is the goal (moksha) and the other is the path (devotion). As devotees who are on the path of moksha, we worship both these principles, as they exist inseparably from one another. The *Isha Upanishad* clearly tells us that those pursuing one at the expense of the other find themselves in the darkest circles of hell, or Asurya Loka. Here, hell is not so much a place; rather, it is the experience of illusion, confusion and a sense of alienation from the most basic essence of oneself.

When devotees worship both the principles of Purusha and Prakriti, it results in these two aspects of the divine being forming a unified whole, the supreme truth.

Then how do we distinguish between them and understand them? In Hinduism, the universal can be found in the personal. It is believed that the entire cosmos exists within us, and as such, Purusha and Prakriti too exist within us. They are representative of two of the highest realities of our existence. They are the known and the unknown, the manifested and the unmanifested; they are equivalent to the father and the mother.

A well-known symbolism of the Purusha–Prakriti shakti is found in Ardhanarishvara (depicted as half-male and half-female). In the tantric texts, this union is shown through the Shiva *lingam*, wherein the cylindrical part is Purusha and the circular base is Prakriti. Similarly, the yantra of Purusha–Prakriti, a mystic diagram, represents their union through a triangle with a dot in the middle. The triangle is Prakriti, or the feminine part, and the dot is Purusha, or the masculine part. As the central deities of Hinduism, they are to be found in every incarnation and embodiment of all Hindu gods and goddesses. As the *Vishnudharmottara Purana* states:

> *Prakriti* and *Vikriti* (come into existence) through (the variation in) the form of the Supreme Soul. That form of him which is scarcely to be seen was called *Prakriti*. The whole universe should be known as the *Vikriti* (transformation) of Him, endowed with form. Worship and meditation (of the Supreme Being) are possible (only when He is) endowed with form. The form of the Supreme deity, as he manifests himself should be worshipped according to rites. Because the invisible condition is apprehended with great difficulty by the corporeal beings, by the Supreme Lord, through His

own will was shown that (form) and the gods (too) point out (that) form (of Him) in His various manifestations. For this reason God is worshipped and endowed with form. That form is full of significance; hear this from me ready to speak.[1]

To understand Prakriti, we must first understand Purusha, for she exists within the duality that arises between the two. Purusha is the supreme cosmic being; he represents the indivisible and the infinite cosmic reality. Nothing exists beyond him; he is the source and the support. We try to grasp the nature of Purusha, but these secrets are shrouded in mystery even in our scriptures. In the Vedas, we know him as both Brahman and a form of Brahman, wherein he sacrifices himself to build the world and its varied beings. With no beginning and no end, it is Purusha.

Now the power behind Purusha is Prakriti, the Universal Mother to the Universal Father. Prakriti herself is the embodiment or the essence of the materiality of creation and all of its dynamism. She is the energy behind its activity, movement, liveliness, awareness and diversity. In her most primal form, she is stable and silent. However, from this form also comes the wild and chaotic energy of nature, the fire of manifestation, and when the chaos is put back in order, it gives us creation. In the Vedic scriptures and the Puranic *katha*s (or stories), we have countless descriptions of Prakriti's fierce and warrior-like forms, existing beside her pleasant and benevolent forms—Uma and Lalita beside Kali and Chandi or even Durga. The transformative and violent goddess destroys pre-existing structures, causing everything to plunge into a state of chaos, only to rebuild effective structures.

Prakriti's energetic manifestation is an eternal reality that exists both independently and co-dependently. As Mula-Prakriti, she is independent and complete, while in her manifested form, she is dependent on Purusha because the unleashing of her power is through him. She is pure energy, or shakti, as Prakriti but she is also matter. Her name means 'natural', or one that is in its original state. Devi Prakriti is thus Mother Nature. She is the mother of all and represents the universal womb, which carries all forms and where all is manifested.

I think one of the most beautiful explanations of the nature of Prakriti comes from understanding the mental states she is representative of and her materiality, or *chit-shakti*, that arises from the 23 tattvas that make up the universe, all integral parts within her. These tattvas are in the order of their gradual development. We have the five base elements or *mahabhuta*s (fire, water, earth, air and sky/space). This is why she is associated and identified with the Ganga, as an intrinsic manifestation of her flowing out upon the earth for blessing everyone. In the *Devi Mahatmya* from the *Skanda Purana*, she is described as follows:

> She (the River-Goddess) is another form of mine in a watery form. She is the very soul of welfare. She is the greatest Prakriti, the mainstay of many Cosmic Eggs. She is the personified form of pure learning and compassion. She possesses three Shaktis, viz. those of will, knowledge and action. She is of the nature of Nectar and bliss. She is the pure form of Dharma. I am sportingly sustaining this support of all the worlds, perfect in form, like the Absolute Brahman for the sake of protecting the universe.[2]

She is in the five physical organs of the body (the five essential organs of action), the five sense organs of the body (eyes, ears, nose, tongue and skin) and the five subtle organs of the mind (seeing, hearing, smelling, tasting and touching). Finally, she is present in *manas* (perceptual mind), *aham* (ego/individuality), *buddhi* (thinking mind/intelligence) and *atman* (the self).

The building blocks of the universe, the three essential modes or *guna*s, are *sattva* (pure), *rajas* (neither pure nor impure) and *tamas* (impure). Everything on earth is a permutation of these three basic gunas. As the mother of the universe, Prakriti becomes the source of all that is pure and also all that is impure, in an inclusive embodiment of existence.

I believe it is important to understand that in their purest and highest aspects, Purusha and Prakriti are nearly indistinguishable; this is what gave rise to the idea that the ultimate reality, the supreme truth, is one—the Brahman. A single reality with no distinction. In the nature of existence, they begin to separate as they descend and become two distinct parts of the ultimate truth. On the material plane, there is a gulf between the two, making it nearly impossible to recognise any similarities, let alone a union of nature and form. In the mortal world, Purusha and Prakriti are present in everything.

In humans, Purusha is the soul and Prakriti is the mind and the body, and they come together to make a human being, or *jiva*. The soul is considered to be pure and light and rising towards the heavens, whereas the body is considered to be dense and impure, bound to the cycle of birth and death. Purusha and Prakriti in our body give us the duality of existence—good and bad, lightness and darkness, knowledge and ignorance, and purity and impurity.

The 23 tattvas exist in their most perfect balance within human beings, giving them the opportunity to live and manifest their lives and destinies to their fullest potential. They have the fundamental capabilities of creating, preserving, destroying, concealing and revealing in their life. They also have the impurities of existence, which can make it difficult to connect with the self (atman or pure consciousness). In this sense, they have to overcome a varied number of challenges to reach the supreme truth.

In each manifestation of our gods and goddesses, Purusha and Prakriti chart out a path to attain this ultimate reality. This could be through Parvati and Shiva, Radha and Krishna, or Sita and Rama; the path of Prakriti is the path to the divine union. Hence, Devi Prakriti is invoked in the manifestation of the divine union of Shiva and Shakti.

Chhinnamasta

ॐ हं छिन्नमस्तायै नमो नमः॥
प्रत्यालीढपदां सदैव दधतीं छिन्नं शिरः कर्त्रिकां
दिग्वस्त्रां स्वकबन्धशोणितसुधाधारां पिबन्तीं मुदा।
नागाबद्धशिरोमणिं त्रिनयनां हृद्युत्पलालङ्कृतां
रत्यासक्तमनोभवोपरि दृढां वन्दे जपासन्निभाम्॥

I meditate on Devi Chhinnamasta.
She is standing with her left foot drawn out
and right foot drawn back;
holding a severed head and a sword.
The one who is clothed by the directions;
and who is drinking the nectar of blood
flowing out from her own headless trunk.
The one who has a gem bound by a serpent on her head;
who has three eyes; and whose heart is adorned with lotus.
The one who is firmly standing above the tendencies of the mind
that is in love with the material world,
symbolized by a copulating couple,
signifying her transcendental nature beyond the world.

—Shri Chhinnamasta Sahasranamavali

The pictorial representation of Chhinnamasta, the goddess without a head, evokes tantric mysticism. She is the sixth *mahavidya*, part of a group of fearsome goddesses from the Hindu tradition of tantra, and her form as one without a head indicates her ability to transcend the mind and its erratic function towards an ecstatic union with the divine. This most straightforward explanation of Devi's form, however, hasn't always been the response. In fact, for centuries, Chhinnamasta has received many adverse reactions and misinterpretations from certain sects of Hinduism because of her association with the mystic traditions of Tibetan Buddhism and Tantric Hinduism. She is also known as Prachandachandika, another manifestation of Devi.

During a conflict between the gods and demons, the gods realised they were outmatched and sought the help of Mahashakti, the Supreme Goddess. Pleased by their devotion, she summoned Prachandachandika to assist them. After vanquishing the demons, Prachandachandika, consumed by unrelenting fury, severed her own head and drank her own blood.[1]

In the yogic tradition, being without one's head is a metaphor for transcending one's identity. It is the release of the bodily consciousness, bringing the practitioner closer to supreme consciousness. It implies overcoming our human attachment to desire and the interminable whirlpool of thoughts—positive and negative—driving forward our desires, our actions and, ultimately, our lives. For the yogi, one's headless-ness is representative of a clear inner self, one that is in communication with the Divine as a perfectly detached witness. The body then becomes maya—part of the illusion.

The idea represented by Devi Chhinnamasta—of the absence of the head—is a spiritual metaphor adopted in the Jnana Yoga tradition, Advaita Vedanta tradition and Zen tradition. The goddess assumes different forms and undergoes a metamorphosis that is recorded and noted in Buddhism as well. According to David Frawley's story of Ganapati Muni, who lived the truth of Chhinnamasta and experienced transformation:

After years of intense yogic practice he experienced the opening up of his skull, the loosening of the suture at the top of the head. After that a light and energy radiated from the top of his head. He lived in the state transcending the ordinary mind-body complex, not just as an idea, but as a physical fact.[2]

Chhinnamasta is emblematic of a spiritual awakening, the ultimate journey that we take as humans. It is perhaps a 'sacrifice of the mind', but this sacrifice is at the altar of the divine, a necessary step for our union with it. With Chhinnamasta, perhaps the question really is one of iconography. Why the need for such vivid picturisation when there is a simple enough solution esoterically? In the Hindu tradition, idols and images of the god were visual reminders of their attributes and representations; they provided a dramatic impact on our inner mind, which sometimes did not even require any words or further explanations. It was a more immediate and intimate passing of complex esoteric knowledge. Yet, interestingly, this ineffable form of inexpressible knowledge is seen as the enlightenment in the Buddhist tradition, where Chhinnamasta assumes the name Chhinnamunda or Vajrayogini. The mantra associated with Vajrayogini tells us:

ॐ ॐ ॐ सर्वबुद्धडाकिणीये वज्र वर्णनीये
वज्र वैरोचनीये हूं हूं हूं फट् फट् फट् स्वाह

According to Miranda Shaw, 'Chhinnamunda is a female Buddha, which means that as a fully enlightened being, she occupies the vantage point of ultimate truth.'[3]

Chhinnamasta embodies various symbolism within Hindu and Tantric Buddhist traditions. She severed her head herself, which symbolises the ultimate sacrifice and selflessness, demonstrating the abandonment of ego and personal desires in pursuit of spiritual enlightenment. This act represents transcending the physical form and worldly attachments, guiding followers towards spiritual liberation and the realisation of their innate nature beyond material constraints. This act of severing her head by herself carries profound symbolism, representing both the shedding of illusion and the source of inner essence. It signifies the removal of maya, the veil of delusion, along with physical attachments, false beliefs, ignorance and ego. The scimitar wielded by the goddess further symbolises the severance of these obstacles, leading to emancipation, wisdom and self-realisation. Chhinnamasta's portrayal also embodies keen perception, enabling devotees to attain a consciousness that transcends the limitations of physical attachment, the body and the mind, through her self-sacrifice.

The flowing streams of blood represent the eternal cycle of life, death and rebirth, highlighting the transformative power of spiritual energy and the ongoing process of cosmic renewal. Chhinnamasta has also been termed as 'the goddess of contradictions', depicted as both the one being devoured and the devourer, symbolising the entirety of existence through this act of consumption. The dichotomy of receiver and giver, or object and subject, collapses into a singular entity within her. Her epithets, as listed in her *nama-stotram*, evoke a sense of awe and fury, with a few names expressing erotic or tranquil attributes, contrasting sharply with Chhinnamasta's fierce nature and appearance.

Standing atop a copulating couple signifies mastery over desires and the imperative of transcending sensual cravings for spiritual evolution. Adorned with a garland of severed heads, Chhinnamasta signifies the attainment of spiritual wisdom and enlightenment, leading devotees on the journey to self-realisation and freedom from the cycle of birth and death.

The iconography of Chhinnamasta also draws one's

attention to her agency and independence as a deity. She holds her head in her left hand, implying that she cut it off herself. Besides this being an utterly gory and somewhat terrifying depiction, it points to a sense of contentment rather than suffering, of a joy transcending any form of pain, for the goddess is happily lapping up her own blood. This joy is manifested in having overcome earthly matters, desires and circles of suffering. This might be the most energetic form of the goddess, potent in its meaning, beautifully evoking the power of transformation.

Notably, the head held in the hand of the goddess seems far from lifeless, which signifies consciousness as moving past the bounds of the form. Even in her terrifying aspect, she represents the deep transformation possible between the macrocosm and the microcosm. She is in fact closely associated with Kali, another popular form of Devi, to the point that their names are used almost interchangeably. The goddess is also related to the warrior goddess Bhairavi, who resonates with the fundamental shakti of the goddess. Her fundamental goal is to free all from the limitations of a human incarnation. So if Chandi destroys the demonic entities, Chhinnamasta destroys the most important enemy of spirituality—the ego.

Chhinnamasta is thus a colossal power that heralds spiritual inner visions, which are inherent to our inner being, separated in this human form from the divine. Her purpose is to bring an end to the illusions of the material world to give us a clear glimpse into the perfect divine knowledge. Thus, in this manner, in the Hindu spiritual tradition, the goddess represents *atma-yajna*, or self-sacrifice, a manifestation of the ultimate surrender of oneself to the Divine through the 'sacrifice of the mind'.

Lalita

प्रातः स्मरामि ललितावदनारविन्दं
बिम्बाधरं पृथुलमौक्तिकशोभिनासम्।
आकर्णदीर्घनयनं मणिकुण्डलाढ्यं
मन्दस्मितं मृगमदोज्ज्वलभालदेशम्॥

*Early in the morning, I remember
the lotus face of Devi Lalita Tripurasundari,
her lips are red like that of bimba fruits,
and her nose is adorned with a large pearl,
Her eyes are large, they stretch up to her ears,
and her ears are decorated with gem-studded earrings,
her face is lit with a gentle smile
and her forehead is shining with kasturi or the musk of the deer.*

—Shri Lalita Pratah Stotrapanchakam

There are many goddesses in the yogic tradition, but preeminent among them is Lalita, known as the sensuous goddess. She is also called Kameshvari. A fascinating detail about the many goddesses in Hindu mythology is the contradictions within a single manifestation. For instance, Devi Lalita is an exquisitely sensory goddess. She is independent and strong-willed and a devoted wife to Lord Shiva, the mother of Ganesha and Kartikeya, as well as the mother of all existence. She represents a perfect state of harmonious balance and her form radiates compassion for all beings. Devi Lalita is portrayed as a voluptuous woman, who is shown holding five arrows of long-stemmed flowers, a bow made of sugarcane, a noose and a goad. It is important to note that many of these symbols are also attributed to Kama, the god of desire, making Devi Lalita in many ways the mother of desire. As Frawley elaborates on her beauty:

> Sundari is called Lalita or 'she who plays'. The entire universe exists for the delight of awareness, which is the play of the Divine Mother. Creation arises in joy, abides in joy, and returns to joy. We are but transient figures in her eternal play, who have yet to understand the source of the energy that moves us. Our sorrow and suffering is a delusion, a misconception born of ignorance and the ego. Because we attempt to control or possess joy from the standpoint of the separate self, we divide ourselves from true joy which is universal. The Goddess, as the image of joy, shows us the way out of our error, which is not to deny ourselves happiness but to discover the true happiness that we seek, which is in being one with all. Lalita awakens the receptive soul to the bliss that underlies all things.[1]

In her iconography, the five long-stemmed flowers held by Devi indicate the five human senses, and the sugarcane bow in this context becomes our mind through which they are dispensed. If our senses are focused on the goddess and our thoughts are directed towards the Divine, then we live a life of spiritual bliss. However, if we are distracted in our spiritual journey and our senses are overwhelmed by the illusions of the material world, the goddess prods us to the correct path with her goad.

In *Brahmanda Purana*, there is a part called Lalitopakhyana ('the Glory of Lalita'). When Shiva, engaged in his ascetic practices, experienced a sudden and uncontrolled flash of lust, his anger flickered and he opened his third eye to see Kamadeva, the god of love and desire, frolicking nearby, having struck the lord of the universe with one of his arrows. Shiva incinerated the god and resumed his meditation, but from his ashes arose the demon Bhanda, flaming with the desire for power, wealth and sensual indulgence. Whenever he met with one of his enemies, he drained half of their power and took it within himself. In no time, the demon became a powerful king, and soon, even the gods in the Devaloka began to worry about the demon's great appetite for power. Indra then began praying to Devi Lalita for inner strength to defeat Bhandasura's blind hunger. On the banks of the sacred Bhagirathi, Indra persevered in intense penance.

> The important fact that the text informs us is that Varahi is a bali devata, which means Goddess Varahi is the receiver of Lalita's offerings. Here, bali means any kind of offerings or sacrifice offered to Goddess Lalita. This text further says that Varahi is the 'father form' while Goddess Kurukulla is the 'mother form' of the devata, Lalita Paramesvari.[2]

Rishi Shukracharya, the sage of the asuras, noticed Indra's actions and alerted Bhanda, who assembled his army and marched onto the Himalayas to disrupt Indra's tapas. On observing the demon's approach to disturb Indra's meditation, Devi Lalita threw around him a protective barrier, preventing anyone from crossing over. The devatas realised that the demon's army was too strong for them, and they decided to dig a fire pit and offer the goddess a human sacrifice to win her favour. As they prayed to the goddess, a circular mass of blazing light appeared above the *havan* fire. At its centre was a spinning wheel, within which Lalita appeared, as beautiful as the glowing sun. The gods immediately recognised the goddess as the life force of the cosmos, the basis of beauty and desire, adorned in bright red and smiling upon them with a loving glance. The goddess promised to protect the devas from the demon Bhanda, and she set out to meet him in battle. The *Brahmanda Purana* describes the marvellous sight of this powerful military force of Shakti and demi-goddesses riding into war against evil, led by the extraordinary Lalita, the source of all cosmic energy.

Bhanda, on hearing about this all-female army, laughed, not understanding the significance of what was to befall him. He was warned by many that it was Shakti (divine power) that granted victories and that he should not underestimate this attack just because they were women. He was reminded of Goddess Kali being the fiercest warrior of all. However, Bhanda, in his pride, could not be persuaded; after all, he could effortlessly absorb half his enemy's strength. Who could possibly defeat him? In each phase of the ensuing battle described in the *Brahmanda Purana* is an allegory to spiritual purification, the legend being a poetic path to a union with the divine.

In the yogic tradition, we have the description of a ring of fire, which has been described as a golden disc protecting the innermost truth. This is the final frontier that one passes through at the time of their death, glimpsing the enlightened truth. There are in fact many gifted yogis who have described this, claiming that it looks like the light emanating from a thousand rising suns. The Gayatri mantra evokes this truth when it says, 'We meditate on the inner sun, the most splendid light in all the worlds. Please illuminate our hearts and minds, and make our lives radiant!'

After emerging victorious in the fatal battle, Devi Lalita brought Kama back to life, more handsome than before. Kama was grateful to Lalita for restoring his life and asked her how he could serve her. Lalita laughed and told him that he had her blessings and her protection and that he should go about his business, enchanting the entire world.

> Her other names Dandini and Dandanatha indicate that she heads and controls the whole army with her *danda*. Another meaning is if anybody does any harm to her devotees she will punish the person with her danda. In the Lalita-Sahasranama, Varahi is described as mounting on 'Kiricakra' chariot and standing in front of Paramesvari. According to the Puranas, Goddess Paramesvari is said to have created from her own self two energies Varahi and Mantrini, and therefore Varahi is Lalita herself. In the hierarchy Mantrini and Varahi are second to Goddess Lalita. In the Lalita-Sahsranama, śl. 70 says: kiricakra ratharudha dandanatha puraskrta. Here the term kiricakra according to Srividya tradition indicates Varahi has Pancavarnatmaka. That means her bijamantra is only of five letters.[3]

Goddess Lalita conquers not with anger or force, but with love. Those who come with a spirit of innocent love are immediately welcomed in her innermost chambers, where the spirit of surrender leads to the greatest of spiritual wealth. When we approach the Mother with that kind of pure devotion, she scoops us up in her arms and grants us victory.

Shakambhari

उद्यदिनद्युतिमिन्दुकिरीटां तुङ्गकुचां नयनत्रययुक्ताम्।
स्मेरमुखीं वरदाङ्कुशपाशाभीतिकरां प्रभजे भुवनेश्वरीम्॥

*Salutations to Devi Bhuvaneshwari
who holds the moon on her crown,
which shines as brilliantly as the rising sun,
who has high breasts and three eyes,
whose hands show the varadamudra and abhayamudra and
who holds an ankusha (a hook) and a pasha (a noose)
in her hands.*

—Shri Bhuvaneshwari Dhyanam

Also known as Bhuvaneshwari, Devi Shakambhari is an incarnation of Parvati and is believed to be a form of the divine mother, particularly of the natural world—our environment or Prakriti. I think an easy way to understand what is most certainly a rather complex manifestation of Mahadevi is to look at Shakambhari through the lens of benevolence and devotion and her role as an incredibly nurturing mother. When the child is hungry, she provides them with crop, nutrition and rich soil. In fact, she is the one who is worshipped during dark periods of famines.

Shakambhari is typically depicted in a benign form, adorned with various attributes symbolising fertility, abundance and sustenance. She is often portrayed with a green complexion, highlighting her association with nature, fertility and the abundance of vegetation. Usually depicted with four arms, she holds symbolic items in each of them. She holds a trident (trishula) in her upper right hand, symbolising her control over the three gunas—sattva, rajas and tamas. She holds a lotus flower (*padma*), representing purity and auspiciousness, in her upper left hand. Shakambhari is often depicted carrying a variety of fruits, vegetables, grains and herbs in both her lower hands, which symbolises her role as the provider of food and nourishment to all living beings.

She is sometimes depicted with a crescent moon adorning her forehead, representing feminine energy and the cycle of time. She is also adorned with a garland of bees in other portrayals, symbolising the importance of pollination in agriculture and the interconnectedness of all living beings in the ecosystem. In some traditions, Devi Shakambhari is depicted riding a lion. However, unlike other goddesses' lions, hers is often depicted as being vegetarian, reflecting her role as the protector of wildlife.

Her iconography is often set against a lush backdrop of forests, fields and abundant vegetation, highlighting her association with nature and fertility. Overall, Devi Shakambhari celebrates her role as the goddess of vegetation and nourishment, embodying the abundance and fertility in the natural world, and devotees worship her to seek blessings for agricultural prosperity, abundance of food and overall well-being.

The many names of Shakambhari provide us with more clues as to the realm of her power and what this form of Adi Shakti truly stands for. She is Parvati, the mother of the entire universe; she is also Ishvari, the feminine energy of the Trimurti; she is Jwala, Chintpurni, Kamakhya, Chamunda, Mansa, Naina and Bala Sundari. She is soft and benevolent and violent and fierce, all in the name of protecting her creation. It is perhaps the result of this overlapping association with a variety of Devi's forms that has resulted in there being a few Siddha Peethas that are attributed to Shakambhari, such as Sakrai Peetha and Sambhar Peetha in Rajasthan and Saharanpur Peetha in Uttar Pradesh.

Kinsley shares the fifth origin tale of the Mahavidyas from the *Devi Bhagavata Purana* in his book.[1] In this story, the gods, overwhelmed by the hardships caused by demonic oppression, sought the aid of Mahadevi. She appeared in a form adorned with countless eyes that shed tears upon witnessing the dire condition of the gods, humanity and the earth. This compassionate display earned her the name Shatakshi, meaning 'she of a hundred eyes'. To alleviate the drought-stricken earth, she nourished its beings by providing fruits and vegetables from her own body, which led to her being called Shakambhari, 'the one who sustains with vegetation'.

Shakambhari itself translates to 'she who bears vegetables' and is derived from the word *shaka*, which means vegetables, and *bhari*, which means the bearer. Further, the root of the word *bhr* means to nourish. There is a legend that goes back to a demon named Durgamasura, who was the son of Ruru, born in the family of Hiranyaksha. He believed that he had to have the knowledge of all the Vedas. He worshipped Lord Brahma and lived on nothing but air for a thousand years. He continued praying, and as his *tejas* grew, the gods and demons began to fear his power. Brahmadeva was finally pleased with him and he came to grant him his boon. The demon asked him for knowledge of all the Vedas and on hearing this, bound by the relation of god and devotee, Brahmadeva granted him this boon.

However, in doing so, the entire knowledge from the world disappeared; the sages forgot the Vedas; the daily rituals, bathing, sacrifices and *japa*s were all stopped. A cry of universal distress arose on earth. The sages began to wonder how they managed to forget all the knowledge of the Vedas. As the distress continued to grow on earth, the gods too became weaker as they were no longer receiving their sacrificial offerings, and the demons began invading the Devaloka, the city of heaven. The gods took refuge at Mount Sumeru and began meditating, calling upon the Great Goddess. The sages and gods chanted hymns of Maheshwari and prayed to her. Devi Shakambhari went to the Shivalik Hills where the gods were worshipping her. Tears continued to roll down from the eyes of the goddess for nine days and nights after seeing the sad state of the earth as a result of the absence of the Vedas. Gradually, she blossomed into the essence of all beauty, as bright and luminous as a thousand suns. The tears shedding from her innumerable eyes transformed into abundant rivers as they fell on the earth. Devi then transformed her appearance, showing eight hands, each of which held foods such as grains, cereals, vegetables, greens, fruits, herbs, etc. The gods and the sages all hailed her as the auspicious one, and she gave them her bounty of delicious vegetables, fruits and roots.

Ushas

सह वामेन न उषो व्युच्छा दुहितर्दिवः।
सह द्युम्नेन बृहता विभावरि राया देवि दास्वती॥
अश्वावतीर्गोमतीर्विश्वसुविदो भूरि च्यवन्त वस्तवे।
उदीरय प्रति मा सूनृता उषश्चोद राधो मघोनाम्॥
उवासोषा उच्छाच्च नु देवी जीरा रथानाम्।
ये अस्या आचरणेषु दध्रिरे समुद्रे न श्रवस्यवः॥
उषो ये ते प्र यामेषु युञ्जते मनो दानाय सूर्यः।
अत्राह तत्कण्व एषां कण्वतमो नाम गृणाति नृणाम्॥

O Ushas, the daughter of the sky, dawn upon us with prosperity,
dawn with great glory and riches, O bounteous one.
Bring steeds and cows, bestow wealth of every sort,
O Ushas, awaken me with the sounds of joy.
May Ushas dawn today, on whose arrival
chariots are harnessed and ships are sent out to sea.
Even Kanva, the chief of Kanva's race,
proclaims the glories of the heroes' names.

—*Rig Veda*, Book 1, Chapter 48, Verses 1–4

*U*shas, whose name translates to 'dawn' in Sanskrit, embodies the concept of the first light that heralds the beginning of a new day, symbolising renewal, vitality and the cyclical nature of time. Almost all cultures have a venerated position for the goddess of dawn. Ushas is one of the oldest goddesses, part of the Vedic canon of divinity. In the *Rig Veda*, Devi Ushas is rather closely associated with divine consciousness and is the goddess who bridges the final gap between *atma* and *paramatma*.

Ushas is often portrayed riding a chariot drawn by seven horses symbolising the seven colours of the rainbow and the seven days of the week. This imagery highlights her association with light, beauty and the cosmic order. Additionally, Ushas is often depicted with celestial beings and divine attendants, emphasising her divine and transcendent nature.

अच्छा वो देवीमुषसं विभातीं प्र वो भरध्वं नमसा सुवृक्तिम्।
ऊर्ध्वं मधुधा दिवि पाजो अश्रेत्प्ररोचना रुरुचे रण्वसंदृक्॥

O worshippers of Ushas, offer your salutations to the divine dawn.
The radiant sight has illuminated the world in an excellent manner.

—*Rig Veda*, Book 3, Chapter 61, Verse 5

In Puranic literature, there is a story about how Lord Brahma created Prajapati, who could not multiply. On Shiva's advice, Brahma created Ushas, the first divine woman, who is said to be the daughter of the sky. This myth of the goddess draws a strong parallel with that of Saraswati; Ushas is believed to be an early form of Saraswati. Added to this is the fact that she is often worshipped as the goddess of the Vedas, inspiring beautiful hymns and shlokas. Vedic poets describe the goddess as a bright apparition. It is this symbolism that speaks to her status as the goddess of dawn. Ushas is known by many names, including Ahana and Dyotana which mean 'illuminating'. In the *Rig Veda*, she was called Yuvati ('the one who is eternally young'), Shukravasah ('the one robed with light'), Subhage ('the blissful one'), Sumangali ('the most auspicious'), and Shreshtatama ('the most excellent one').

As the goddess of dawn who is also worshipped as the

daughter of the sky, Ushas readily assumes the form of the sky. Over the ages, she has easily transitioned from the abstract brightness and brilliance of the sky to a personified goddess. The *Rig Veda* speaks to the presence of dual goddesses Ushas and Nakta, one representing dawn and the other representing night, and together, the goddesses inspire humans to lead righteous lives.

ऋतावरी दिवो अर्कैरबोध्या रेवती रोदसी चित्रमस्थात्।
आयतीमग्न उषसं विभातीं वाममेषि द्रविणं भिक्षमाण:॥

The possessor of truth is recognized by the rays of the sun;
the possessor of wealth is situated between the Earth and
Heaven;
Agni, soliciting alms of the radiant advancing Ushas,
may you obtain your desired treasure (of oblations).

—*Rig Veda*, Book 3, Chapter 61, Verse 6

The interesting thing about the Vedic gods is how they are largely portrayed as friends of mankind who are actively involved in the day-to-day functioning of the world, unlike the gods of the Puranic texts who guide and chart pathways but don't seem to actively participate in the lives of mankind. This might largely be because of the evolving nature of the gods, who were simply deities responsible for the elements in the Vedic period and have, over time, adopted more complex roles in the creation and destruction cycles of the universe. Ushas, as the daughter of Dayus and the sister of Agni and Indra, is thus also seen as the link between heaven and earth, which is perhaps the reason why she was first attached to the idea of guiding divine consciousness.

In another tale, Ushas is the sister of Aditya; other legends claim that she is the wife of Surya who, in the Vedic era, represented the supreme truth or light. As the goddess of dawn, she has her shining chariot drawn by seven cows who bring the first light of the day. She is believed to be connected with the Ashvins, the twin deities of health and well-being.

Devi Ushas' iconography depicts her in crimson robes as she is veiled in gold, the colour of auspiciousness. In this depiction, she is likened to a young bride or wife, whose beauty grows with each passing day. She breathes life into humans in what is often described as a form of rebirth, which is both in her power as someone bringing in the new day and as someone who stands at the gateway of a spiritual awakening.

As the goddess of divine consciousness, Ushas takes away the darkness of ignorance and illusion. Darkness, as defined in this context, is symbolic of hopelessness, and the dawn of Ushas destroys this hopelessness with light, inspiration, prosperity and happiness. When one experiences grief, sadness and despair in the mortal world, it is Ushas who comes forth, rejuvenating us with her creativity, hope and light. How does dawn emerge then? Simple. Through the truth, through seeking the absolute truth; the one who seeks it opens themselves to seeing the Supreme Brahman and rejecting the falsehoods and maya of the world. Their thoughts, actions and words have to be in keeping with the truth, and when this becomes an organic, unconscious act, one is primed to see the divine. Thus, as much as Ushas is the goddess of divine consciousness, Nakta is the goddess of ordinary consciousness, one that arises from the world of illusion.

समानो अध्वा स्वस्रोरनन्तस्तमन्यान्या चरतो देवशिष्टे।
न मेथेते न तस्थतुः सुमेके नक्तोषासा समनसा विरूपे॥

Common, unending is the path of the sisters,
guided by the radiant sun, they travel it alternately;

combined in purpose, though of different forms, night and dawn, neither they obstruct each other, nor do they stand still.

—*Rig Veda,* Book 1, Chapter 113, Verse 3

Despite representing two polarities, there is no conflict between the sisters; where Ushas is the daughter of Aditi, the mother of undivided consciousness, Nakta is the daughter of Diti, the mother of divided consciousness. Their path is circular and never-ending, and Ushas, being one half of this cycle, is depicted as rosy-hued and bright, much like the rising sun, radiant in its lustre.

Shashthi

ॐ ह्रीं षष्ठी देव्यै स्वाहा
नमो देव्यै महादेव्यै सिद्धयै शान्त्यै नमो नम:।
शुभायै देवसेनायै षष्ठीदेव्यै नमो नम:॥
वरदायै पुत्रदायै धनदायै नमो नम:।
सुखदायै मोक्षदायै षष्ठीदेव्यै नमो नम:॥
शक्ते: षष्ठांशरूपायै सिद्धायै च नमो नम:।
मायायै सिद्धयोगिन्यै षष्ठीदेव्यै नमो नम:॥
पारायै पारदायै च षष्ठीदेव्यै नमो नम:।
सारायै सारदायै च पारायै सर्वकर्मणाम्॥

Salutations to the Goddess, the great Goddess,
the one who grants spiritual success and peace.
I bow again and again to the auspicious one,
Devasena, and to Goddess Shashthi.
The one who grants boons, offsprings and wealth;
who bestows happiness and liberation.
Salutations to the one who embodies the
sixth part of Shakti and grants spiritual attainments.
Salutations to the mystical, accomplished yogini;
who helps in crossing over and overcoming obstacles.
Salutations to the essence and bestower of all deeds.

—Devi Shashthi Stotram, Verses 1–4

*G*oddess Shashthi is among the lesser-known folk goddesses of India. She is that form of Shakti who is particularly known as a goddess who looks after, protects and is a benefactor to children. I think it is perhaps as an extension of this function of being a benefactor and protectress that she is also sometimes considered the goddess of reproduction and, in nature, of vegetation and fruitfulness.

The name Shashthi literally translates to 'the sixth' and also because she is taken to be one-sixth of Prakriti or nature. She is also believed to be the sixth incarnation of Mother Earth. The etymology of the name hints towards the sixth day after the birth of a child. Shashthi plays the role of custodian for infant welfare. Thus, the goddess is worshipped on the sixth day of the lunar fortnight. In eastern India, she is the most venerated, especially in West Bengal and Odisha. The cultural impact of the goddess can also be observed in the literary genre Mangalkavyas, especially in the *Shashthi-mangal* that is devoted to her reverence and the exploits of the goddess.

She is often depicted as a beautiful motherly figure, riding on a cat and nursing one or more infants upon her breast. In certain rural cultures, the goddess is worshipped and evoked by pregnant women who are about to give birth and by midwives assisting in the birthing process. Yet, the interesting stories associated with her names inform us about an intriguing tale, as David Gordon White states:

> Sasthi's 'six-ness' manifests itself in a number of ways: she is the spouse (or sister) of the six-headed Skanda; she is the sixth in a series of deities including Skanda and his 'four brothers'; like Skanda, she has six heads; and also like Skanda, she is worshipped on the sixth day of the lunar month and the sixth day after childbirth. She continues to be worshipped down to the present day, at childbirth as well as in puberty and marriage rites, in north India. In Bengal, where her cult is particularly prominent, Sasthi is worshipped as

a bird-headed goddess and is portrayed together with anywhere from one to eight infants.[1]

Rural goddesses or folkloric goddesses take on a more symbolic manifestation than an actualised physical manifestation that one comes to expect of the Trimurti and the gods and goddesses of Devaloka. These deities have accessibility to them that is best explored through the symbolic and the everyday; they are quick, it would seem, to answer the prayers of their devotees. Shashthi is thus symbolically represented in a variety of forms that are mostly related to the feminine, such as an earthenware pitcher, a banyan tree, or a portion of the red stone beneath the tree. There are spaces outside the home called Shashthitala, which are consecrated for the goddess' worship because she is truly significant to the future of the family and its expansion and well-being.

Many scholars believe that the roots of Shashthi worship and the goddess herself can be traced to the early folkloric traditions of the 8th and 9th centuries BCE. She is in the scriptures associated with Skanda, the Hindu god of war, and she is mentioned as being the foster mother of the god. However, later texts contradict this by identifying her as Devasena, the consort of Skanda.

> In fact, Sasthi had two principal names in this period: the 'Sasthi of Women in Childbirth' (sutika-sasthi) and the 'Winged Sasthi' (paksa-sasthi)—for Sasthi, too, is a bird goddess. A significant number of coins, sculptures, and inscriptions from the Kushan and Yaudheya periods picture the six-headed Sasthi, often on the reverse of coins upon which Skanda is figured on the obverse; and she is figured in Kushan-age 'Vrishni triads' from the Mathura region, flanked by Skanda and Visakha in a way that replicates the Balarama–Ekanamsa–Krisna trinity.

> In addition, Kushan images of the six-headed Sasthi may have inspired the iconography of the *caturvyuha* ('four sheaths') forms of the emerging high gods Visnu and Siva of the same period.[2]

There are certain depictions where Shashthi is shown as an attendant of Skanda and is said to be both the cause and the cure of diseases in the mother and the child. It is in worshipping her on the sixth day after childbirth that one prevents her wrath and ensures the well-being of both the mother and the child. In most of her depictions, she is golden-skinned, or shown as a fair young woman, pleasant to look at and brimming with youthfulness and fertility. She is bedecked in jewels and silk garments, radiating an auspicious glow of positivity.

> The fifth-century text *Kashyapa Samhita* calls Shashthi by the epithet Jataharini ('one who steals the born') and provides a list of the malevolent activities in which Shashthi is believed to engage, including her practice of stealing foetuses from the womb and devouring children on the sixth day following birth. For this reason, the text recommends that she be propitiated through worship in her honour on this day and on the sixth day of every fortnight thereafter.[3]

With the passage of time, the characterisation of Shashthi as a goddess gradually began to shift. Now, the perception became more inclined to Shashthi being a benevolent figure who bestowed protection on her devotees.

This pattern of goddesses being demonised in history has surfaced quite often. A similar change in perspective can be noted in the depiction of the Buddhist goddess Hariti as well as Jara in the epic Mahabharata. Initially, they too were ostracised as malevolent goddesses but later became popular figures who were revered as protectors and saviours. There have been numerous mentions of Shashthi in ancient texts; the Vayu Purana is one such text of the fifth century, which lists Shashthi as one among the then 49 significant goddesses, while another Puranic text refers to Shashthi as the one worthiest of worship among mother goddesses. Despite constant references, White questions the classification of Shashthi as a folk goddess, which challenges the traditional universality of her worship since the Kushana era.

During the Kushana rule, between the first and third centuries, the goddess is depicted as being two-armed and six-headed, much like the god of war Skanda. As White writes:

> If nearly every Hindu in India has been worshipping Sasthi since Kushan times, hers is no more a 'folk' cult than those of the great Goddesses Durga or Laksmi: in fact, the *Manava Grihya Sutra*, which describes a ritual to her called the Sasthi-Kalpa, identifies her with Sri, the great Goddess of royal sovereignty.[4]

Coins from this period show the god and goddesses on either side, speaking to their significance in the lives of the people. Another practice observed that comes into play in the worship of Goddess Shashti is during the sixth day of each lunar month when she is meditated upon. It is said that women who have trouble with conception or during the pregnancy or even those who would simply like to start a family should seek her protection and worship Devi so that she may shower them with her blessings.

There are various interpretations and meanings associated with the deity. Devotees believe that Devi Shashthi helps newborns to bear the burden of the sins of their past lives. Her symbolism is represented in the forms of an earthenware pitcher, a banyan tree, or a red stone beneath the tree. Her depiction glorifies a mother figure who is responsible for safeguarding and protecting children.

However, as the earlier representations explored the darker aspects, it was believed that she could also harm a newborn child and the mother in the form of puerperal fever, even causing their deaths if she was not propitiated and pleased appropriately. Nonetheless, this terrifying symbolism was surpassed by the promulgation of more positive beliefs. She became an emblematic deity that comforted women who desired to conceive and mothers who would seek protection for their children.

Vindhyavasini

किं मया हतया मन्द जातः खलु तवान्तकृत्।
यत्र क्व वा पूर्वशत्रुर्मा हिंसीः कृपणान् वृथा॥

O Kamsa, what will be the use of killing me?
The Lord, who has been your enemy
from the very beginning and who will
certainly kill you, has already been born.
Thus, do not unnecessarily kill other children.

—*Devi Bhagavata Purana*, Book 10, Chapter 4, Verse 12

*D*evi Vindhyavasini is a regional goddess associated with the Vindhyachal region, namely as a personification of the Vindhya mountain range. She has often been mentioned in several ancient scriptures and the Puranas, including the Mahabharata, *Vamana Purana*, *Markandeya Purana*, *Matsya Purana*, *Devi Bhagavata Purana*, *Harivamsa Purana*, *Skanda Purana* and *Brihatkatha*.

The famed war between Goddess Durga and the demon king Mahishasura, which was discussed earlier, was believed to have occurred in the Vindhya mountains. As a result, Goddess Vindhyavasini holds a deeply spiritual and contemporary meaning in terms of female empowerment and the destruction of the ego.

[...] Vindhyavasini's diverse mythological associations made her a highly effective means of absorbing others.

Her mythology not only linked her to a wide region but connected her to other goddesses, and to Visnu, Indra, and the pastoral deity Krishna. Unlike Uma, her power was not controlled or diminished by a more powerful husband. Vindhyavasini was thus capable of providing the nuclear origin for a cult of the unmarried, virgin Great Goddess, who was understood as the single Adisakti, the world's primeval power. Vindhyavasini's modern devotees still maintain that she is Adisakti and say that Uma is but an incarnation of this power. Thus, as Uma claims to absorb Vindhyavasini, so Vindhyavasini claims to absorb Uma.[1]

A legend in the *Devi Bhagavata Purana* recounts the episode of Lord Rama visiting Vindhyachal and its surrounding areas along with Sita and Laxman during his 14-year-long *vanavasa* (exile). This myth gives us spiritual pilgrimage spots, such as the Sita Kund, Sita Rasoi, Rama Ghat and the Rameshwar temple, marking key milestones of Lord Rama's heroic journey. The temple of Vindhyachal was also surrounded by thousands of temples in the medieval ages; these temples were places of worship for the Shakti cult, holding as much importance in the South as the cave-dwelling temples in the Himalayas did in the North.

The *Vindhya Mahatmya* thus differs from the *Devi Mahatmya* and its appendix in four major ways. First, the *Vindhya Mahatmya* depicts Vindhyavasini not as one among many expressions of the Great Goddess but as the most transcendent form of Mahalaksmi. Second, Vindhyavasini/Mahalaksmi in manifest form as Vindhyavasini is composed primarily of *rajas*. Third, in ultimate form she is extolled in terms resonant within Advaita tradition: *brahman, bindu,* and so on. Finally, although the *Devi Mahatmya's angas* do explain how to envision various goddesses, as well as detailing certain practices concerning the text's recitation, the *Vindhya Mahatmya* is far more explicit about the worship of the Goddess. Furthermore, unlike the *Devi Mahatmya*, it specifically enjoins that Tantric and Smarta methods be employed to conjure and honour her as the power within and beyond all.²

Vindhyavasini is closely related to Parvati, as the southern counterpart of the North Indian Goddess, and is reminiscent of both Parvati (*parvat-ki*) and Shailputri (the daughter of the mountains). However, the uniqueness of Vindhyachal in the Shakti cult stems from the fact that this is the only place where Devi is worshipped as per the tenets of both *vamachara* and *dakshinachara*. These refer to the left- and right-hand paths of worship, respectively, associated with tantric scriptures; while the former indicates tantric sects that don't engage in heterodox practices, the latter describes tantric practices considered heterodox in nature.

The two *mahatmyas* also treat the Sumbha and Nisumbha myth quite differently. The *Devi Mahatmya* devotes six of its thirteen chapters (5–10) to the story of Sumbha and Nisumbha's defeat, but without once mentioning Vindhyavasini or Krishna. Moreover, the location of the battle is said to be the Himalaya mountains. The eleventh chapter opens with the gods singing a lengthy hymn of praise to the victorious Goddess. Pleased, she offers them a boon, whereupon they ask for the pacification of all miseries and the destruction of their enemies. In response, she graciously promises to incarnate herself in the future whenever demons arise, beginning thus:

When the twenty-eighth era in the Vaivasvat Manu interval has come,

> Two more great demons, also [named] Sumbha and Nisumbha, will be born.
>
> Then, born in the house of the cowherd Nanda, appearing from the womb of Yasoda,
>
> I will slay these two, dwelling on the Vindhya mountain.[3]

Another notable fact in the worship of Shakti in Vindhyachal is the importance afforded to the individual devis part of the Tridevi. Each goddess is prayed to independently—Lakshmi, Kali and Saraswati. The specific temples dedicated to them are located in trine, creating a highly spiritual energy field known for its potency in the meditative tradition called Trikona.

Beautiful descriptions of lush forested areas surrounding Vindhyachal, which are inhabited by lions, elephants and other wildlife, indicate an Eden-like paradise. Since then, much of this forested area has been encroached upon by human cities, except in select areas such as Kali Khoh, Sita Kund and Ashtabujakaram. There are accounts of the temple's existence in the Middle Ages—namely, the memoirs of Col. Sleeman—that tell us how the worship of Goddess Vindhyavasini was open to and favoured by both Hindus and Muslims of the region.[4]

The structure of the Vindhyachal temple, which is one of the Shakti Peethas—where Devi Sati's *pind* (body part) fell on earth—is no longer the one that was there in ancient times. This Shakti Peetha is considered the most important, for this was where Devi chose to reside after her birth. It is believed that when Krishna—it was prophesied that he would bring an end to Kamsa—was born as the eighth child of Devaki and Vasudeva, Devi Mahamaya also took birth at the same time in the home of Nanda and Yashoda. Lord Vishnu had appeared before Vasudeva and instructed him to take the baby boy to Yashoda and bring her daughter to Devaki. When Kamsa tried to kill the baby girl the next morning, she escaped from his hands and turned into her divine form, informing him of his folly—the one who would kill him was already born and safe and away from his prison.

Mohini

धान्वन्तरं द्वादशमं त्रयोदशममेव च।
अपाययत्सुरानन्यान् मोहिन्या मोहयन् स्त्रिया॥

*During his thirteenth incarnation,
the Lord made the other gods drink the amrita or nectar
while deluding the asuras in the form of a charming woman.*

—*Devi Bhagavata Purana*, Book 1, Chapter 3, Verse 17

Mohini, the goddess of enchantment, was an incarnation of Lord Vishnu. He took on the deceptively attractive and irresistible female form to defeat the asuras after the Samudra Manthana, as they were after the amrita or the elixir of life that had come out of the sea. According to another legend, Mohini even seduced Lord Shiva into a union to fend off a future catastrophe. She is also often closely associated with Krishna, having adopted this form in the South Indian folktale that tells of the Mahabharata hero Aravan. Interestingly, Devi Mohini is known for her ability to change her gender as per the necessity of the time, and in the process, she enriches the understanding of Hindu folklore.

The name Mohini means 'erotic magic' or 'spell'. In this regard, she is also associated with the legend of Dasa Mahavidyas. As Kinsley notes, the Mahavidya goddesses intertwine the themes of sex and mortality, symbolising enlightenment for the *sadhaka*.[1] These depictions encourage the seeker to confront life's ultimate realities, stripping away comforting illusions about one's transience and inevitable mortality. By doing so, they help the sadhaka transcend the veil of maya, the illusion born from self-obsession.

The origin of the name comes from the word *moha*, which means 'delusion personified' or 'to enchant and perplex'. The root word 'moha' also means to have desire or to be desirous; desire here has the ability to override the self-awareness of the rational mind; in a way, it is turning away from consciousness to sense gratification.

In the *Devi Bhagavata Purana*, Mohini is one of the 24 avatars of Lord Vishnu. She is often mentioned as one of the most delightful forms of Vishnu. However, many scholars believe that the goddess cannot truly be called an avatar, since that requires the descent of Vishnu's energy on earth to establish dharma. After accomplishing the purpose of the birth, the avatar merges once again with Lord Vishnu's primal essence.

The Mohini avatar appeals to feminine energy because it is capable of driving all reason out of one's mind. However, this is rarely considered a purpose of establishing dharma and Mohini is thus more a manifestation of God than an avatar. While unravelling the Mohini form of Vishnu, it is important to understand that Mohini is perhaps a manifestation that comes into play when Vishnu, as the Preserver, has to intervene to maintain the balance of the universe. The way in which Radha is Krishna's pleasure (*raas*), Mohini can be thought of as Vishnu's purpose and potency.

The emergence of Mohini dates back to the Samudra Manthana episode, as narrated in the Mahabharata. When the amrita emerged, the asuras stole it to prevent the devas from keeping it all for themselves. To avoid a war and its collateral damage, Vishnu assumed the form of Mohini and offered to mediate between the devas and the asuras. Both sides, taken by the beauty and eroticism of the woman, were unable to understand anything that was occurring before them. Meanwhile, Mohini continued giving the amrita to the devatas until not a single drop was left for the asuras. As the last of the devas were getting the amrita, i.e., Suryadeva and Chandradeva, a demon stole the *kalasha* (urn) to take the last of the immortality elixir for himself.

In that instant, Vishnu assumed his form and, with his Sudarshana Chakra, severed the head of the demon from his body; the head then became Rahu, always ravenously hungry, and the body became Ketu, who is consistently detached from all things. The asuras lost their rational mind to the illusion of Mohini and hence moved away from divine consciousness. As seen in this legend, Mohini also refers to the illusion and trappings of the material world that keep us in a cycle of loss. Yet, interestingly, if we compare Devi Mohini to Maya, we would notice the similarities and dissimilarities, with reference to how unique the conception of illusion, or maya, became in Hindu mythology.

Another tale from the *Vishnu Purana* tells us a story of the time when Shiva granted Bhasmasura the boon that gave him the ability to turn everything he touched into ash. It was a destructive power but a weapon of great intensity; having received this boon, the demon wanted to try it on Shiva. To protect himself, Shiva ran away from the demon, with Bhasmasura chasing after him through all planes of the universe. It was an impossible situation where no one could intervene, lest they stood in the way of destruction themselves.

Lord Vishnu then appeared before Bhasmasura in the form of Mohini. The demon immediately fell in love and proposed to marry the goddess, who laughed at the ease with which he had offered marriage and said that she had vowed to only marry a man who could match her ability to dance. As a bhakta of Shiva, the demon would perhaps be a good dancer, thought Mohini. To impress her, he initiated a competition.

The goddess would dance, and Bhasmasura would follow, in a truly wondrous performance. Soon, Mohini began to use various mudras (hand gestures). So intoxicating in nature was this dance that Bhasmasura forgot everything—about chasing after Shiva, his boon, etc. As the goddess frequently started touching her forehead, Bhasmasura followed, instantly turning into a pile of ash. Unable to control his moha (attachment to desire), the asura brought on his own end. It is believed, as stated in the *Vishnu Purana*, that when Shiva laid eyes on Mohini, his seed fell on earth and from this seed, Hanuman was born, who was to assist Rama and serve Vishnu in his every incarnation.

According to the *Brahmavaivarta Purana*, Mohini—an apsara created by Shiva—falls in love with Brahma, the Creator. Despite her attempts to seduce him, Brahma rebuffs her advances, claiming to be too old for her and comparing her to a daughter. Mohini, angered by his rejection, reminds Brahma of his past desires. Vishnu then explains to Brahma that the purpose of this incident was to humble him.

Another folktale from South India recounts the story of Aravan, a hero from the Mahabharata who later became Kuttantavar, a Tamil deity. Before his sacrificial ritual, known as *kalappali*, to secure the Pandavas' victory, Aravan married Mohini. Seeking three boons from Krishna, his guide, Aravan requested to be wed before his sacrifice—an uncommon request. In the legend, Krishna assumes the form of Mohini to fulfil Aravan's wish. After the sacrifice, Mohini mourns Aravan's death, symbolising widowhood, before reverting to the original form. This narrative forms the focal point of an 18-day annual festival held at Koovagam during the Tamil month of Cittirai (April–May). In this festival, transgenders, or hijras, enact the marriage ceremony, embodying the role of Mohini–Krishna.

Dasa Mahavidyas

गायन्ती दोलयन्ती च बालभावान्मयि स्थिते।
सेयं सुनिश्चितं ज्ञातं जातं मे दर्शनादिव।।
कामं नो जननी सैषा शृणु तं प्रवदाम्यहम्।
अनुभूतं मया पूर्वं प्रत्यभिज्ञा समुत्थिता।।

*Now I recollect all what I felt before at Her sight
and recognize that She is the Bhagavati.
I will now communicate these very things to you.
Hear attentively that She is this Lady and She is our Mother.*

—*Devi Bhagavata Purana,*
Book 3, Chapter 3, Verses 66–67

The Dasa Mahavidyas refer to a group of 10 tantric goddesses, known as the Mahavidyas, who embody different forms of Shakti, the divine feminine. Each goddess has unique characteristics and origin stories. With the rise of tantrism, the goddesses gained significant prominence in both textual and visual representations, and theology became distinctly centred around the goddess. By the 15th century, the tantric goddesses had established a strong presence and unique identities.

Modern scholars translate *'maha'* as supreme and *'vidya'* as knowledge, but this doesn't fully capture the complex nature of these tantric goddesses. Some are fierce and fearsome, while others are graceful and enchanting. For instance, one goddess carries her own severed head, while another has the power to mesmerise.

The order and names of the Dasa Mahavidyas can vary, but the list commonly includes Kali, Tara, Tripura Sundari, Bhuvaneshwari, Bhairavi, Chhinnamasta, Dhumavati, Bagalamukhi, Matangi and Kamalatmika. Scholars believe Kali, Tara and Chhinnamasta to be the most prominent, and they are worshipped individually. Kinsley describes Kali as representing the 'personified wrath' of Sati, Durga and Parvati in various myths.[1]

The Mahavidyas are often connected to Shiva's consort, Sati, and their origins relate to events leading up to Daksha's sacrifice. According to the *Devi Bhagavata Purana*, there is a disagreement between Shiva and Sati regarding her attendance at Daksha's yajna. When Shiva refuses to let her go, Sati reveals her supernatural abilities, transforming into Kali—naked, dark-skinned, and wearing a garland of skulls. Frightened, Shiva tries to escape, but Sati's 10 forms appear, surrounding him, and he eventually grants her permission to attend the sacrifice.

Kinsley further points out that these manifestations are not just female equivalents of the Dashavatara. They are not portrayed as warriors, and their fierceness is not related to preserving cosmic order. Instead, their purpose is to intimidate Shiva and assert dominance over him, which significantly alters the traditional story of Sati.

The principal aim of the tantra is to overcome differences that would be stifling to individuals. The Dasa Mahavidyas facilitate the escape of such artificial shackles because they themselves are 'social antimodels', notes Kinsley.[2] These goddesses, who once thrived on the fringes, advocate different types of transgressive practices that flaunt or undermine the distinctions between the categories of pure and impure. This is what created the composite worship of a hybrid group of goddesses. The integration of the devis from diverse regions and with different doctrines gives prominence to marginalised goddesses such as Matangi, Dhumavati and Bagalamukhi. Each goddess has her own point of origin and many versions. They retain their ethnic trait, making them fascinating and creating a fabric that is fundamentally inclusive.

Determining the exact timeline of the Mahavidyas' formation is challenging. They appear to have emerged after the Ashta Matrikas and Chausath Yoginis, indicating they belong to a later era. Their earliest mention can be found in the Mahakala Samhita from the 12th century. Despite their secretive nature, they are widely represented in regions from north to east through temples, life-size painted icons and popular calendar art.

Some scholars suggest a link between Brahmanical Hinduism and local deities, attributing the Mahavidyas' development to a consistent and complementary interaction between the two traditions.[3] The origin, aspects and features of the Dasa Mahavidyas begin with the description of Goddess Kali. According to the Kalikula (the family of Kali) system in Shaktism, she is the supreme deity and the devourer of time (kala), followed by Tara.

The overlap of form and function in the description of each Mahavidya is because of the cultural differences between Sanskrit and pan-Hindu ideologies.[4]

Tripura Sundari is named next as she is the Supreme Deity according to the Srikula belief in Shaktism; followed by Bhuvaneshwari, Bhairavi, Chhinnamasta, Dhumavati, Bagalamukhi, Matangi and Kamalatmika.

Goddess Kali is considered to be the Adi Shakti who controls universal power, time, life, death, and both rebirth and liberation. Etymologically, she is the feminised variant of Mahakala, another name for Lord Shiva, and a deity common to Tantric Buddhism as well. Both Mahakala and

Kali represent the ultimate destructive power of Brahman—knowledge that can destroy the boundaries of known time and space.

The remaining Mahavidyas are a unique manifestation of Goddess Kali. They may emanate from her but each has their own cosmic personalities that include mythology as well as religious iconography. For example, Tara, considered the second of the Mahavidyas, is common to Buddhist as well as Jain cosmology. She is worshipped as a yogini, a formal term of respect for female Hindu or Buddhist spiritual teachers in the Indian subcontinent, Southeast Asia and Greater Tibet.

The Shaktas believe the Dasa Mahavidyas are 10 different cosmic facets of the divine mother; in Tantra, the Mahavidyas are an incarnation or manifestation of Mahakali.

Kali

Kali, a pivotal figure in Hinduism and Tantra, embodies ultimate power, time, destruction and transformation, being the ultimate manifestation of Shakti, the primordial cosmic energy and mother of all living beings. In various devotional and tantric sects, she is venerated as a ferocious form of the divine feminine, inspiring both awe and reverence. Tantric rituals often involve confronting Kali on cremation grounds, symbolising the courage to face mortality and embrace change. Interestingly, in West Bengal, she is approached with the innocence and love of a child, showcasing her multifaceted nature. Within Shaktism, Kali is Mahakali, the devourer of time and the ultimate form of Brahman. The Mahavidyas, including Kali, symbolise various aspects of the divine feminine, with Kali representing primal ferocity as Adi Shakti. Mythologically, Kali's emergence is linked to Durga, arising from her anger during her battle with the demons.

Tara

Among the Mahavidyas, Tara almost always follows Devi Kali. She is indeed more akin to Kali in appearance than any of the other Mahavidyas.[5] In the *Kalika Purana*, she is described as a fierce deity, holding her desired weapons. According to Tantric texts within Jain and Buddhist literature, she became popular only after the development of Jainism and Buddhism. In Buddhist lore, Tara figures as the counterpart, the Shakti to the Lord who has directed his gaze in compassion (Avalokiteswara). Her personality in Tibetan Buddhism is that of overwhelming her devotees with compassion, whereas in Hindu traditions, her characteristics are closer to those of Goddess Kali.

Tripura Sundari

The Srikula tradition from the Srividya school of Vedic Hinduism believes Tripura Sundari to have created the supreme and divine triad of deities. Srividya largely views the goddess as 'benign (*saumya*) and beautiful (*saundarya*)', in contrast to the Kalikula traditions of focusing on her 'terrifying (*ugra*) and horrific (*aghora*)' manifestations. In many South Indian shrines, she is worshipped as Goddess Lalita. According to Tantra, she has a body like a crystal, covered in tiger skin, with a garland of snakes around her neck. Holding a trident and a drum, she rides a large bull decorated with jewels, flowers and ashes. Tripura Sundari occupies a very special place in the Shakta scripture known as the Tripura Rahasya.[6] The goddess is described as having 'beauty of the three worlds' and as the 'Tantric Parvati' or the 'Moksha Mukta'.

Bhuvaneshwari

The Mahavidya Bhuvaneshwari represents the cosmic notion of the primordial space as the embodiment of the physical world. She is associated with the underlying dynamic energy that has created the worlds, particularly the visible, with the might to empower even the sun god. She is represented carrying all three worlds. Praying to the goddess of all three worlds promotes cosmic vision and liberates one from the restriction of narrow beliefs by bestowing one with universal understanding. She is worshipped as the patron goddess of Bhubaneswar by the Brahmin community in Odisha. Devotees make promises of saris to the Goddess for granting their prayers; in this respect, they pray to gain material success and well-being from a goddess who is so strongly identified with the physical world.[7]

Bhairavi

According to Tantra, Bhairavi is a primary yogic goddess associated with the cosmic fire. She is the fierce Shakti who purifies internal speech and thought through the heat of the divine fire. Bhairavi is part of the holy trinity of Bhuvaneshwari and Tripura Sundari, whose actions are interconnected and represent different stages of consciousness. Traditional texts present Bhairavi as radiating more powerfully than a thousand suns. She has three eyes and wears a crown of precious stones in the shape of a crescent moon. Dressed in red garments, she wears a necklace of skulls around her neck even though her expression is kind and happy, signified by the abhayamudra and varadamudra.

Chhinnamasta

As an individual goddess, Chhinnamasta is worshipped as Devi in Vedic Hinduism and as Chhinnamunda in Buddhist Tantric traditions. The name Chhinnamasta is also used as a generic name for goddess icons who do not have heads. The legends of Chhinnamasta emphasise her self-sacrifice, coupled with a maternal element of sexual dominance and self-destructive fury. Within the esoteric tantric tradition, she is worshipped and depicted as part of the Mahavidyas group in temples. The Goddess is treated as a motherly figure of regal authority and power. Unlike other Hindu deities who are depicted facing the devotee, Chhinnamasta is shown looking at herself through her own severed head, suggesting that devotees look within themselves. In accordance with the Rasa theory of the *Natyashastra*, the naked Chhinnamasta positioning herself on a copulating couple has elements of heroism (*vira rasa*) and terror (*bhayanaka rasa*) as well as the erotic (*sringara rasa*).

Dhumavati

In the *Mahabhagavata Purana*, a tale recounts the creation of the Mahavidyas, where Sati insists on attending Lord Daksha's yajna. In the manifestation of Dhumavati, she engulfs Lord Shiva, compelling him to open his third eye, reducing her to ashes. Dhumavati symbolises misfortune, frustration and poverty, often deemed inauspicious in mainstream Hinduism and likened to the Vedic goddess Nirriti (the goddess personifying death, decay and sorrow). Known as the mother of non-existence, Dhumavati represents a trance-like repose amidst cosmic dissolution. Adorned in white, resembling a widow, she rides a horseless chariot with a crow emblem, bearing two trembling hands, one granting boons or knowledge and the other holding a winnowing basket.

Bagalamukhi

Devi Bagalamukhi is the female personification of Devi and is worshipped as an incarnation of Goddess Parvati. She has been mentioned in the *Tantrasara of Abhinavagupta* as clad in yellow, with her left hand holding the opponent's tongue and striking him with a mace she holds in her right hand. In North India, Bagalamukhi is commonly known as Maa Pitambari because of her association with the colour yellow, which is symbolic of a mythological lake on the shores of where the goddess appeared when Lord Vishnu prayed for protection against a cosmic storm.

Matangi

In southern India, Matangi, a form of the Hindu goddess Saraswati, is revered as the minister to Tripura Sundari, representing both orthodox and inner knowledge. She embodies the leftover divine essence and governs speech and learning, symbolising the power of the spoken word and listening. Matangi's origin story involves a boon from Tripura Sundari to the sage Mantaga, her father. She is depicted in the ancient Sanskrit poem 'Shyamaladandakam' as having an emerald complexion and playing a ruby-studded veena. Matangi's association with Madurai's Meenakshi and the green colour symbolises deep knowledge and Mercury's influence in Hindu astrology. She is worshipped primarily for acquiring supernatural powers, especially gaining control over enemies, and mastery of the arts, with her presence felt at the Kamakhya temple complex, a significant centre for tantra worship.

Kamalatmika

Kamalatmika, the last of the Dasa Mahavidyas, embodies Vishnu's energy in Shaktism. Her shrine is in Kamakhya, and she is worshipped as a *yoni*. She is depicted as a formidable goddess bringing bliss and prosperity, and is described as having a molten-gold complexion and three serene eyes, and is seated on a lotus and adorned with pearls. Mythologically, she emerges from the churning ocean of milk, symbolising immortality, and is bathed by four elephants, who symbolise fertility and divine authority. Devi Kamalatmika is also known as Tantric Lakshmi, representing refinement beyond the material world yet rooted in it, symbolised by the lotus. Her portrayal reflects a blend of fierceness and benevolence, embodying both power and grace.

Sapta Matrikas

प्रेतसंस्था तु चामुण्डा वाराही महिषासना।
ऐन्द्री गजसमारुढ़ा वैष्णवी गरुड़ासना॥
माहेश्वरी वृषारुढ़ा कौमारी शिखिवाहना।
ब्राह्मी हंससमारुढ़ा सर्वाभरणभूषिता॥
इत्येता मातर: सर्वा सर्वयोगसमन्विता:।

*I pay obeisance to the Matrikas,
who are endowed with powers.
Devi Chamunda, who abides with ghosts and spirits,
Devi Varahi, who is seated on a buffalo,
Devi Aindri, who is mounted on an elephant,
Devi Vaishnavi, who is seated on Garuda,
Devi Maheshwari, who is mounted on a bull,
Devi Kaumari, who is mounted on her peacock,
Devi Brahmi, who is mounted on a swan and adorned with ornaments,
They all are mothers (Matrikas), who are endowed with powers.*

—*Durga Saptashati*, Devi Kavacham,
Verses 9, 10 and 12

Matrikas, meaning 'mothers', are an early group of goddesses who are often depicted and worshipped together. Another term, Matrigana, meaning 'the collective group of divine mothers', is also used. This collective veneration of goddesses is a notable aspect of Hinduism and is primarily seen among female divinities rather than male ones. Other similar groups of goddesses include Ashta Lakshmi, Navadurgas, Dasa Mahavidyas, Nityakala Devis, and Chausath Yoginis, but the Matrikas are the oldest of these.

Scholars have traced the earliest mentions of the Matrikas to the epic Mahabharata, dating back to around the first century CE. Although their exact number isn't specified, the passages suggest there were many, as noted by Kinsley. These references highlight the inauspicious and dangerous qualities of the Matrikas. For instance, Indradeva sends them to kill the war god Kartikeya when he is born, but they are moved by their maternal instincts upon seeing him and ask to become his mothers, because of which they are also known as Krittikas.[1]

Their physical appearance, including long nails, protruding lips, and sharp large teeth, emphasises their threatening nature. Further, they reside in locations like burning grounds, trees, crossroads, caves and mountains. These goddesses speak various languages, hinting that they may have originated from different regions, initially linked to non-Brahmanical traditions common in outlying areas. They might also have been related to village goddesses connected to illnesses.

By the early medieval period, the Matrikas became more defined in their names and numbers, with mentions in both the Puranas and Tantras. Their character evolved to include associations with male gods and protective roles, and they began to be considered emanations of the great Devi. The *Devi Mahatmya* recounts Durga summoning the Sapta Matrikas, or 'seven mothers', for help against the demon Raktabija, and they emerge from her to aid her. They also assist in defeating Shumbha and Nishumbha. Chapter 11 of the *Devi Mahatmya* provides detailed descriptions of the Matrikas, including Brahmani on a chariot pulled by swans, Maheshwari riding a bull with a trident and serpent,

Kaumari with a peacock and spear, and Vaishnavi holding a conch, discus, club and bow.

The Matrikas are regarded as the female counterparts of male deities with corresponding names. For instance, Brahmi or Brahmani is linked to Brahma, Maheshwari to Maheshwara (another name for Shiva), and Vaishnavi to Vishnu. They share the same forms, weapons and mounts as their male versions. Given that Devi was formed from the combined energies of the gods, this theory of the origin of the Sapta Matrikas makes sense. The weapons given to Devi to conquer the asuras were infused with her divine energy, Shakti, rather than being mere replicas, thus making the created one also the creator.

In another interesting myth, the Sapta Matrikas come to Shiva's aid during his battle with Andhaka, a fearsome asura who, like Raktabija, can replicate himself with each drop of his blood. Faced with an ever-growing number of Andhakas, the male gods sent the Sapta Matrikas to intervene and control the asura's blood to prevent further multiplication.

A senior monk of the Ramakrishna Order and an author, Swami Harshananda provides an esoteric interpretation of the Matrikas in his study. He suggests that Brahmi symbolises *nada*, or the primal energy 'before the first throb occurs', which is also known as 'the unmanifest sound' or 'the origin of all creation'.[2]

Vaishnavi's energy establishes the universe's structure, providing it with definite space, harmony, beauty and order. Maheshwari represents the force that gives each created being a sense of individuality. She resides within all hearts and animates them. Harshananda describes Kaumari as 'the ever-youthful deity', representing the 'aspiring force of the evolving soul'. She is also known as Guru Guha, with 'guru' meaning teacher and *guha* meaning cave. Varahi embodies the power of assimilation and enjoyment, enabling living beings to have food and physical pleasures. Aindri signifies 'the destructive force against all that opposes the cosmic law'. Harshananda concludes by explaining that 'Chamunda symbolises focused awareness and the power of spiritual enlightenment in the heart, which consumes the relentless activity of the mature mind'.

Considering the iconography, the Matrikas are typically portrayed in human form, riding the mounts associated with their male counterparts. Varahi has the head of a boar. She is often depicted alongside Ganesha, the son of Parvati, and Virabhadra, a fierce form of Shiva, in panels within Shiva temples. The Matrikas also have their own dedicated shrines. Their arrangement is determined by the desired outcome, according to Harshananda. For instance, when seeking the protection of a village, Brahmi is placed at the centre. At times, the Matrikas are also depicted sitting on lotus thrones, with their attendants and mounts accompanying them.

There are multiple instances connecting the Matrikas with children. Originally, these goddesses were not seen as nurturing figures; instead, they were fearsome deities known for attacking children. Scholars suggest this belief may stem from the superstition that women who died without having children or during childbirth became vengeful spirits targeting other people's offspring. Over time, the Matrikas assumed protective roles, as seen in their iconography, where they are often depicted with children either beside them or seated on their laps. Early sculptures show diverse female figures with animal or bird heads, either holding or surrounded by children.

Maheshwari

Associated with Maheshwara (Shiva), Maheshwari signifies

the power that gives individuality to beings. Like Shiva, she rides Nandi, the bull, and has four arms holding a trident, prayer beads, a pellet drum, and a drinking vessel. She wears a matted crown, or *jatamukuta*, and has a third eye on her forehead.

Aindri

Linked to Indradeva, Aindri represents the power to destroy cosmic law. She has four arms and three eyes (sometimes described as having 1,000 eyes) and wields Indra's thunderbolt. Her vahana is a white elephant, similar to Indra's mount, and she resides near the wish-fulfilling tree Kalpavriksha.

Kaumari

Connected to Kumara or Kartikeya, the god of war, Kaumari symbolises valour and courage. She rides a peacock and is often depicted with four arms holding weapons like a spear, an axe, and a bow. Sometimes she is portrayed with six heads, mirroring her consort Kartikeya.

Brahmi

Associated with Brahma, Brahmi symbolises order, symmetry and beauty in the universe. Like Brahma, she has four heads and holds a water pot and a japamala. Also known as Brahmani, her mount is a white swan, and she is often seen seated on a lotus.

Varahi

Varahi is related to Varaha, Vishnu's boar form, representing the power of assimilation. She has the face of a boar and a skin tone similar to a storm cloud. Varahi wears a conical basket-shaped crown and rides an elephant.

Chamunda

Chamunda, the most formidable of the Sapta Matrikas, is associated with Shiva and embodies spiritual awakening. Often depicted as being gaunt, with prominent ribs, a sunken belly, and skulls in her hair, she is also characterised by protruding fangs and a scorpion near her navel, symbolising death and disease. In rural Karnataka, Chamunda—also known as Chamundi, Chowdeshwari or Mahishasuramardini—is singled out from the Sapta Matrikas and revered as Matri, Amma or Thayi, the divine mother. Sometimes, she holds a central position among the Sapta Matrikas, as seen in the Chowdeshwari temple near T. Narasipura, where sculptures of the goddesses were discovered in the nearby forest.

Vaishnavi

Vaishnavi, linked to Vishnu, symbolises protection. She is often depicted riding Garuda, the king of birds, and holding a chakra and a conch, which are associated with Vishnu's oceanic connections.

∞

In Tamil Nadu and Karnataka, regions with shared historical and religious ties, the Sapta Matrikas are predominantly worshipped in rural shrines and temples. They hold significance in agriculture, often depicted in terracotta images on irrigation bunds. Their identity was established by the 5th century CE, typically associated with Shiva or his form Virabhadra. Unlike their counterparts in the North, the Sapta Matrikas in the South have distinct attributes and are not directly derived from male deities, except for Chamunda. This portrayal underscores their collective power, blending fierceness, gentleness and seduction.[3]

In rural Karnataka, the Sapta Matrikas, revered as divine mothers known as Matrgalu or Saptamatrgalu, are worshipped for fertility, prosperity and well-being. Unlike the classical Sapta Matrikas, the rural notion of the Sapta-Kannigal (seven virgins) or Sapta-Matru (seven mothers) in South India is relatively simple despite local variations in the manner in which they are evoked and worshipped. It is noticed that the tradition of grouping goddesses, a common practice in villages, is to demonstrate their collective power, emphasising the independence of feminine divinity as omnipotent mothers, in contrast to their classical counterparts who are primarily viewed as the energy of their male consorts. Associated with fertility and various aspects of human life, the rural Sapta-Kannigal are typically linked with guarding village boundaries and serving as tutelary deities. They are often depicted anthropomorphically or symbolically, with clay figurines commonly installed in village sanctuaries or under trees. Some communities associate them with other deities like Muniappan or Mariamman.

The formation of groups of goddesses often arises from community wishes or as a fulfilment of vows. In gratitude, families or individuals worship Sapta-Kannimar through rituals, typically requiring priestly services. These goddesses, characterised as aggressive, demand specific forms of worship, including offerings of cooked rice, chicken or mutton, and country liquor. Adorned with jasmine flowers, turmeric and vermilion, they are worshipped either as burnt bricks submerged in water or as stones under trees. Among forest tribes like the Irulas in Tamil Nadu, Sapta-Kannimar are revered as patron deities. Ritual practices associated with the cult of Sapta Matrikas vary greatly among communities, but generally, direct viewing of the goddesses is forbidden due to perceived malevolence. According to local belief, they may cause 'death and decay'. Ritual worship is deemed necessary to seek their blessings for village prosperity and individual happiness. In Karnataka, religious pilgrimages, or *jatra*s, involving fasting, fire walking and self-mortification, are integral to the worship tradition.

In the former North Arcot district of Tamil Nadu, the Sapta-Kannigal are believed to protect tanks and irrigation bunds, though they are also associated with death, prompting their shrines to be placed outside villages. Devotees often dress as the seven goddesses during annual festivals, where divination and spirit possession play central roles in the ritual worship. However, worship of the Sapta-Kannigal extends beyond village shrines. As Jayalakshmi Yegnaswamy states:

> In Tamil Nadu and Karnataka the seven goddesses under the name Saptamatas or Saptamatrika are depicted in relief on the inner wall of the village step wells to protect the water source. The earlier mention of the Saptamatrika is in the epic *Mahabharata* where they are connected to seven sages. Known in the Purana as Akasa Matrika the seven divine mothers are also associated with the sky and cosmic forces. In the rural south they are known as Akasa Kannigals, protectors of the entire village from natural disasters. As tutelary deities they are worshipped in symbolic manner and as Kaval Deivam or guardian deities the divine heptads are placed at the entrance to the villages where they are offered customary worship in diverse kinds of rituals in Tamil Nadu and Karnataka.[4]

The worship of Sapta Matrikas is associated with healing, evident in shrines like Guthalamma in Mandya, where they are invoked for curing diseases and protection from death. In Karnataka, the Kolaramma Temple in Kolar, built around 1040 by Rajendra Chola, is renowned as a shrine dedicated to the Sapta Matrikas. Additionally, in sacred groves (*devarkadu*), the Sapta Matrikas are linked to ancestor worship, as seen in the Kodagu district where various mother goddesses, including those connected to the Sapta Matrikas, are venerated. Similar practices are observed in rural Tamil Nadu and parts of north Karnataka, where rituals blend tantric and folk traditions to invoke blessings or harm upon enemies. Overall, the diverse roles and regional identities of the Sapta Matrikas reflect the intricate blend of magic and reverence within rural communities, serving to maintain balance in their existence.

Chausath Yoginis

ॐ ऐं क्लीं श्रीं हसौः चतुःषष्टीयोगिनेभ्यो नमः।

*With the sounds aem, kleem, shreem and hasauh,
I offer salutations to the sixty-four Yoginis.*

—*Chausath Yogini Yantra*

Who exactly are these 64 yoginis? Kinsley, who has studied the Dasa Mahavidyas extensively, calls them females with magical powers. It is accepted that belief in the Chausath Yoginis, who belong to the Shakti cult (primarily in the tantric sect), started somewhere in the 5th or 6th century CE. They found prominence in the 9th century CE and flourished till the 12th century. Another significant scholar, Vidya Dehejia, states that the yogini tradition is tantric in nature and thus connected to rural and tribal traditions.[1]

It is believed that the yoginis are village goddesses, or *grama* devis, who protect the villages. Over time, these grama devis assumed greater powers and they gained new forms, and as a group, they started imparting magical powers to their worshippers.

While deconstructing the evolution of the Chausath Yogini cult, it became clear that this cult may have had its roots in the earliest of the prehistoric periods. With the passage of time, the discovery of tantric literary texts belonging to the 6th century BC, along with archaeological remains of temples, brought to prominence the vivacity of worship and reverence that these goddesses might have enjoyed across the country all through the 9th century. The same might also find resonance with the folk continuum of Yakshi worship, where each deity would be worshipped as a local protector.

In the early medieval period, a group of lesser-known goddesses emerged in various parts of India, although many of the temples dedicated to them have since been lost. Scholars are currently engaged in uncovering the identities and significance of these goddesses. Among them, the yoginis have retained a captivating allure, their mystique gradually being demystified through scholarly pursuits. Tantric texts, now undergoing translation and analysis, offer insights into the diverse descriptions, rituals and traditions associated with the yogini cult. However, much remains to be comprehended about their nature and significance, with the likelihood that some aspects may elude accurate interpretation.

The term 'yogini' carries a broad meaning in Indian culture, often blurring the lines between goddesses and women. It has been used to denote attendants, sorceresses or even demons, but in Tantra, it refers to women who undergo specific rituals to become yoginis. According to Indian Tantra scholar N.N. Bhattacharyya, yoginis could have originally been women or priestesses believed to be possessed by goddesses, eventually elevated to the status of deities.[2]

Dehejia discusses ancient Indian texts that depict yoginis, *dakini*s and *sakini*s as female deities or spirits possessing supernatural abilities, including the ability to transform people into animals, eliciting both reverence and fear. Referring to the Chausath Yoginis mentioned in the Puranas, Dehejia suggests they may represent various aspects of the

Great Goddess, embodying her complete presence. Unlike many Hindu goddesses, yoginis are typically worshipped collectively, devoid of spousal associations with male deities, indicating their independence. Dehejia proposes that the Chausath Yoginis served as patron deities for the followers of the unorthodox Kaula Marga,[3] a tantric tradition, with their earliest mention in the 9th-century *Agni Purana*, highlighting their significant influence despite being treated as outsiders with no established mythology. Their worship is also noted in texts such as the *Lalita Sahasranama*, appended to the *Brahmanda Purana*, reflecting their association with Shakta practices.[4]

The yoginis are depicted in diverse forms, often as life-size sculptures found in open-air temples scattered across central and northern India. These magnificent stone sculptures exhibit varying expressions, ranging from serene to fearsome, and are typically voluptuous in appearance. Each temple houses its own group of yoginis, reflecting unique characteristics and identities, with some temples situated near ancient capitals, suggesting a belief in their protective and dynastic roles.

The iconography of the yoginis lacks uniformity, with individual groups displaying distinct features, sometimes accompanied by inscribed names on pedestals. Many yogini sculptures exhibit their anthropic elements, featuring animal heads such as those of horses, lions, birds and snakes, alongside diverse body types, from aged figures with drooping breasts to heavily ornamented ones adorned with multiple necklaces and garlands. Despite these variations, yoginis are typically depicted with halos and multiple arms.

Interpreting the Yogini cult requires understanding its contextual significance. Their temples' circular walls likely enclosed spaces for Mahayajna rituals, aiming to appease the yoginis for occult powers. In sculptures like that of

Kamada in Madhya Pradesh's Bhedaghat temple, tantric rites, such as yoni puja, are illustrated, rare in explicitness even within tantric texts. The act, depicted with anatomical accuracy, symbolises reverence for the female form and its potential for enlightenment. This practice, according to cultural activist Pupul Jayakar, centres on worshipping women and their sexual organs as embodiments of divine power, a concept supported by Shaw.[5] Such rituals, possibly linked to *guhyapuja* (secret worship), underscore the belief of women being manifestations of goddesses requiring devoted veneration.

The names and nature of the yoginis also hint at their personality. While Takari means a particular part of a woman's pudenda, Lampata translates to lustful or licentious. Some other names include Vibhatsa ('the dreadful one') and Bhisani ('the terrifying one'). Rauravi refers to the yogini who makes loud sounds or has the voice of a jackal. There is also Garbhabhakshi, who is the eater of the foetus.

Judging by their names, it appears that they originated in villages and were folk divinities. Some of their names indicate a Sanskrit root, while others do not; several are grammatically incorrect.

Yoginis, diverse and nameless, exhibit a range of unique characteristics, from animal faces to voluptuous figures, to distinct weapons or objects. Some exude fierceness and sensuality, while others dance with abandon. Among them, the winnow-bearing yogini from Kanchipuram holds a winnow and a head of corn, challenging gender norms with the sacred thread across her chest. Another yogini from Kanchipuram, her hair splayed in a wild halo, rides a corpse, with snake armlets and a human-hand earring. In Hirapur, Odisha, the kettledrum-carrying yogini balances on a mouse. An unknown yogini from the same region possibly depicts Yamuna standing atop a tortoise, while the anklet-adjusting yogini stands sensually atop a dog. Antakari from Bhedaghat, Madhya Pradesh, has a menacing face surrounded by snakes and skulls, while Shri Erudi, theriomorphic with a horse's face, embodies sensuality. Shri Vaishnavi from eastern India, mounted on Garuda, wields a spear and a sword, her fingers poised at her mouth as if to make a sound.

The depiction of the feminine anthropomorphic body accompanied by animal heads perforates the diaphanous boundaries between the literal, the metaphorical and the divine.[6] The yogini evokes the divine through historical narratives such as in *Hatha Yoga Pradipika*[7], which records her presence as Devi, superimposed by the Yogini Chakra.

The Chausath Yogini Yantra, represented by Padma Mandala containing eight petals, symbolically refers to the Ashta Matrikas associated with eight great siddhis. It follows the worship of the Ashta Matrikas as endowments, such as 'Animan—the ability to become microscopic in size, Mahiman—the power to enlarge, Laghiman—the power to command lightness at will, Gariman—the assumption of excessive weight, Prakamya—an irresistible will that compels others to abide by one's wishes, Isistva—the control over mind and body of all beings, Vaisitva—the control over natural elements, and Kamavasayita—the fulfilment of one's desires'.[8]

According to the Kaula Tantra tradition, these Ashta Matrikas, in turn, manifest as eight divine shaktis, resulting in the Chausath Yoginis being worshipped as part of the pantheon of Hinduism, and also in Buddhism and Jainism. Along with the iconographic portrayal of the Chausath Yoginis comes the portrayal of the wandering Bhairavas, who are also portrayed in Buddhist and Jain iconographic delineation.

[...] there is little doubt that the cult was originally esoteric. Even after it was brought within the fold of tantric Hinduism, it remained a secret cult, and was never a popular religious phenomenon.[9]

Yellamma

रेणुका सूनुयोगी च भक्तानामभयङ्करी।
भोगलक्ष्मीर्योगलक्ष्मीर्दिव्यलक्ष्मीश्च सर्वदा।।
कालरात्रि महारात्रि मद्यमांसशिवप्रिये।
भक्तानां श्रीपदे देवि लोकत्रयविमोहिनि।।

*Renuka, the one who ensures her devotees are fearless;
the goddess of pleasure, yoga and divine prosperity;
the goddess of night, who's fond of meat and wine;
the goddess who bewitches all three worlds.*

—*Renuka Stotram*, Verses 16–17

The cult of Yellamma is rooted in mythology. She is presented as Renuka, who is an obedient wife of the Brahmana sage Jamadagni. Once, Renuka got aroused by the love play of Malaprabha and joined him in the river. This enraged Jamadagni, who ordered his five sons to kill her. The youngest son, Parashurama, agreed and also killed all four of his brothers for disobeying their father. But once he beheaded Renuka, he realised he had made a mistake, as it was Devi Yellamma in disguise. He repented by worshipping Yellamma's head, and all his brothers came back to life but as eunuchs.

In an alternate version of the tale, when Renuka got distracted by the nymphs in the river Malaprabha, she returned home very late, which sparked suspicion in Rishi Jamadagni about her fidelity, leading him to order his sons to punish her. When four of his sons refused, the sage cursed them to become eunuchs, while his fifth son, Parashurama, beheaded Renuka. Surprisingly, Renuka's severed head multiplied and travelled to various regions, inspiring devotion from her eunuch sons and others. Scholars suggest that myths often justify rituals and reflect social customs and values. Devotees of Yellamma used to re-enact events from Renuka's life during the full moon, including the ritual during Nagna Puja where women would strip naked on the full-moon day of Magha and walk towards the local Yellamma temple to be initiated as a *devadasi* ('religious prostitute'). However, this ritual was banned in the mid-1980s for propriety's sake.[1]

Yellamma is also revered as the matron deity by sex workers. She further extends her blessings to a group of devotees known as Jogathis or transgender persons who are 'married' to the goddess, akin to the Aravanis of Tamil Nadu. These eunuch servants of Yellamma adopt the identity of the 'third sex' by tightly binding their genitals and living their lives accordingly. They encompass a diverse group, including effeminate homosexual men and cross-dressing transgender individuals, transcending the typical norms associated with eunuch cultures worldwide.

For centuries, eunuch priests have been devoted to various goddesses, including Yellamma. The marginalised and uneducated worshippers of Yellamma, residing on the fringes of society, commit themselves, along with their families, to serving the goddess and partaking in prostitution. Curiously, if a young girl's hair becomes tangled, it is interpreted as a sign from Yellamma, prompting her ritual dedication to the goddess' service.

The initiation of *jogti*s (female) and *jogta*s (male) volunteers into Yellamma's service involves an elaborate ceremony, including bathing in three holy ponds and receiving guidance from the head priest and community elders. They are instructed to empathise with the plight of the poor and the marginalised and contribute to societal welfare. Twice a year, on full-moon days, they perform nude rituals to honour Yellamma's immense power and renew their allegiance to her shrine, often adorning themselves minimally or with neem leaves. However, these practices have attracted media scrutiny, leading to restrictions on this traditional form of worship.

By the 10th century, the institution of devadasi, or temple women, had become deeply rooted in the history of the Deccan. This tradition, linked to divine kingship, underwent a transformation in the 20th century, notably seen in Bharatanatyam, a ritual dance originally performed by temple dancers who served as consorts to the presiding deity. These devadasis, skilled in various arts, were granted a unique status, where their expressions of sexuality were elevated to artistic and spiritual levels, freeing them from conventional marital obligations.

However, whether the Devadasi tradition has origins in the Yellamma cult remains unclear. Devadasis were typically women dedicated to male deities in temples, trained in music and dance, and known for their courtesanship. In the Vijayanagara Empire (1350–1565), the cult of Goddess Pampa, absorbed into the Devaraja cult through her marriage to Virupaksha, exemplifies this tradition. Despite the collapse of the empire, the influence of Goddess Pampa persisted, with Virupaksha remaining the tutelary deity of the Vijayanagara kings. Similarly, in South India, the cult of Yellamma, known by various names, such as Jogamma and Holiyyamma, endured, highlighting her significance in the region's religious landscape.

Temples dedicated to Yellamma are found in various regions, including Saundatti in Belgaum, Chandragutti in

Shimoga, and Huligi in Bellary, Karnataka. Additionally, her devotees can be found in Maharashtra, Andhra Pradesh and Tamil Nadu. Adorned with turmeric, vermilion and cowry shell ornaments, Yellamma's followers, both male and female, display diverse attire preferences, with some opting for elaborate accessories, and others choosing simplicity. Some male devotees aim to emulate the eunuch sons of Renuka, known as Jogappas; they are distinct from the traditional hijra eunuchs. Despite challenges in concealing their masculinity, Jogappas often adopt feminine mannerisms to attract admirers, enduring societal ridicule with resilience. Among Yellamma's devotees are also hijras who, typically moving in groups, engage in musical performances and dance to earn alms. Revered for their auspicious presence, hijras are often invited to bless weddings and childbirth ceremonies, receiving monetary rewards in return.

Jogathis, the devotees of Devi Yellamma, often carry her bust made of brass in a metal vessel or bamboo basket atop their heads, miraculously stable without any visible support, which is believed to be a blessing from the deity. These vessels are elaborately adorned with flowers, sometimes using different coloured cloths. Witnessing Jogathis dance with these icons balanced on their heads is a mesmerising sight, accompanied by rhythmic drum beats. Sadly, superstition and economic hardship drive some parents in northern Karnataka to dedicate their young daughters, aged between 8 and 10 years, to Yellamma, perpetuating a controversial tradition influenced by societal challenges and religious beliefs.

The Venkatasani and Jogini traditions, where girls are dedicated or 'married' to Devi Yellamma, persist in certain regions of Andhra Pradesh, notably among the Dommara tribe, who ritually dedicate their eldest daughters. This practice, cloaked in religious sanctity, has unfortunately led to the exploitation of these girls, who often end up in prostitution to sustain their families' livelihoods. The exploitation continues in other forms too, as the Dommaras receive infant girls of other castes to dedicate them as Venkatasanis, especially from Madigas and Malas.

In Tamil Nadu, the worship of Mariamman, the goddess of fertility, holds significant importance, sought after for blessings of fertility, well-being and abundance, especially in agricultural communities where rain is vital for crops. Some adherents associate her with Devi Renuka, the mother of Parashurama, believed to bring rain to refresh the earth. In certain sects of Tamil Nadu and Andhra Pradesh, devotees engage in rituals to invoke rain, with women drumming and men self-flagellating in public spaces, a practice believed to stir the goddess' intervention. Offerings, particularly *pongal* (a dish of rice cooked in boiling milk), are presented at temple precincts, while in the summer months, devotees travel long distances to fetch water infused with turmeric and neem leaves to ward off illnesses.

Many rural shrines feature modest depictions of Mariamman, often just a plain granite stone adorned with lemon garlands, while cobras dwelling in anthills nearby are appeased with offerings of milk and eggs. Rituals primarily focus on averting diseases such as smallpox and chickenpox, with Mariamman regarded as a manifestation of Kali, known as Mahamayi or Shitala Gauri, believed to have emerged from the poison ingested by Shiva. Mariamman temples are typically administered by non-Brahmana priests, although the Arulmigu Mariamman Temple, situated along the Kaveri river in Samayapuram, Tamil Nadu, is a notable exception.

Salabhanjika

शृणु कल्याणि! मद्-वाक्यं, कवचं देव-दुर्लभं।
यक्षिणी-नायिकानां तु, संक्षेपात् सिद्धि-दायकं॥
ज्ञान-मात्रेण देवशि! सिद्धिमाप्नोति निश्चितं।

Listen, O Kalyani! My words, the divine and rare armour.
Of the Yakshini and the leader; it grants success in brief.
By mere knowledge, O Divine One! One surely attains success.

—*Yakshini Kavach*

There are frequent representations of Salabhanjika in ancient Indian art and literature, highlighting its significance as a woman-and-tree motif. It is a beautiful display of the aesthetic sense in the ornamentation of temple facades under a tree, generally with one arm touching the branches of the tree.

Originally representing a recreational activity for women called *udyana krida* (playing in the garden), the concept of Salabhanjika later transformed into a special festival, influenced by the legend of Buddha's birth in a sal forest. This festival celebrates the graceful motif of a woman, known as Salabhanjika, depicted bending the branch of a sal tree while standing beneath it with crossed legs, often accompanied by elegant hand gestures. The Salabhanjika motif stands out among various popular depictions of beautiful women in early Indian art, appearing on pillars and gateways.

A legend states that Queen Mahamaya gave birth to Gautam Buddha in the lush grove of Lumbini. The Buddhist scripture *Lalitavistara Sutra* recounts the playful activities of Queen Mahamaya in the sal grove and the miraculous birth of Siddhartha. The sal tree, under which Buddha was born, holds profound sacred symbolism and is revered by Buddhists. Scenes depicting sal-krida and Buddha's nativity have been captured in Indian art, notably on stone slabs.

For instance, at Nagarjunakonda, Mahamaya is depicted standing cross-legged under a sal tree, holding its branch with her right hand, while a lady stands beside her. Four Brahmanas, holding golden cloth marked with seven footprints, approach the lady to proclaim Buddha's birth. This illustration, reflecting Hinayana art, signifies Buddha's presence through the footprints, with a lady worshipping them and a female attendant standing behind Mahamaya. Various symbols like the cauri, umbrella, *triratna* and lotus further represent Buddha's physical presence in the scene.

During the Maurya–Shunga and Satavahana periods, the form of Salabhanjika became particularly favoured by artists as a motif. Artworks from various regions, such as Sanchi, Bharhut, Kaushambi, Mehrauli and Amaravati, dating back to the Shunga–Satavahana period between the 2nd century BCE and the 1st century CE demonstrate its popularity.

The Salabhanjika motif gained widespread popularity during the Kushan period, characterised by women with rounded breasts, wearing diaphanous clothing or almost nothing with waistbands. These figures were often heavily adorned with jewellery and depicted standing on various mounts such as dwarfs, crocodiles, elephants, swans or lotuses. Carved onto the brackets of *torana*s (gateways) and the pillars of railings, they served both decorative and symbolic purposes, representing worldly allure and contrasting with the symbolism of domed stupas, which stood for the transient nature of life and inevitability of death. These depictions symbolise the worldly attractions that Buddha renounced on his path to enlightenment. The types of Salabhanjika depicted in nativity in the Hinayana phase were not carried forward in the Mahayana phase.

During the Gupta period, the prevalence of the Salabhanjika motif diminished, with Mahayana art opting not to include representations of Buddha's nativity scene. The Gupta period became important as it marked the departure of Salabhanjika motifs from earlier traditions of emphasising physical beauty. Instead, Hindu art during this period replaced it with anthropomorphic depictions of river goddesses, such as Ganga and Yamuna on their mounts of crocodiles and tortoises, engraved on temple lintels. In the post-Gupta period, the Salabhanjika motif underwent further transformation.

According to J. Ph. Vogel, the term 'Salabhanjika' in various Indian traditions may have a connection to the sal tree. In the Buddhist tradition, the sal tree holds importance due to its association with the birth of Buddha, while Hindu and Jain traditions utilise the wood of the same tree for sculpting statues and artistic objects. The term Salabhanjika does not appear in Vedic or Pali literature, nor in major Indian epics. Instead, it emerges in classical Indian literature of the early 1st millennium CE, such as Ashvaghosha's *Buddhacharita* (circa 100 CE).[1]

The term *salastri*, denoting a woman shaped out of the sal tree, appears in the Hindu text *Natyashastra*, specifically from verses 2.83 to 2.84. This indicates that the terminology was influenced by traditional practices and the prevalent art of carving wooden statues during that period. Despite a decline in its artistic popularity, the motif of the Salabhanjika continued to hold significance in Indian literature throughout the early and late medieval periods, from the 8th to 12th centuries CE. Prominent literary figures such as Bana, Rajashekhara, Govardhanacharya and Shriharsha made references to the term Salabhanjika in their works, underscoring its importance in both literary and sculptural contexts. This indicates that the concept of the Salabhanjika remained deeply ingrained in Indian culture, transcending its depiction in art to become a prominent theme in literature during this period. The motif no longer retained its original form and meaning, instead symbolising the charming body of heroines or *nayika*s.

During the medieval period (13 CE–18 CE), the term Salabhanjikas either denoted life-size or miniature female figures crafted from stone, marble or bronze, or symbolised the 'nayika', a charming beauty, prevalent in Sanskrit dramas and Kavya literature. However, during this era, there was a notable decline in the representation of the earlier forms of the Salabhanjika.

A stone fragment unearthed from the Ghositarama monastery's site and now exhibited in the Allahabad University Museum features a rare panel divided into two horizontal sections, providing insights into the surroundings of Buddha's miraculous birth. While the upper part of the panel is significantly damaged, it still depicts Indra receiving the bodhisattva emerging from the womb on a piece of cloth. Remarkably, Buddha is represented not in human form but through sacred symbols, which are characteristic of early Indian art, and showcases the exceptional craftsmanship of the Kaushambi school of sculpture.

Prajnaparamita

ॐ पिकु पिकु प्रज्ञवर्धनी ज्वाला ज्वाला
मेधवर्धनी धीरि धीरि बुद्धिवर्धनी स्वाहा।

O flame of wisdom, may you enhance intelligence and knowledge.
With steadiness and clarity, may you nourish our intellect.

—Sadhanamala

*P*rajnaparamita is the mother of the Bodhisattvas. In Mahayana literature, the pinnacle of enlightened wisdom is personified as a goddess. While all Buddhist goddesses represent *prajna* (wisdom), Prajnaparamita embodies perfection, being the ultimate manifestation of wisdom. The *Prajnaparamita Sutras*, attributed to the 4th-century scholar Asanga and named after Devi Prajnaparamita, are pivotal philosophical texts within Buddhism. These sutras are not only reflections of wisdom but are also revered as the very embodiment of Prajnaparamita herself.

> She is unstained, the entire world cannot stain her.
> [...] she leads away from the blinding darkness [...]
> She cannot be crushed. She protects the unprotected
> [...] She is the antidote to birth-and-death.[1]

In Indian Mahayana Buddhism, the worship of the *Prajnaparamita Sutras*, often represented in the form of books, held significant importance, a concept indicated within the sutras themselves. For instance, the *Ashtasahasrika Prajnaparamita Sutra* instructs followers to worship the sutra on an altar adorned with flowers, lamps, incense and other offerings. Moreover, the *Prajnaparamita Sutras* assert their own significance as the highest object of study and worship, surpassing even the reverence for stupas, Buddha relics and other sacred objects. This elevation is attributed to Prajnaparamita's transcendent knowledge, which perceives all phenomena as illusory and unborn.

The *Prajnaparamita Sutras* not only present the physical book form as sacred but also equate it to Buddha's physical form *(rupakaya)* and his teachings *(dharmakaya)*. This viewpoint elevates the importance of the physical scriptures to a level akin to the veneration of relics and the teachings themselves.[2]

A transformation in this reverence occurred when both the *Prajnaparamita Sutras* and the concept of Prajnaparamita as transcendent wisdom became personified as a specific deity, Devi Prajnaparamita. This evolution into a bodhisattva-goddess figure likely took place around the 7th or 8th century CE. Devi Prajnaparamita serves as an embodiment of wisdom and compassion, guiding practitioners on the path to enlightenment. This development marks a significant shift in the worship and understanding of Prajnaparamita, emphasising her role as a divine figure worthy of devotion and reverence.

Iconographically, the goddess is typically depicted with a radiant golden complexion and either two or four arms. She is wearing exquisite garments, adorned with gems, and often crowned with a jewelled tiara, symbolising her embodiment of divine enlightened knowledge. Thangkas, traditional Buddhist paintings on cloth or silk, portray her with a deep orange hue, often holding a palm leaf manuscript. Additionally, she typically carries a vajra, a double-headed thunderbolt, in one of her rear hands, while her front hands make the two-handed gesture of teaching.

Prajnaparamita's ascension within the Buddhist pantheon, transitioning from a peripheral figure to the central focus of reverence, marks a significant evolution. This transformation occurs as wisdom, embodied in the female form of Prajnaparamita, becomes deified. According to Shaw, the Prajnaparamita philosophy hinges on the notion that the one who gives birth surpasses the one who is born.[3] The *Ashtasahasrika Prajnaparamita Sutra* contains verses that personify the concept of 'the perfection of wisdom', or prajna, as a maternal figure and teacher. Described as the perfect wisdom that transcends birth and dissolution, she is revered as the Great Mother, the eternal source of enlightenment. Prajnaparamita is portrayed as the one who gives 'birthless birth' to all Buddhas, symbolising the origin of enlightenment itself. She is hailed as the 'mother' of all beings who attain enlightenment, as it is her wisdom that leads to liberation.

The *Ashtasahasrika Prajnaparamita Sutra* further asserts that Buddhas owe their very existence to her, emphasising the profound role of Prajnaparamita in the enlightenment of all beings. The notion of the perfection of wisdom personified as a nurturing mother figure is also echoed in the *Dà zhìdù lùn*, or *The Treatise on the Great Prajnaparamita*, as translated by Kumarajiva.

In Tantric Buddhism, also known as Vajrayana, the concept of Prajnaparamita, along with the feminine deity Devi Prajnaparamita, acquired deeper esoteric meanings. According to James B. Apple, Prajnaparamita came to symbolise the prototype and essence of all female figures involved in tantric practices. She is often depicted with symbolic representations such as the ritual bell (*ghanta*) and the lotus (padma), and is associated with yoginis or female practitioners of yoga.[4]

Tantric contemplative rituals known as sadhanas, or 'means of achievement', involve practitioners who visualise the deity while reciting mantras. Prajnaparamita is central to these practices, serving as a focal point for meditative concentration and spiritual attainment. Additionally, Tantric Buddhism views Prajnaparamita as inherently present in all women, promoting an attitude of reverence and respect towards the feminine form. This inclusive attitude towards women as embodiments of Prajnaparamita is advocated even by Mahasiddha Laksminkara in her *Adhvayasiddhi*, highlighting the profound reverence for and recognition of the feminine principle within Tantric Buddhism.

Prajnaparamita emerges as a radiant embodiment of pure spirit and wisdom, marking a significant departure from the earthly origins of her predecessors in the Buddhist tradition, such as tree spirits or yakshinis. This transformation from deities associated with nature and fertility to the mother with transcendent wisdom signifies a profound evolution within Mahayana Buddhism. It reflects a notable shift towards the reverence for wisdom and enlightenment as central principles of the tradition.

Devi Prajñaparamita, much like the philosophical concept she embodies, represents a revolutionary shift in Buddhist thought. While Prajnaparamita is said to transcend conventional categories, her gender plays a central role in her character. There are profound metaphorical resonances between motherhood and the matrix of wisdom and reality that she symbolises. In assigning gender to a generative principle, the feminine gender is a logical choice, as the womb is universally recognised as the most tangible source of generation in human experience.

Furthermore, there is a symbolic significance in the femaleness of Prajnaparamita. Just as male bodies biologically derive from female ones, it follows in the religious sphere that male Buddhas would have a female source. Therefore, the femaleness of Prajnaparamita carries the weight of both logical reasoning and observable natural phenomena, reinforcing her status as the nurturing source of wisdom and enlightenment in Mahayana Buddhism.

At times, Hindu female deities are associated with Prajnaparamita through shared mantras, such as Saraswati and Vasudhara. For example, the *Vasudharadharani* contains mantras that invoke Prajnaparamita, illustrating the interconnectedness of these divine figures. In certain depictions, the Buddhist Saraswati is holding the *Prajnaparamita Sutra*, further highlighting their association.

Scholars have noted similarities between Prajnaparamita and other Buddhist deities like Cunda (or Cundi) and Tara. According to Jacob Kinnard, Devi Prajnaparamita is part of a group of 'prajna deities', associated with wisdom, alongside figures like Manjushri and Cunda. These deities are often depicted holding sutras and making the *dharmachakrapravartana mudra*, symbolising the turning of the wheel of dharma. Cunda, known as the 'mother of the seventy million Buddhas', shares the epithet 'mother of Buddhas' with Devi Prajnaparamita.[5] Their artistic representations often overlap, leading scholars to suggest intentional ambiguity. Similarly, Tara is considered an emanation of Prajnaparamita in Tibetan Buddhism. Referred to as the 'mother of all Tathagatas', Tara embodies the nurturing essence of enlightenment, as evidenced in texts such as the *Tantra Which is the Source for All the Functions of Tara, Mother of All the Tathagatas*.[6]

Similarly, Manjushri is often portrayed with symbols reminiscent of Prajnaparamita, including a book, lotuses adorned with books, and a sword symbolising the keenness of wisdom. Some depictions even pair Prajnaparamita and Manjushri together, as seen in the mandala of the Jnanapada Guhyasamaja Tantra tradition, highlighting their complementary roles in the pursuit of enlightenment.[7]

Isakki Amman

रौद्रायै नमो नित्यायै गौर्यै धात्र्यै नमो नमः।
ज्योत्स्नायै चेन्दुरूपिण्यै सुखायै सततं नमः॥

*I offer my salutations to you,
who is terrible, eternal, beautiful and motherly,
who is not only radiant but joy herself.*

—*Durga Saptashati*, Chapter 5, Verse 10

Along many wayside shrines and within some temple precincts in the state of Tamil Nadu are a number of statues, both seated and standing, known as *ammans*. Ammans are normally subsidiaries of a male shrine and serve as another name for a Tamil goddess, who could be crossing the boundaries of folk, tribal and mainstream Devi. Generally, she would be a cultic goddess. There are a number of ammans in Tamil Nadu—from Pechi to Pathirakali to Mariamman.

Pathirakali Amman is akin to Kali, also known as the elder Durga. She is a village deity who is believed to protect the villagers from evil. Mariamman, on the other hand, is the goddess of rain, who is worshipped by the Dalit community of Tamil Nadu. Puttaarthi Amman is another goddess who is worshipped in Tamil Nadu; she is said to protect children from illnesses. But here, I will concentrate on Isakki Amman.

The goddess embodies a fusion of mythology and ritual, harnessing the inherent energy present in all aspects of nature. This energy can be potentially threatening due to its overwhelming nature. It is believed to be capable of causing great harm if left untamed. Consequently, natural forces are often viewed as malevolent entities personified as goddesses that must be appeased through worship. Isakki Amman is a prominent folk goddess in southern Tamil Nadu. Isakki's manifestation is depicted through intricate metaphysical imagery, reflecting the complexity of her nature. She is characterised by a prevalent fear of dense jungles and the unpredictable aspects of nature. The name 'Isakki' is derived from 'yakshi', which is commonly associated with Buddhist culture. According to tradition, yakshis are believed to dwell in forests.

It is believed that 'yakshas' are unique, for they belong in the nominal space between humans and superhumans. While some yakshas are considered malevolent and require appeasement, others are associated with prosperity and abundance. Another set of supernatural beings are 'bhutas'. The cult of *yaksha-bhuta*s is believed to transform into yakshas after death.

In pre-modern belief systems, invoking the spirits of the deceased was a means of protection against evil forces. Yakshas and yakshis represent concepts like abundance and prosperity. Yakshis, in particular, were revered as fertility spirits with the ability to ward off malevolence through miraculous means. The cult of Isakki Amman serves as a continuation of ancient animistic beliefs and popular traditions. This convergence of beliefs has resulted in the development of a unique theological framework, where the Buddhist or Jain influences on the Isakki cult are absent.

Isakki Amman personifies the raw and uncontrollable forces of nature. Her fierceness represents the untamed aspects of the natural world. Through specific ritual worship, devotees seek her blessings and protection, aiming to appease her. A common ritual practice involves offering votive terracotta images of Isakki, known as Vuruvam Kodutthal. These terracotta figures, resembling yakshis and nagas, reflect ancient religious beliefs, transcending geographical boundaries. Typically worshipped by communities belonging to Scheduled and Backward Classes, Isakki Amman's terracotta image is often adorned with vibrant yellow hues and draped in colourful attires such as a red silk cloth and green blouse, which contrasts with her dark complexion. However, it is her wild laughter and the portrayal of a distorted human figure trapped within her jaws, ensnared by her long incisors, which identify her.

Despite her depiction as a fierce devourer, Isakki Amman is also revered as a maternal figure by her devotees and sculptors and painters alike. To her devotees, she embodies both the destructive force and a maternal figure, signifying a complex transformation in mythological perception and iconography. Often depicted holding a child and wielding a sacred weapon called *sulam*, she is also known by alternate names like Neeli and Iyakki. Moreover, major temple entrances are frequently guarded by a demi-goddess named Duvarashakthi. While Isakki Amman is initially viewed as a benevolent mother, her underlying destructive nature is very much part of her persona.

As a formidable deity in mythology, Isakki Amman is revered and worshipped in numerous small temples scattered on the outskirts of villages, with larger shrines being relatively uncommon. These temples have a simple structure, comprising a single thatched room with roofs made of coconut or palm leaves. The deity is often represented by a stone or pedestal adorned with a colourful cloth, such as red, green or yellow.

There is a dedicated annual festival, known as Kodai, Pongal or Thiruvizha, which takes place on the last or second Tuesday of the Tamil month of Aadi (July–August) and includes various important rituals such as divinations, fire-walking and the spirit possession dance, Samiattam. During the festival, the story of Isakki unfolds through performances. Offerings made to the goddess during worship include silk cloth, flower garlands, sandal paste, milk, oil, camphor and incense sticks.

The primary devotees of the formidable goddess Isakki belong to the non-Brahmin communities. In the multi-caste village temples dedicated to Isakki Amman, the local priests are typically men hailing from the Tamil-speaking Kambar community residing in the southern regions of Tamil Nadu. Although they consume non-vegetarian food, they refrain from beef and pork. Further, they have traditionally been involved in musical performances at various other temples. Some of these priests adorn themselves with tufts of hair, ear studs and sacred threads, and they apply sacred ash, sandalwood paste and vermilion on their foreheads and chests as part of their religious observances.

Many Isakki temples are under the control of the Dalit community, where a member from their community serves as the priest. In some instances, women too serve as priestesses of Isakki. Typically, the decision to construct an Isakki temple arises from the counsel of a priest when worshippers voice their concerns during Kodai ceremonies at popular temples, such as those in the villages of Muppandal or Palavoor.

Establishing Isakki shrines may be prompted by various other factors as well. The Goddess herself may request the construction of a temple through divine communication, or a shrine may be erected to appease her if her anger is aroused by the cutting of trees. If a pregnant woman dies, a stone pillar may be installed for Isakki worship. In some regions, Isakki worship is becoming more integrated into mainstream Hinduism. Temples dedicated to Isakki Amman, such as the one in Thandiarkulam village in Tirunelveli, Tamil Nadu, can be valued at millions. While certain traditional rituals in Isakki temples are declining, new practices are being incorporated, such as Kavadi Edutthal and Alagu Kuthuthal, originally associated with the worship of Lord Murugan but now also observed during Kodai at Aalamootamman Isakki Temple.

The temples are constructed using a tradition known as Pidimun Edutthal, wherein devotees gather sand from revered temples. This process involves a devotee collecting sand from beneath the statue or pedestal, which is then placed in a clay pot and handed to the priest for blessings. Afterwards, the devotee takes the sand back to their village and deposits it in a specially prepared foundation pit for the pedestal. The process also involves burying offerings such as eggs and live fowl under the Isakki statue.

Karakattam is an ancient folk dance unique to Tamil Nadu. During the performance, young women dance to various rhythms of the naiyandi melam (a type of drum) while balancing a painted pot on their heads. They execute intricate foot movements on their toes in synchrony with the beats. This dance form is often showcased during Isakki temple festivals. Isakki Amman embodies the fierce aspect of the goddess, representing untamed energy and demonic power. In various myths, legends and rituals, Isakki is profoundly venerated as the dynamic force underlying all aspects of existence. Worship practices for Isakki take diverse forms but are unified in their goal of appeasing and seeking blessings from the divine, which manifest as life force, offering health, protection, agricultural prosperity, marital bliss and fertility.

Bharat Mata

गायन्ति देवा: किल गीतकानि
धन्यास्तु ये भारतभूमिभागे।
स्वर्गाऽपवर्गाऽस्पद हेतुभूते
भवन्ति भूय: पुरुषा: सुरत्वात्।।

*The Gods themselves sing that
people born in the land of India,
which is the path to heaven and salvation,
are more blessed than even Gods.*

—*Vishnu Purana*, Bharat Prashasti,
Book 11, Chapter 3, Verse 24

The development of the concept of Bharat Mata or Mother India has had a singular trajectory over the years. Hinduism has undergone significant evolution over centuries, shaped by societal, political, economic and psychological factors. From this dynamic environment, numerous deities have emerged, often serving the specific needs or aspirations of the people. One such manifestation is Bharat Mata, representing the Indian subcontinent as a divine entity.

The earliest association of the Goddess with India's sacred geography dates back to the *Rig Veda*, where the rivers Bharati, Ila and Saraswati were revered as maternal figures because of their distinct qualities of nurturing, healing and, in certain instances, the gift of speech. In the *Rig Veda*, the supplicant addresses the goddesses as 'water goddesses', acknowledging their healing properties, the purifying nature of water and its capability to cleanse sins and evils. Referring to them as the 'seven mother streams', the vivid description continues with their inexhaustible nourishment, likening them to sources of pleasure and abundance.

आ यत्साकं यशसो वावशाना: सरस्वती सप्तथी सिन्धुमाता।
या: सुष्वयन्त सुदुघा: सुधारा अभि स्वेन पयसा पीप्याना:॥

May the seventh, Saraswati, who is the mother of the Sindhu and other rivers that flow abundantly, fertilize the soil, bestow food, and nourish people by its waters.

—*The Rig Veda,* Book 7, Chapter 36, Verse 6

Thus, the connection between the Goddess and India's sacred waters and land is established. By the Gupta period, the iconography of Devi Ganga and Yamuna, each depicted holding the holy waters in a pot, also became established. In the 5th century, in *Devi Mahatmya* within the *Markandeya Purana,* Devi embodies the entire creative principle with dynamic attributes. Particularly noteworthy is her connection with the symbolic, poetic and physical aspects of the land. Despite being associated with the earth, Devi is not confined to it. Devi's manifestations are closely linked to her immanence and are often associated with battles and blood sacrifice. Myths such as those of Madhu–Kaitabha, Mahishasura and Shumbha–Nishumbha illustrate her role as Devi Durlabha, who is accessible to her devotees when male agency fails.

By the 12th century, the *Devi Bhagavata Purana* solidified Devi's powers into a comprehensive portrayal of a personified Bharata. This Purana is pivotal as it assigns Devi both conceptual and physical presence; when Himavan asks Devi about her favourite places, she specifically mentions

Devi's *sthal*s (sites) located across Bharat. This highlights the dual identification of the Goddess' body with the sacred land.

Firstly, in the Sati myth, as parts of her body fell to the ground, they created Shakti Peethas, sanctifying the land and embodying the Divine Feminine. Secondly, the notion of active sacrifice depicted in the Sati myth is crucial in shaping the ethos of Bharat Mata. Additionally, Devi reveals her cosmic form, described with natural phenomena symbolising various parts of her body. This evolution from the *Rig Veda's* association of the holy earth with river goddesses to the Puranic depiction of an all-encompassing feminine principle illustrates a significant transformation. Specific sites associated with Devi's power became holy, such as the transition of mythical rivers like Ila and Bharati to the revered Ganga and Yamuna. The *Brahmavaivarta Purana* further emphasised this sanctity, with Vishnu proclaiming Ganga's purifying role in cleansing the sins of the people of Bharata.

∽

The concept of Bharat Mata again gained prominence during the late 19th and early 20th centuries, coinciding with the rise of the nationalist movement in India. As the movement sought symbols of unity and identity, the idea of the Earth Goddess was transformed into that of Bharat Mata.

The origins of the popular national imagery of Mother India can be traced back to Raja Ravi Varma's oil painting of Bharat Mata, where she is depicted as a young goddess adorned in regal attire, holding symbols representing war, peace and state power. This hybrid iconography, blending Indian and European symbols, reflects a notion of self-rule characterised by power-sharing rather than complete independence.

The artist's nationalist prints, widely distributed during this era, often portrayed Draupadi as a representation of India. It was believed that tales of great kings and fierce heroines would evoke a sense of Hindu identity and uphold traditional societal values threatened by Western influences. The introduction of new printing technologies enabled the mass production and distribution of Varma's mythological artworks, which replaced local deities with pan-Indian iconography, contributing to the formation of a unified national consciousness.

Bankim Chandra Chatterjee, an Indian novelist and poet, first visualised Bharat Mata in his 1880 book *Anandamath*, portraying her as the embodiment of the Indian land. This concept was further popularised by Indian artist Abanindranath Tagore through his 1905 painting titled *Bharat Mata*. In Tagore's depiction, Bharat Mata appeared as a four-armed goddess adorned in saffron attire, with a radiant halo surrounding her head, symbolising her divine stature. Early representations also included images of India's map overlaid with the form of a goddess, reminiscent of Durga or Lakshmi.

Tagore's iconic watercolour painting represented a different strand of nationalist thought rooted in Orientalist ideals of spirituality and austerity. Depicted as a married woman dressed as a Vaishnava ascetic in saffron robes, she holds symbols representing various sections of Indian society. This Hinduisation of national imagery faced resistance, especially from Muslim groups. Varma's portrayal of Bharat Mata on calendar pictures further served to glorify the Hindu ruling classes and advance their interests in the anti-colonial movement.

Dehejia notes that during the freedom struggle, Tagore's portrayal of Bharat Mata wasn't religious but rather a symbol of artistic expression.[1] It served as a visual representation of India, pivotal in nurturing nationalist sentiments and fostering unity among its people. Rajeswari Sunder Rajan further emphasises how the concept of Mother India was used to empower women and serve as a unifying emblem for national identity.[2] Her worship materialised with the inauguration of the Bharat Mata temple in Varanasi by Mahatma Gandhi in 1936, amidst escalating communal tensions.[3]

Gandhi saw the temple as a means to promoting unity, featuring a marble relief map of India depicting its geographical features. Subsequent temples, like the one built in Haridwar in 1983, continued this legacy, with a dedicated floor to Bharat Mata showcasing a detailed map of India with the Goddess at its centre. Diana L. Eck further explained how this map-goddess emblem became symbolic of Indian identity, embraced within nationalist and later Hindu nationalist narratives.[4] The imagery of Bharat Mata evolved over time, reflecting changing socio-political contexts. For example, while pre-Independence associations with swadeshi cloth symbolised nationalism, contemporary constructions—such as the statue of Bharat Mata, the presiding deity of the Sahara Group, on a chariot driven by four fierce-looking lions adorning its headquarters in Lucknow—depict Bharat Mata in new contexts.

During the freedom struggle, Bharat Mata's image evolved according to the political climate. In posters from the 1920s and 1930s, she emerged from the map of India as a self-generative form, demanding sacrifices from her subjects. Freedom fighters like Bhagat Singh pledged their lives to her, which were accompanied by depictions of them offering their severed heads or revealing her image within their chests. Mother India, depicted with multiple arms and wielding nationalist symbols, symbolises the struggle for independence. However, Gandhi's use of passive and spiritual values for political resistance and Tagore's ascetic ideals of Bharat Mata did not gain popularity in popular imagery.

Bharat Mata is a continuing leitmotif. Contemporary artists continue to engage with the iconic imagery of Bharat Mata in their work. While M.F. Husain's *Bharat Mata* drew a lot of outrage and made things difficult for him, in contrast, artists like Tyeb Mehta and Atul Dodiya offered critical analyses through their fragmented and emotive imagery. Mehta's portrayal of Kali and Mahishasuramardini alongside a falling figure challenges earlier heroic depictions, while Dodiya's 'Tearscape' series presents grotesque figures on a map of India, reflecting themes of loss and dispossession.

These contemporary interpretations mark a departure from earlier artists like those of the Bengal School or Husain, who celebrated the Divine Feminine's authority and beauty. Artists like Manjit Bawa, Mrinalini Mukherjee, K.G. Subramanyan and Jogen Chowdhury offered fresh perspectives on the concept of Bharat Mata, challenging conventional norms and prompting reflection on whether their work represents an anomaly, subversion or reinforcement of existing beliefs.

These contemporary depictions of the Goddess as Bharat Mata continue to challenge traditional interpretations of Indian icons, questioning notions of beauty, symbolism and pedestalisation. They not only challenge the idealisation of the state but also question the enduring relevance of mythic beliefs, thereby challenging the foundation of indigenous art that merges myth with the envisioned nation.

Notes

Preface

1. Avalon, Arthur, *The Serpent Power: The Secrets of Tantric and Shaktic Yoga*, Dover Publications, Mineola, NY, 1974.
2. In Hinduism, bhog is the food offered to the gods during any puja. It is later served for free to all those who came for the puja. A most common form of bhog is khichdi, served with a semi-dry vegetable, sweet tomato chutney and *payesh* (rice pudding).
3. *The Wonder That Was India* by A. L. Basham, *Hindu Goddesses* by David Kinsley, *Shakti* by Nilima Chitgopekar, *Devi: The Great Goddess* by Vidya Dehejia, *Devi: The Goddesses of India* by John Stratton Hawley and Donna Marie Wulff, and others.
4. *Devi: The Goddesses of India*, John Stratton Hawley and Donna Marie Wulff (eds.), University of California Press, Berkeley and Los Angeles, CA, 1996.
5. The various weapons and attributes of the goddess amongst her accoutrements.

Mahadevi

1. Daljeet, 'Goddess Durga in Indian Miniatures', *Cult of the Goddess*, ArputhaRani Sengupta (ed.), D.K. Printworld, New Delhi, 2015, 287.
2. Ibid. 286
3. Gupta, Mahendranath, *The Gospel of Sri Ramakrishna*, Swami Nikhilananda (trans.), Ramakrishna Vivekananda Centre, New York, NY, 1942, 961.

Sati

1. Kinsley, David, *Tantric Visions of the Divine Feminine: The Ten Mahavidyas*, Motilal Banarsidass, New Delhi, 1998, 16.
2. Asnani, Rajesh, 'Rajasthan: Roop Kanwar Forced Sati Case in Final Stage', *The New Indian Express*, 9 September 2019, https://tinyurl.com/2sxvjek2. Accessed on 14 August 2024.

3. Thapar, Romila, 'History', *Sati: A Symposium on Widow Immolation and Its Social Context*, Seminar no. 342, 1988, 14–19.
4. Harlan, Lindsey, *Religion and Rajput Women: The Ethic of Protection in Contemporary Narratives*, Munshiram Manoharlal Publishers, 1994, 120–121.
5. Courtright, Paul B., *The Goddess and the Dreadful Practice*, Oxford University Press (forthcoming).
6. Kinsley, David, *Tantric Visions of the Divine Feminine: The Ten Mahavidyas*, Motilal Banarsidass, New Delhi, 1998, 37.

Parvati

1. Tripathi, G. C., 'Goddess of Orissa', *Cult of the Goddess*, ArputhaRani Sengupta (ed.), D.K. Printworld, New Delhi, 2015, 513.
2. *Pranatoshini-tantra*, Basumati Sahitya Mandir, Calcutta, 1928, 378, Benard (trans.), 35–36. This version is also present, with slight modifications, in Sri Swami Ji Maharaja Datiya, *Sri Chinnamasta Nityarchan*, Kalyan Mandir Prakashan, Prayag, 1978, 5.
3. Vedavyas, *Skanda Puranam*, Kashi Khand, 27: 182–184, Gurumandal Series No. XX, Calcutta, 1961, 4.

Durga Mahishamardini

1. Chattopadhyay, Pramodkumar, *Tantrabhilasir Sadhusanga*, Bishwabani Prakashani, Calcutta, 1983, 199–200.
2. 'Durga Saptashati: A Glorious Song to the Divine Mother', *The Art of Living*, https://tinyurl.com/5cmkr375. Accessed on 14 August 2024.

Navadurgas

1. Kurtz, Stanley N., *All the Mothers Are One: Hindu India and the Cultural Reshaping of Psychoanalysis*, Columbia University Press, New York, NY, 1992, 91–131.

Girija

1. Kempton, Sally, *Awakening Shakti: The Transformative Power of the Goddesses of Yoga*, Sounds True Inc, Boulder, CO, 2013.
2. Nandagopal, Choodamani, 'Divine Marriage of the Goddess', *Cult of the Goddess*, ArputhaRani Sengupta (ed.), D.K. Printworld, New Delhi, 2015, 396.
3. Ibid.

Gajalakshmi

1. Sengupta, ArputhaRani, 'Gaja-Lakṣmi: Coexisting Goddess in Buddhist Art and Culture', *Cult of the Goddess*, ArputhaRani Sengupta (ed.), D.K. Printworld, New Delhi, 2015, 309–357.
2. Menzies, Jackie, *Goddess: Divine Energy*, Art Gallery of New South Wales, Sydney, 2006, 41.
3. Coomaraswamy, Ananda, *Rajput Painting*, Oxford University Press, London, 1916, 45.

Kali

1. Kinsley, David, *Tantric Visions of the Divine Feminine: The Ten Mahavidyas*, Motilal Banarsidass, New Delhi, 1998, 75.
2. *Devi: The Goddesses of India*, John Stratton Hawley and Donna Marie Wulff (eds.), University of California Press, Berkeley and Los Angeles, CA, 1996, 11–12.
3. Agamavagisha, Krishnananda, *Tantrasara: Part I*, Basumati Sahitya Mandir, Calcutta, 1934, 374.
4. *Devi: The Goddesses of India*, John Stratton Hawley and Donna Marie Wulff (eds.), University of California Press, Berkeley and Los Angeles, CA, 1996, 25.
5. *She Rises Like the Sun: Invocations of the Goddess by Contemporary American Women Poets*, Janine Canan (ed.), The Crossing Press, Freedom, CA, 1989, 153.

Chamunda

1. *The Agni Purana: Part II*, N. Gangadharan (trans.), Motilal Banarsidass, New Delhi, 1954, 397–399.
2. Avalon, Arthur, *Hymn to Kali: Kalpuradi-Stotra*, Luzac & Co., London, 1922, 28.
3. Handiqui, Krishna K., *Yasastilaka and Indian Culture*, Jaina Samskriti Samrakshaka Sangha, Sholapur, 1968, 56.

Sharada

1. Ahmad, Junaid, and Abdul Samad, 'Sarda Temple and the Stone Temples of Kashmir in Perspective: A Review Note', *Pakistan Heritage*, 2015, Vol. 7, 112, https://tinyurl.com/4ssmtmte. Accessed on 14 August 2024.
2. Ibid. 113

3   Ibid. 116

Vagadevi

1   Kinsley, David, *Hindu Goddesses: Vision of the Divine Feminine in the Hindu Religious Tradition*, Motilal Banarsidass, New Delhi, 1998, 12.
2   Daljeet, 'Goddess Durga in Indian Miniatures', *Cult of the Goddess*, ArputhaRani Sengupta (ed.), D.K. Printworld, New Delhi, 2015, 287.
3   Kinsley, David, *Hindu Goddesses: Vision of the Divine Feminine in the Hindu Religious Tradition*, Motilal Banarsidass, New Delhi, 1998, 13.

Aranyani

1   Tripathi, Gaya C., 'Goddess of Orissa', *Cult of the Goddess*, ArputhaRani Sengupta (ed.), D.K. Printworld, New Delhi, 2015, 513.

Bhudevi

1   Nagar, Shanti Lal, *Varaha in Indian Art, Culture and Literature*, Aryan Books International, New Delhi, 1993, 38.
2   C. Sivaramamurti, *Sri Lakshmi in Indian Art and Thought*, Kanak Publishers, New Delhi, 1982, 81.

Momai

1   Westphal-Hellbusch, Sigrid, and Heinz Westphal, *Hinduistische Viehzüchter im nord-westlichen Indien: Die Rabari* (in German), Duncker & Humblot, Berlin, 1974, 162. It has been translated by the author.
2   Fischer, Eberhard, Temple Tents for Goddesses in Gujarat, India, Niyogi Books, New Delhi, 2014, 183.

Jyestha

1   *Roles and Rituals for Hindu Women*, Julia Leslie (ed.), Motilal Banarsidass, New Delhi, 1992, 114–115.
2   Ibid. 115

Kamadhenu

1   Kanwar, Purnima B., 'Bhudevi and the Gaia Hypothesis: Revival of a Cult', *Cult of the Goddess*, ArputhaRani Sengupta (ed.), D.K. Printworld, New Delhi, 2015, 522–538.
2   Ibid.

Kamakshi

1. Kakati, Banikanta, *The Mother Goddess Kamakhya*, Publication Board Assam, Guwahati, 1989, 16.
2. Dutta, Birendranath, 'The Cult of the Mother Goddess in North-East India', *Cult of the Goddess*, ArputhaRani Sengupta (ed.), D.K. Printworld, New Delhi, 2015, 495.
3. Kinsley, David, *Tantric Visions of the Divine Feminine: The Ten Mahavidyas*, Motilal Banarsidass, New Delhi, 1998, 17.

Lajja Gauri

1. Bolon, Carol R., *Forms of the Goddess Lajja Gauri in Indian Art*, College Art Association, Inc., New York, NY, and The Pennsylvania State University Press, University Park, PA, 1992, 4.
2. J. Kedareswari, 'Sammakka Saralamma Jathara: Medaram Goddess Cult in Andhra Pradesh', *Cult of the Goddess*, ArputhaRani Sengupta (ed.), D.K. Printworld, New Delhi, 2015, 415.
3. Bolon, Carol R., *Forms of the Goddess Lajja Gauri in Indian Art*, College Art Association, Inc., New York, NY, and The Pennsylvania State University Press, University Park, PA, 1992, 5.

Manasa

1. Chakrabarti, Asis K., 'Folk Goddesses of Bengal', *Cult of the Goddess*, ArputhaRani Sengupta (ed.), D.K. Printworld, New Delhi, 2015, 481.
2. Ibid. 453
3. Coomaraswamy, Ananda K., and Sister Nivedita, *Myths of the Hindus and Buddhists*, Dover Publications, Inc., New York, NY, 1967, 330.

Matangi

1. Kinsley, David, *Tantric Visions of the Divine Feminine: The Ten Mahavidyas*, Motilal Banarsidass, New Delhi, 1998, 213.
2. Ibid. 222

Mumba

1. Graham, Maria, *Journal of a Residence in India*, Asian Educational Services, New Delhi, 2000, 14.
2. Vicziany, Marika, and Jayant Bapat, 'Mumbadevi and the Other Mother Goddesses in Mumbai', *Modern Asian Studies*, Vol. 43, No. 2, 2009, 511–541.

3   K. Raghunathji, *The Hindu Temples of Bombay*, Fort Printing Press, Bombay, 1895.

Renuka

1   Kamat, K. L., 'Given to the Goddess: Cult of Yellamma', *Cult of the Goddess*, ArputhaRani Sengupta (ed.), D.K. Printworld, New Delhi, 2015, 404.
2   Devdasis were women who dedicated their lives to the worship and service of a deity or a temple.
3   Daniélou, Alain, *The Myths and Gods of India: The Classic Work on Hindu Polytheism*, Inner Traditions International, Rochester, VT, 1985, 172.

Sandhya

1   Doniger, Wendy, *On Hinduism*, Oxford University Press, New York, NY, 2014, 278.
2   Ibid. 278–279
3   Ibid. 280–281

Santoshi

1   *Devi: The Goddesses of India*, John Stratton Hawley and Donna Marie Wulff (eds.), University of California Press, Berkeley and Los Angeles, CA, 1996, 22.
2   Ibid. 4
3   Lutgendorf, Philip, 'A Superhit Goddess: *Jai Santoshi Maa* and Caste Hierarchy in Indian Films (Part One)', *Manushi*, Vol. 131, Nos. 10–16, 2002, 24–37.
4   *Devi: The Goddesses of India*, John Stratton Hawley and Donna Marie Wulff (eds.), University of California Press, Berkeley and Los Angeles, CA, 1996, 4.
5   Das, Veena, 'The Mythological Film and Its Framework of Meaning: An Analysis of *Jai Santoshi Ma*', *India International Centre Quarterly*, Vol. 8, No. 1, 1981, 43–56.
6   *Devi: The Goddesses of India*, John Stratton Hawley and Donna Marie Wulff (eds.), University of California Press, Berkeley and Los Angeles, CA, 1996, 105.

Aditi

1. R. Nagaswamy, 'Vedic Goddess', *Cult of the Goddess*, ArputhaRani Sengupta (ed.), D.K. Printworld, New Delhi, 2015, 189.

Annapurna

1. Banerjee, Asitkumar, *Bangla Sahityer Sampurna Itibrtta* (in Bengali), Modern Book Agency, Calcutta, 2001, 147–149.

Gayatri

1. Bansal, Sunita Pant, *Hindu Gods and Goddesses*, Smriti Books, New Delhi, 2005, 68.
2. Ibid.
3. Sharma, B.N., *Iconography of Sadasiva*, Abhinav Publications, New Delhi, 1976, 25–29.

Katyayani

1. Coburn, Thomas B., *Encountering the Goddess*, Sri Satguru Publications, Delhi, 1992, 35.
2. Swami Nikhilananda, 'Svetasvatara Upanishad, Chapter 4, Verses 9–10', *The Upanishads: A New Translation*, Advaita Ashrama, Kolkata, 2023.
3. *The Laws of Manu*, Wendy Doniger and Brian K. Smith (eds.), Penguin Books, London, 1991, 128.

Ganga

1. Sinha, Gayatri, 'Gender and Nation: From Bharati to Bharata Mata', *Cult of the Goddess*, ArputhaRani Sengupta (ed.), D.K. Printworld, New Delhi, 2015, 549.
2. *Devi: The Goddesses of India*, John Stratton Hawley and Donna Marie Wulff (eds.), University of California Press, Berkeley and Los Angeles, CA, 1996, 150.

Hariti

1. Langenberg, Amy Paris, 'Pregnant Words: South Asian Buddhist Tales of Fertility and Child Protection', *History of Religions*, Vol. 52, No. 4, 2013, 350, https://doi.org/10.1086/669645. Accessed on 1 November 2024.

2. Sarkar, Radha Banerjee, 'Hariti, Buddhist Deity', Indira Gandhi National Centre for the Arts, 31 July 2014, https://tinyurl.com/cyyzbkcw. Accessed on 29 October 2024.
3. Ibid.
4. Langenberg, Amy Paris, 'Pregnant Words: South Asian Buddhist Tales of Fertility and Child Protection', *History of Religions*, Vol. 52, No. 4, 2013, 347, https://tinyurl.com/4hbfurwy. Accessed on 29 October 2024.

Prakriti

1. Kramrishch, Stella, *The Vishnudharmottara Part III: A Treatise on Indian Painting and Image-Making*, Calcutta University Press, Calcutta, 1928, 67–68.
2. Tagare, G.V., 'The Greatness of Ganga', *The Skanda Purana*, Chapter 27, Verses 7–9, Motilal Banarsidass, New Delhi, 1950.

Chhinnamasta

1. Kinsley, David, *Tantric Visions of the Divine Feminine: The Ten Mahavidyas*, Motilal Banarsidass, New Delhi, 1998, 148.
2. Frawley, David, *Tantric Yoga and the Wisdom Goddesses*, Lotus Press, Twin Lakes, WI, 1994, 16.
3. Shaw, Miranda, *Buddhist Goddesses of India*, Princeton University Press, Princeton, NJ, 2015, 404.

Lalita

1. Frawley, David, *Tantric Yoga and the Wisdom Goddesses*, Lotus Press, Twin Lakes, WI, 1994, 88.
2. Rangarajan, Haripriya, 'Goddess Varahi in Saktism and Tantric Saktism', *Cult of the Goddess*, ArputhaRani Sengupta (ed.), D.K. Printworld, New Delhi, 2015, 204.
3. Ibid. 202

Shakambhari

1. Kinsley, David, *Tantric Visions of the Divine Feminine: The Ten Mahavidyas*, Motilal Banarsidass, New Delhi, 1998, 35.

Shashthi

1. White, David Gordon, *Kiss of the Yogini*, The University of Chicago Press, Chicago, IL, 2003, 41.
2. Ibid.
3. *Encyclopaedia of Hinduism (Vols. 31–45)*, Nagendra Kumar Singh (ed.), Anmol Publications, New Delhi, 2000, 861–872.
4. White, David Gordon, *Kiss of the Yogini*, The University of Chicago Press, Chicago, IL, 2003, 41.

Vindhyavasini

1. *Devi: The Goddesses of India*, John Stratton Hawley and Donna Marie Wulff (eds.), University of California Press, Berkeley and Los Angeles, CA, 1996, 51.
2. Ibid. 67
3. Ibid.
4. Sleeman, W.H., *Rambles and Recollections*, J. Hatchard and Son, London, 1844.

Mohini

1. Kinsley, David, *Tantric Visions of the Divine Feminine: The Ten Mahavidyas*, Motilal Banarsidass, New Delhi, 1998, 246.

Dasa Mahavidyas

1. Ibid. 37, 73
2. Ibid. 251
3. Ibid. 22–38
4. Caldwell, Sarah, *Oh Terrifying Mother*, Oxford University Press, New Delhi, 1999, 10.
5. Kinsley, David, *Tantric Visions of the Divine Feminine: The Ten Mahavidyas*, Motilal Banarsidass, New Delhi, 1998, 92.
6. An ancient treatise considered one of the prime texts on the Advaita school of classical Indian metaphysics.
7. Kinsley, David, *Tantric Visions of the Divine Feminine: The Ten Mahavidyas*, Motilal Banarsidass, New Delhi, 1998, 143.

Sapta Matrikas

1. Chitgopekar, Nilima, *Shakti: An Exploration of the Divine Feminine*, DK Books, New Delhi, 2021, 144.

2   Ibid. 146–147
3   Yegnaswamy, Jayalakshmi, 'Saptamatrka in Rural South India', *Cult of the Goddess*, ArputhaRani Sengupta (ed.), D.K. Printworld, New Delhi, 2015, 421–429.
4   Ibid. 424

Chausath Yoginis

1   Dehejia, Vidya, *Yogini Cult and Temples*, The National Museum, New Delhi, 1986.
2   Bhattacharyya, N.N., *History of the Tantric Religion*, Manohar Books, New Delhi, 1992.
3   Kaula is an esoteric system of Shaiva Tantra in which adherents, called Kaulas, utilise transgressive or 'left-handed' practices to achieve the harmonious fusion of Shiva (represented by the initiated man referred to as the Siddha) and Shakti (represented by the initiated woman, the Yogini).
4   Dehejia, Vidya, *Yogini Cult and Temples*, The National Museum, New Delhi, 1986.
5   Jayakar, Pupul, *The Earth Mother*, Penguin Books, New Delhi, 1989; Shaw, Miranda, *Passionate Enlightenment: Women in Tantric Buddhism*, Princeton University Press, Princeton, NJ, 1994.
6   Dehejia, Vidya, 'The Yogini Temples of India', *Art International*, Vol. 25, Nos. 3–4, 1982.
7   The *Hatha Yoga Pradipika* is a classic 15th-century Sanskrit manual on Hatha Yoga written by Svatmarama. It is among the most influential surviving texts on haṭha yoga, being one of the three classic texts alongside the *Gheranda Samhita* and *Shiva Samhita*.
8   Dehejia, Vidya, 'The Yogini Temples of India', *Art International*, Vol. 25, Nos. 3–4, 1982, 10.
9   Ibid. 8

Yellamma

1   Kamat, K.L., 'Given to the Goddess: Cult of Yellamma', *Cult of the Goddess*, ArputhaRani Sengupta (ed.), D.K. Printworld, New Delhi, 2015, 404–413.

Salabhanjika

1   Vogel, J. Ph., 'The Woman and Tree or *Salabhanjika* in Indian

Literature and Art', *Acta Orientalia Vol. 7*, Akadémiai Kiadó, Budapest, 1929, 202–209.

Prajnaparamita

1. Conze, Edward (trans.), 'The Perfection of Wisdom in Eight Thousand Lines & Its Verse Summary', *Ashtasahasrika Prajnaparamita Sutra*, 129, The Huntington Archive, Columbus, OH, https://tinyurl.com/46pxafrc. Accessed on 3 November 2024.
2. Kinnard, Jacob N., *Imaging Wisdom: Seeing and Knowing in the Art of Indian Buddhism*, Routledge, London, 1999, 114–148.
3. Shaw, Miranda, *Buddhist Goddesses of India*, Princeton University Press, Princeton, NJ, 2006, 187.
4. Apple, James B., 'Prajnaparamita', *Encyclopedia of Indian Religions*, Arvind Sharma (ed.), Springer Publishing, 2023.
5. Kinnard, Jacob N., *Imaging Wisdom: Seeing and Knowing in the Art of Indian Buddhism*, Routledge, London, 1999, 114–148.
6. Beyer, Stephan, *The Cult of Tara: Magic and Ritual in Tibet*, University of California Press, Berkeley and Los Angeles, CA, 1973, 13.
7. Cummings, Cathleen A., 'Guhyasamaja Tantra', *The Circle of Bliss: Buddhist Meditational Art*, Serindia Publications, Inc., Chicago, IL, 2003, 432–448.

Bharat Mata

1. Chitgopekar, Nilima, *Shakti: An Exploration of the Divine Feminine*, DK Books, New Delhi, 2021, 331.
2. Ibid.
3. 'What Makes Bharat Mata Mandir of Varanasi So Special', *India Today*, 1 August 2018, https://tinyurl.com/95829jkr. Accessed on 3 November 2024.
4. Eck, Diana L., *India: A Sacred Geography*, Harmony Books, New York, NY, 2012, 27.

Acknowledgements

The idea for this book was born from one of my previous books, *Shakti: 51 Sacred Peethas of the Goddess*. I wish to gratefully acknowledge my commissioning editor, Dibakar Ghosh, for inspiring the concept and for believing in me.

Devi and Her Avatars has enriched me tremendously. I would like to begin by acknowledging and thanking my family: my sister, Dr Tripti Pande Desai, and my daughter, Dr Mandakini Devi, who energised me at various stages of the writing process. I am also grateful to my editor, Shatarupa Dhar, whose sensitive and thoughtful editing brought an organic feel to my text.

My young colleagues Tezal Dahiya and Rashmi Kapoor constantly helped me connect the dots. I also thank my office staff members Kushal Singh and Ravinder Rawat, without whom I would be lost. My team at the Visual Arts Gallery—Suprabha Nayak, Aditi Tandon and Saurabh Rai—helped and supported me in numerous ways. Most importantly, my husband, Mukul Joshi, is my pillar of strength.

Bibliography

Agamavagisha, Krishnananda. *Tantrasara: Part I.* Basumati Sahitya Mandir, 1934.

Ahmad, Junaid, and Abdul Samad. 'Sarda Temple and the Stone Temples of Kashmir in Perspective: A Review Note'. *Pakistan Heritage*, https://tinyurl.com/4ssmtmte.

Asnani, Rajesh. 'Rajasthan: Roop Kanwar Forced Sati Case in Final Stage'. *The New Indian Express*, https://tinyurl.com/2sxvjek2.

Avalon, Arthur. *Hymn to Kali: Kalpuradi-Stotra.* Luzac & Co., 1922.

Avalon, Arthur. *The Serpent Power: The Secrets of Tantric and Shaktic Yoga.* Dover Publications, 1974.

Banerjee, Asitkumar. *Bangla Sahityer Sampurna Itibrtta.* Modern Book Agency, 2001.

Bansal, Sunita Pant. *Hindu Gods and Goddesses.* Smriti Books, 2005.

Basham, A. L. *The Wonder That Was India.* Picador India, 2019.

Benard (trans.). *Pranatoshini-tantra.* Basumati Sahitya Mandir, 1928.

Beyer, Stephan. *The Cult of Tara: Magic and Ritual in Tibet.* University of California Press, 1973.

Bhattacharji, Sukumari. *The Indian Theogony: A Comparative Study of Indian Mythology from the Vedas to the Puranas.* Cambridge University Press, 2007.

Bhattacharyya, N. N. *History of the Tantric Religion.* Manohar Books, 1992.

Bolon, Carol R. *Forms of the Goddess Lajja Gauri in Indian Art.* College Art Association, Inc. and The Pennsylvania State University Press, 1992.

Brockington, J.L. *The Sacred Thread.* Edinburgh University Press, 1996.

Brown, C. Mackenzie. *The Devi Gita: The Song of the Goddess: A Translation, Annotation, and Commentary.* State University of New York Press, 1998.

Caldwell, Sarah. *Oh Terrifying Mother: Sexuality, Violence and Worship of the*

Goddess Kali. Oxford University Press, 1999.

Campbell, Joseph. *The Power of Myth.* Doubleday, 1988.

Canan, Janine (ed.). *She Rises Like the Sun: Invocations of the Goddess by Contemporary American Women Poets.* The Crossing Press, 1989.

Chakrabarti, Kunal. *Religious Process: The Puranas and the Making of a Regional Tradition.* Oxford University Press, 2018.

Chattopadhyay, Pramodkumar. *Tantrabhilasir Sadhusanga.* Bishwabani Prakashani, 1983.

Chattopadhyaya, Debiprasad. *Indian Philosophy: A Popular Outline.* People's Publishing House, 1964.

Chaturvedi, B.K. *Saraswati: Gods and Goddesses of India.* Books For All, 1998.

Chitgopekar, Nilima (ed.). *Invoking Goddesses: Gender Politics in Indian Religion.* Shakti Books, 2002.

Chitgopekar, Nilima (ed.). *Shakti: An Exploration of the Divine Feminine.* DK India, 2021.

Clooney, Francis X. *Divine Mother, Blessed Mother: Hindu Goddesses and the Virgin Mary.* Oxford University Press, 2005.

Coburn, Thomas B. *Encountering the Goddess: A Translation of the Devi-Mahatmya and a Study of Its Interpretation.* Sri Satguru Publications, 1992.

Conze, Edward (trans.). 'The Perfection of Wisdom in Eight Thousand Lines & Its Verse Summary'. *Ashtasahasrika Prajnaparamita Sutra,* The Huntington Archive, https://tinyurl.com/46pxafrc.

Coomaraswamy, Ananda. *Rajput Painting.* Oxford University Press, 1916.

Coomaraswamy, Ananda K., and Sister Nivedita. *Myths of the Hindus and Buddhists.* Dover Publications, Inc., 1967.

Courtright, Paul B. *The Goddess and the Dreadful Practice.* Oxford University Press.

Cummings, Cathleen A. *The Circle of Bliss: Buddhist Meditational Art.* Serindia Publications, Inc., 2003.

Daniélou, Alain. *The Myths and Gods of India: The Classic Work on Hindu Polytheism.* Inner Traditions International, 1985.

Darian, Steven G. *The Ganges in Myth and History.* Motilal Banarsidass, 2001.

Das, Veena. 'The Mythological Film and Its Framework of Meaning: An Analysis of Jai Santoshi Ma'. *India International Centre Quarterly,* Vol. 8, No. 1, 1981, 43–56.

Dehejia, Vidya. *Devi: The Great Goddess.* Prestel Verlag, 1999.

Dehejia, Vidya. 'The Yogini Temples of India'. *Art International,* Vol. 25, Nos. 3–4, 1982.

Dehejia, Vidya. *Yogini Cult and Temples: A Tantric Tradition.* The National Museum, 1986.

Doniger, Wendy. *On Hinduism.* Oxford University Press, 2014.

Doniger, Wendy, and Brian K. Smith (eds.). *The Laws of Manu.* Penguin Books, 1991.

Dowson, John. *A Classical Dictionary of Hindu Mythology and Religion, Geography, History and Literature.* Trübner & Co, 1879.

'Devi Mahatmyam'. *Shree Shree Ma An andamayi Ashram,* https://tinyurl.com/2v2743dh.

'Durga Saptashati: A Glorious Song to the Divine Mother'. *The Art of Living,* https://tinyurl.com/5cmkr375.

Eck, Diana L. *Devi: Goddesses of India.* Motilal Banarsidass, 2008.

Eck, Diana L. *India: A Sacred Geography.* Harmony Books, 2012.

Fischer, Eberhard. *Temple Tents for Goddesses in Gujarat, India.* Niyogi Books, 2014.

Flood, Gavin. *The Blackwell Companion to Hinduism.* Blackwell Publishing, 2003.

Frawley, David. *Tantric Yoga and the Wisdom Goddesses.* Lotus Press, 1994.

Gangadharan, N. (trans.). *The Agni Purana: Part II.* Motilal Banarsidass, 1954.

Graham, Maria. *Journal of a Residence in India.* Asian Educational Services, 2000.

Gupta, Mahendranath. *The Gospel of Sri Ramakrishna.* Ramakrishna Vivekananda Centre, 1942.

Gupta, Subhadra Sen. *Devi.* Rupa Publications, 2017.

Gupta, Swarupa. *Cultural Constellations, Place-Making and Ethnicity in Eastern India, c. 1850–1927.* Brill Academic Publishers, 2017.

Handiqui, Krishna K. *Yasastilaka and Indian Culture.* Jaina Samskriti Samrakshaka Sangha, 1968.

Harding, Elizabeth U. *Kali: The Black Goddess of Dakshineswar.* Nicolas-Hays Inc., 1993.

Harlan, Lindsey. *Religion and Rajput Women: The Ethic of Protection in*

Contemporary Narratives. Munshiram Manoharlal Publishers, 1994.

Hawley, John Stratton, and Donna Marie Wulff (eds.). *Devi: The Goddesses of India*. University of California Press, 1996.

Huntington, John C., and Dina Bangdel (eds.). *The Circle of Bliss: Buddhist Meditational Art*. Serindia Publications, Inc., 2003.

Jayakar, Pupul. *The Earth Mother*. Penguin Books, 1989.

Kakati, Banikanta. *The Mother Goddess Kamakhya*. Publication Board Assam, 1989.

Kempton, Sally. *Awakening Shakti: The Transformative Power of the Goddesses of Yoga*. Sounds True Inc, 2013.

Keul, István (ed.). *'Yogini' in South Asia: Interdisciplinary Approaches*. Routledge, 2013.

Kinnard, Jacob N. *Imaging Wisdom: Seeing and Knowing in the Art of Indian Buddhism*. Routledge, 1999.

Kinsley, David. *Hindu Goddesses: Visions of the Divine Feminine in the Hindu Religious Tradition*. Motilal Banarsidass, 1998.

Kinsley, David. *Tantric Visions of the Divine Feminine: The Ten Mahavidyas*. Motilal Banarsidass, 1988.

Kramrishch, Stella. *The Vishnudharmottara Part III: A Treatise on Indian Painting and Image-Making*. Calcutta University Press, 1928.

Kurtz, Stanley N. *All the Mothers Are One: Hindu India and the Cultural Reshaping of Psychoanalysis*. Columbia University Press, 1992.

Langenberg, Amy Paris. 'Pregnant Words: South Asian Buddhist Tales of Fertility and Child Protection'. *History of Religions*, Vol. 52, No. 4, 2013, 350, https://doi.org/10.1086/669645.

Leeming, David. *The Oxford Companion to World Mythology*. Oxford University Press, 2005.

Leslie, Julia (ed.). *Roles and Rituals for Hindu Women*. Motilal Banarsidass, 1992.

Lutgendorf, Philip. 'A Superhit Goddess: Jai Santoshi Maa and Caste Hierarchy in Indian Films (Part One)'. *Manushi*, Vol. 131, Nos. 10–16, 2002, 24–37.

Mahalakshmi, R. *Art and History: Texts, Contexts and Visual Representations in Ancient and Early Medieval India*. Bloomsbury Publishing, 2020.

Menon, Ramesh. *Devi: The Devi Bhagavatam Retold*. Rupa Publications, 2010.

Menzies, Jackie. *Goddess: Divine Energy*. Art Gallery of New South Wales, 2006.

Mittal, Sushil and Thursby, Gene (eds.). *The Hindu World*. Routledge, 2007.

Mohanty, Seema. *The Book of Kali*. Penguin Books, 2009.

Mookerjee, Ajit. *Kali: The Feminine Force*. Thames & Hudson, 2008.

Nagar, Shanti Lal. *Varaha in Indian Art, Culture and Literature*. Aryan Books International, 1993.

Palmer, Travis L. 'The Courtship of Shakti: The Hindu Goddess in Myth and Philosophy'. *Goddess Traditions*, University of Tennessee.

Parthasarathy, V.R., and Indu Parthasarathy. *Devi: Goddesses in Indian Art and Literature*. Bharatiya Kala Prakashan, 2009.

Pattanaik, Devdutt. *7 Secrets of the Goddess*. Westland, 2023.

Pattanaik, Devdutt. *Devi, the Mother-Goddess: An Introduction*. Vakils, Feffer & Simons, 2000.

Pattanaik, Devdutt. *Lakshmi: The Goddess of Wealth and Fortune: An Introduction*. Vakils, Feffer & Simons, 2002.

Pintchman, Tracy. *The Rise of the Goddess in the Hindu Tradition*. State University of New York Press, 1994.

Pollock, Sheldon. *The Language of the Gods in the World of Men: Sanskrit, Culture, and Power in Premodern India*. University of California Press, 2009.

Raghunathji, K. *The Hindu Temples of Bombay*. Fort Printing Press, 1895.

Ramachandran, Nalini. *Nava Durga: The Nine Forms of the Goddess*. Penguin Random House India, 2020.

Rao, Subba. *Tales of Durga*. Amar Chitra Katha, 1971.

Rao, T.A. Gopinatha. *Elements of Hindu Iconography (Volume II)*. Indological Book House, 2019.

Sarkar, Radha Banerjee. *Hariti, Buddhist Deity*. Indira Gandhi National Centre for the Arts, https://tinyurl.com/cyyzbkcw.

Sengupta, ArputhaRani (ed.). *Cult of the Goddess*. D.K. Printworld, 2015.

Sharma, Arvind (ed.). *Encyclopedia of Indian Religions*. Springer Publishing, 2023.

Sharma, B. N. *Iconography of Sadasiva*. Abhinav Publications, 1976.

Sharma, Bulbul. *The Book of Devi*. Penguin Books India, 2010.

Shaw, Miranda. *Buddhist Goddesses of India*. Princeton University Press, 2006.

Shaw, Miranda. *Passionate Enlightenment: Women in Tantric Buddhism.* Princeton University Press, 1994.

Shri Guhyakali Sahasranama Stotra'. *Sanskrit Documents,* https://tinyurl.com/4822df56.

Singh, Nagendra Kumar (ed.). *Encyclopaedia of Hinduism (Vols. 31–45).* Anmol Publications, 2000.

Sivaramamurti, C. *Sri Lakshmi in Indian Art and Thought.* Kanak Publishers, 1982.

Sleeman, W.H. *Rambles and Recollections.* J. Hatchard and Son, 1844.

Smith, H. Daniel, and M. Narasimhachary. *Handbook of Hindu Gods, Goddesses, and Saints.* Sundeep Prakashan, 1997.

Sri Swami Ji Maharaja Datiya. *Sri Chinnamasta Nityarchan.* Kalyan Mandir Prakashan, 1978.

Swami Harshananda. *Hindu Gods and Goddesses.* Sri Ramakrishna Math, 2002.

Swami Nikhilananda. *The Upanishads: A New Translation.* Advaita Ashrama, 2023.

Swami Satyananda Saraswati. *Devi Gita.* Motilal Banarsidass, 1991.

Tagare, G.V. *The Skanda Purana.* Motilal Banarsidass, 1950.

Thapar, Romila. 'Sati: A Symposium on Widow Immolation and Its Social Context'. *Seminar no. 342,* 1988.

Tiwari, Kartikey. 'Navratri 2019 Nine Mantras for Maa Durga Puja'. *Jagran,* https://tinyurl.com/5n96hu63.

Tiwari, Shubha (ed.). *Contemporary Indian Dramatists.* Atlantic Publishers and Distributors, 2011.

Vanamali. *Shakti: Realm of the Divine Mother.* Simon & Schuster, 2008.

Varadarajan, Lotika. 'Oral Testimony as Historical Source Material for Traditional and Modern India'. *Economic and Political Weekly,* Vol. 14, No. 24, 1979, 1009–1014.

Vedavyas. *Skanda Puranam.* Gurumandal Series No. XX, 1961.

Vicziany, Marika, and Jayant Bapat. 'Mumbadevi and the Other Mother Goddesses in Mumbai'. *Modern Asian Studies,* Vol. 43, No. 2, 2009, 511–541.

Vogel, J. Ph. 'The Woman and Tree or Salabhanjika in Indian Literature and Art'. *Acta Orientalia Vol. 7,* Akadémiai Kiadó, 1929, 202–209.

Westphal-Hellbusch, Sigrid, and Heinz Westphal. *Hinduistische Viehzüchter im nord-westlichen Indien: Die Rabari* (in German). Duncker & Humblot, 1974.

'What Makes Bharat Mata Mandir of Varanasi So Special'. *India Today*, https://tinyurl.com/95829jkr.

White, David Gordon. *Kiss of the Yogini.* The University of Chicago Press, 2003.

Whitehead, Henry. *The Village Gods of South India.* Oxford University Press, 1921.

Williams, George M. *Handbook of Hindu Mythology.* Motilal Banarsidass, 2016.

Woodroffe, John. *Hymns to the Goddess and Hymns to Kali: Karpuradi Stotra.* Motilal Banarsidass, 2014.